# ANALYZING PSYCHOTHERAPY

# Analyzing
# Psychotherapy
## A SOCIAL ROLE INTERPRETATION

## Melvyn L. Fein

PRAEGER

New York
Westport, Connecticut
London

**Library of Congress Cataloging-in-Publication Data**

Fein, Melvyn L.
    Analyzing psychotherapy : a social role interpretation / Melvyn L. Fein.
        p.    cm.
    Includes bibliographical references and index.
    ISBN 0-275-93966-9 (alk. paper)
    1. Psychotherapy—Social aspects.   2. Social role.    I. Title.
RC480.5.F42    1992
616.89'14—dc20          91-28650

British Library Cataloguing in Publication Data is available.

Library of Congress Catalog Card Number: 91-28650
ISBN: 0-275-93966-9

First published in 1992

Praeger Publishers, One Madison Avenue, New York, NY 10010
An imprint of Greenwood Publishing Group, Inc.

Printed in the United States of America

∞™

The paper used in this book complies with the
Permanent Paper Standard issued by the National
Information Standards Organization (Z39.48-1984).

10 9 8 7 6 5 4 3 2 1

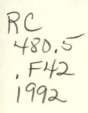

# *Contents*

| | | |
|---|---|---|
| Preface | | vii |
| 1 | Psychotherapy and Role Theory | 1 |
| 2 | The Role Change Process | 27 |
| 3 | A Multitude of Specialties | 49 |
| 4 | Psychoanalysis | 77 |
| 5 | Cultural Therapies | 97 |
| 6 | Ecological Therapies | 119 |
| 7 | The Romantics | 143 |
| 8 | The Academics | 167 |
| 9 | Antitherapies | 189 |
| 10 | Conclusion | 207 |
| | Bibliography | 209 |
| | Index | 219 |

# *Preface*

Recently, after having published a book on role change (Praeger, 1990), I was surprised to discover that many of my associates in sociology, psychology, and social work did not fully seem to comprehend the applicability of the resocialization paradigm to psychotherapy. For me, the implications of a social role perspective were obvious. I had been working with a role-problem outlook for over a decade and found it invaluable in work with clients. I therefore imagined others would too. When it became evident that some colleagues had conceptual allegiances that prevented them from perceiving the connections between role theory and their own work, I resolved to explicate these as best I could. The result is the present volume.

Another motive for writing has been my belief that there is an underlying consistency to psychotherapy that has usually been obscured by the rivalries that exist among competing schools of thought. While it has long been a cliché that there are almost as many therapeutic orientations as there are psychotherapists, this seems to me more a consequence of the absence of a unifying conception than of the nature of the therapeutic enterprise. With time, it has become apparent to me that resocialization bridges many of the gaps that separate clinicians and gives their efforts a coherence they would not otherwise enjoy. I have therefore come to believe that demonstrating the implications of a social-role framework can enable competing therapists to integrate what have seemed to be antagonistic world views and will help them make further advances in developing effective helping technologies. As a bonus, such an awareness may also foster a greater utilization of sociological knowledge. Being a clinical sociologist by training and practice has alerted me to the applicability of sociological insights to psychotherapy, as well as the degree to which these have been neglected by more psychologically oriented practitioners.

Still, an analysis of the full scope of psychotherapy has seemed a daunting prospect. It has consequently been with considerable trepidation that I pondered the task of interpreting the plethora of disparate approaches in use, especially since I am not equally conversant with all. Though I have accumulated over twenty years of experience as a counselor and therapist, I am, and have been, very mindful of not being an expert on every form of therapy. Even so, I have come to the conclusion that my unique background in sociology and mental health has provided me with a wider exposure to the realities of therapeutic practice than most observers enjoy, and hence has furnished me with the possibility of reconciling many of the disparities that exist.

At the beginning of my college career I was a philosophy major, but my first paid employment was in social welfare. A decade later, in the hope of expanding my understanding of client needs, I returned to school to obtain a Ph.D. in sociology, this time concentrating on the socialization of client roles. Along the way, I obtained training through a psychoanalytic training institute, a community mental health center, a master-of-social-work program, countless in-service training sessions, numerous professional workshops, and an unbroken regimen of reading.

Of course, there were many moments during this process when I wondered where I was headed and what all these nonstandard experiences would add up to. In retrospect, it now seems that a part of my unconscious was busily comparing, contrasting, and making correlations. I was, as it were, trying to make sense of the extravagant gyrations of my professional history and attempting to close the lacunae in my personal knowledge.

Moreover, being a practitioner at various times within a welfare system, at a vocational rehabilitation agency, at a psychiatric hospital, at a community mental health center, and in private practice has given me the opportunity to apply what I have learned. These settings also provided me with a chance to observe the activities of a multitude of professionals employing widely divergent treatment philosophies. Furthermore, six years of individual and group therapy, when I was in my twenties and trying to figure out what to do with my life, were of inestimable value. Not only did this provide me with personal direction, it enabled me to understand the inner dynamics of therapy in a manner I am sure is obtainable in no other way. Therapy became for me much more than an academic exercise or an antiseptic change technology directed only toward others.

It is this combination of theoretical and practical experience that I have drawn upon to decide what therapies to include within the compass of this work. What I have attempted is to present a cross-section of the most influential of contemporary treatment strategies. Though it is not possible to do equal justice to all these perspectives, I believe that a serviceable guide to their actual application is feasible. Real depth, however, should not be expected, for this is an effort at analysis and synthesis, not a how-to book on therapy.

Because I have set out to sketch a comprehensive portrait of psychotherapy, it is of necessity less like a snapshot and more like a pointillist painting, that is, a sampling of many small fragments that are intended to add up to a recognizable whole. Though numerous parallels are described and conclusions drawn, not all are presented in the depth some specialists might desire. It is hoped, however, that the theses advanced acquire validity through an accumulation of details. In short, the whole is designed to add up to more than a sum of the parts.

Given such an agenda, it is inevitable that some of my biases will have crept into the analysis. I confess to having definite points of view that color my interpretations, but this is unavoidable in pursuing a unified conception. The only way to have prevented it would have been to assign unrelated individuals to analyze each therapy—a strategy that others have already attempted. This, however, would have resulted in a very different book, one without the singularity of outlook needed to organize diversity.

Because this work embraces such a large portion of my experience, it is impossible to acknowledge everyone who has played a significant part in helping me reach my conclusions. I wish to begin by recognizing the contributions of my family. The encouragement of my mother, Florence Fein, my sister, Carol Schwartz, and my brother, Joel Fein, has been invaluable. I am also acutely aware of the influence of my late father, Samuel Fein, who, I suspect, would have been very pleased to see this work in print. Two persons I must especially thank are Prof. Joanne M. Jacobs, of the Rochester Institute of Technology, and Margaret Balconi, of the Rochester Association for Retarded Citizens. To them I owe a debt for their professional and personal inspiration, as well as for reading and revising my manuscript. My gratitude also extends to my colleagues in the Sociological Practice Association—Beverley Cuthbertson-Johnson, Susan St. John, Michael Hoover, and Philip Robinette—as well as to

Steven Buff, of the American Sociological Association, who have been a vital part of my professional network. Finally, I must mention the many colleagues and clients who over the years have enabled me to learn about psychotherapy. Without their example and patience, most of what I have discovered would still be beyond my ken.

# ANALYZING PSYCHOTHERAPY

# 1

# *Psychotherapy and Role Theory*

## THE PROBLEM

What is psychotherapy? Despite its popularity and the plethora of professionals claiming it as their specialty, nobody seems to be quite sure. While there is no shortage of answers, agreement has eluded those who have asked the question. Disputes about how it works and what it does abound. Some have talked about a procedure for curing mental illness, others of correcting the effects of environmental stress; some stipulate that it is a peculiar interpersonal relationship that helps a person cope, while still others insist it involves a relearning of problem behaviors. Which of these competing views is correct is often the subject of acrimonious argument, with each protagonist insisting that he is right and all others are wrong.

Today there are many "brands" of psychotherapy. It has been estimated that well over 250 of them compete in the marketplace and that this number continues to swell (Corsini, 1981). Among the approaches that command significant numbers of adherents are client-centered therapy, rational-emotive therapy, psychoanalysis, cognitive therapy, transactional analysis, family therapy, stress management, psychodrama, existential therapy, ego psychology, gestalt therapy, Adlerian analysis, object relations, educational approaches, strategic therapy, behavior modification, Jungian analysis, hypnotherapy, reality therapy, Sullivanian psychotherapy, community interventions, trait interpretations, temperament analysis, phenomenology, medical therapy, and labeling theory. Also commanding a significant following are logotherapy, multimodal therapy, primal-scream therapy, play therapy, T-groups, time-limited therapy, art therapy, dance-movement therapy, and para-verbal therapy.

Tedious as this list is, it could be extended several pages longer. No wonder, then, that many practitioners have become more than a little confused. Some have even thrown up their hands in despair, declaring that psychotherapy is whatever psychotherapists do. They may sense that therapy changes something inside the person, but they are perplexed as to precisely what this may be. What especially distresses them is that there is not only diversity, but apparent contradiction. And not only contradiction, but obstinacy about the correctness of very different perspectives. Thus they worry when Freudians declare that there is no psychotherapy without an examination of the psychosexual precursors of contemporary patterns of living, while reality therapists argue with equal passion that only the here and now counts. They are disturbed when gestalt therapists wallow in emotional expressiveness, while cognitivists fervently declare that feelings are secondary to thoughts. And they agonize over the differences between client-centered therapists, who allow their clients to solve their own problems, and strategic therapists, who manipulate their clients in preselected directions.

Some clinicians have sought to penetrate this morass by describing themselves as eclectic and appropriating bits and pieces from many different sources. Because they can't decide where the truth lies, they conclude that it lies nowhere and settle instead for pragmatism. As long as a technique works for them, they are content. Though this may seem to be a reasonable response to confusion, there may yet be undiscovered truths that make sense of the diversity, that explain not only why there are differences, but why there are acrimonious disputes. What follows will suggest that these answers are to be found in a source not commonly exploited by psychotherapists: role theory.

The situation, and the reason for the confusion, may be elucidated by the familiar Jain parable about the blind men and the elephant. The story relates that a group of wandering blind men, being sightless, were accustomed to deciphering the environment through their fingertips. Usually this worked well, but when they encountered an elephant during the course of their travels, each came in contact with a different part of it. One felt its trunk, another its leg, the third its tail, and so forth. In consequence, the first declared, "This creature is a snake; I can feel it coiling around my hand," while the second, with equal vehemence, affirmed that he had touched a tree. The fable recounts that the remaining sages also came to widely divergent conclusions. Since each had chanced upon a distinct part of the creature, each honestly believed in his own interpretation.

Of course, we nonblind observers recognize that all were mistaken. From our vantage point we perceive that none saw the whole picture. Though each made a reasonable deduction from the evidence at hand, each came to the wrong conclusion. Since we can see the whole animal, we realize the truth and draw the intended moral, namely that one must be wary of partial evidence. The point of relating this parable is that it tells us much about the current state of psychotherapy. Many contemporary clinicians are also trapped by partial evidence. While they see a lot, and draw tantalizing conclusions, each encounters only part of a very large phenomenon. Because they are trying to facilitate a complex change process, each notices, and therefore emphasizes, only part of it.

The psychotherapeutic elephant turns out to be essentially a role-change process. It includes many of the factors psychologists, social workers, and psychiatrists have grown accustomed to studying, but it fits them together in a novel way. If role theory is correct, the different schools of therapy have been at odds, not because they have discovered contradictory facts, but because they have not been able to see how their respective truths are related. In short, role theory holds the prospect of a grand synthesis that can place competing schools of therapeutic thought in a shared context. It reconciles many of their apparent inconsistencies, while explaining why they differ in emphasis.

To date, role theory has not been used to embrace the totality of the psychotherapeutic enterprise. While it has not been excluded from the field, it has been allocated a rather limited mission. Instead of providing a comprehensive perspective for psychotherapy itself, it has largely been invoked for specialty tasks. Whether incorporated in Jacob L. Moreno's psychodrama or in specific forms of alcoholism counseling, it has been used to supplement other therapies rather than as an explanatory device for the overall process.

Yet a social-role interpretation of psychotherapy has many advantages. Properly understood, it gives coherence to what is inherently a long-term and multifaceted procedure, and explains why the procedure is of necessity lengthy and difficult to document. Moreover, the mechanisms through which role change operates explain why some therapies are oriented toward the past while others are consumed with the present. They also show why the symptoms tackled involve a bewildering melange of emotions, cognitions, and value commitments. Perhaps most importantly, the facts of role conservation and role dysfunction indicate why psychotherapy is typically painful, often requiring professional participation if success is to be attained.

Role theory achieves these breakthroughs by rendering visible the tangled lineaments of role change. In emphasizing the significance of role loss, it makes clear that an intricate path must be traversed before people can free themselves of the problems that propel them into therapy. It also makes plain that this process is intrinsically psychosocial and that ultimately the changes clients undergo are in what they do and experience, rather than who they are. It is their interpersonal behavior patterns that are altered, not a quality of their personhood.

## DEFINING PSYCHOTHERAPY

Defining psychotherapy sometimes seems to be a cottage industry, with the authors of every new therapy feeling compelled to present a new definition. Those intent on reconciling the differences within the field have similarly felt duty bound to encapsulate what specific therapies have in common. They often crave a precise and comprehensive verbal package that contains the essence of their insights. Others are more pragmatic in their bent and are satisfied to let what therapists do speak for itself, rather than make the enterprise contingent on a linguistic formula.

Perhaps a good way to begin looking for a definition is with a search for central tendencies. Are there underlying patterns that unite ostensibly different therapies? Can a short verbal description highlight the commonalities of diverse treatment strategies? Many have thought so. We must take a look at some of the answers they have put forward.

As John Reisman (1971) has pointed out, definitions of psychotherapy tend to follow consistent channels. They define the process in terms of (1) its goals, (2) the procedures it uses, (3) the practitioners who employ it, or (4) some combination of these. In the description of role change that will be enlarged upon in this book, it is the goals and procedures utilized that will be highlighted. According to Reisman, goals should be logically impermissible in a definition of psychotherapy, because if one does not achieve one's defined objective, then one presumably will not have engaged in the desired activity—and this he considers a logical absurdity. My view is that the effort to attain a goal, and not its accomplishment, is what counts. An activity does not cease to be fishing merely because the person engaging in it fails to catch a fish. Indeed, without a view to the goal of psychotherapy, the process is both blind and pointless.

Another potential pitfall is that in defining the procedures used to implement a change process, one can be very particularistic and try to specify the exact measures used to achieve the goal. Such micromanagement is generally counterproductive. While there may be central techniques that characterize therapy, it is necessary to have flexibility in introducing new procedures; defining some as "politically correct" and some as incorrect is foolhardy. Moreover, it may be that a multitude of procedures used in concert, or sequentially, add up to what is labeled psychotherapy. In this case, it would be a mistake to single one out as *the* element that makes the process therapeutic.

The approach that will be considered utterly unacceptable here is understanding psychotherapy in terms of the practitioner who implements it. This strategy is more a manifestation of the politics of the helping professions than a necessary characteristic of the way they function. If we allow ourselves to be boxed in by assertions that therapy is the preserve of a select few, this artificially limits the technique to those who already claim it. Since many of these have psychological and medical affiliations, permitting them to remain unchallenged is tantamount to acquiescing in their theoretical orientations and it would totally vitiate attempts to interpret psychotherapy from a social-role perspective.

## The Goals of Change

Although most therapists agree that they are trying to change something that is related to the individual (or to individuals), there is considerable discord about what this is. The range of candidates includes a person's personality, his character, his self, the behaviors he is enacting, his adjustments to external stressors, difficulties in the social systems in which he is enmeshed, his problems in living, and mental disorders. Some definitions attempt to incorporate several of these, and some use vague language to fuzz the differences. Thus, Horace English and Ava English (1958) define psychotherapy as "the use of any psychological technique in the treatment of mental disorder or maladjustment" (p. 429). They go on to note that "the term is very general. It includes 'faith cure,' suggestion, hypnosis, psychoanalysis, provision of rest, assurance, advice, consultation designed to relive anxiety, psychodrama, etc." (p. 429).

Other statements of the goals of therapy are more specific. Leland Hinsie and Jacob Shatsky (1947) wrote that therapy is "the art of treating mental diseases or disorders" and asserted that it includes "any measure, mental or physical, that favorably influences the mind or psyche" (cited in Reisman 1971:11). Abraham Maslow and Béla Mittleman (1951) described therapy as "a method which aims to help the impaired individual by influencing his emotional processes, his evaluation of himself and of others . . . and his manner of coping with the problems of life" (p. 179). More recently Jeffrey Zeig and W. Michael Munion (1990) described it as "a change oriented process that . . . explicitly or implicitly focuses on the personality of the client(s)" (p. 14). Raymond Corsini (1989) is more circumspect in his definition. He recognizes that while psychotherapy cannot be defined with precision, a definition should specify that it is

a formal process of interaction between two parties . . . the purpose [of which is the] amelioration of the distress of one of the two parties relative to any of the following areas of disability or malfunction: cognitive functions (disorders of thinking), affective functions (suffering or emotional discomforts), or behavioral functions (inadequacy of behavior). (p. 1)

Corsini goes on to suggest that while not all therapies fit this description it is a good starting point. As we shall shortly see, it also represents a good point of departure for the portrayal of role dysfunction.

*Personality Dysfunction*

Describing psychotherapy as a means for correcting personality dys-function is a popular stratagem. Many of those engaged in therapy are psychologists or psychiatrists who have been trained to believe that their function is to alter the anguished psyche. The term "psychotherapy" itself seems to give warrant to this interpretation. The word obviously has two roots, namely "psycho" and "therapy." "Psyche" refers to the mind; in ancient Greek it referred to the personification of the life principle. "Therapy," also from the Greek, refers to nursing or the provision of a cure. It has distinctly medical origins, although modern authors, such as the Englishes, often extend it to mean returning someone to "normal functioning"; this allows for a nonmedical interpretation that generalizes the term for use with problems in living.

The American Psychiatric Association *Diagnostic and Statistical Manual of Mental Disorders* (3d ed., rev., 1988; hereafter *DSM*), in trying to incorporate personality disorders within its compass, adopts the tactic of defining these disorders in terms of personality "traits." It characterizes these latter as "enduring patterns of perceiving, relating to, and thinking about the environment and oneself [that] are exhibited in a wide range of important social and personal contexts." It goes on to state that "it is only when *personality traits* are inflexible and maladaptive and cause either significant impairment in social or occupational functioning or subjective distress that they constitute *Personality Disorders*" (p. 335). As we shall shortly see, these definitions of "personality trait" and "personality disor-der" are very close to those for the concepts we will designate as "basic, personal roles" and "role dysfunction." Similarly "enduring patterns of perceiving, relating and thinking" are comparable to what we will refer to as "role scripts," and "impairments to social functioning that cause distress" are akin to our "failed roles" and "aborted roles."

Still, despite these parallels, there are difficulties with relying on "personality" to explain what is changed in psychotherapy. The concept places the locus of fault in the wrong place, namely, in the person, and fails to distinguish sufficiently between acquired and inherited characteristics. Furthermore, it focuses too emphatically on the individual and often omits the social aspects of what troubles him.

First, talk about a personality disorder implies that the person seeking psychotherapeutic help is herself impaired. It suggests that there is something wrong with who she is, not with what she does. The notion of a personal trait has similar implications. Since a trait is a quality (not unlike hair color), it suggests that an indelible part of the person, rather than his activities or thoughts, must be changed. If psychotherapy involves altering personality, the inexorable conclusion is that a client will be a different person at the end of the process, and this is simply untrue. A social role, however, is something that is performed by a person and can be altered without casting aspersions on her. She merely has to conclude that her previous interpersonal strategies were faulty not that she was defective as a human being.

Second, personality refers to those aspects of a person that distinguish him from other people. It includes both acquired and inherited factors, that is, characteristics that are learned or constructed, as well as those that are genetically determined. Some apparently genetic traits, such as temperament, are integral to what we mean by personality, yet are difficult, if not impossible, to alter. One's activity level, sensitivity to noxious stimuli, or tendency toward risk taking all seem to derive from biology, not from a decision to act in a particular way. They are physiological and emotional sets that are neither selected by a person nor easy for him to control. In consequence, they are relatively impervious to therapeutic manipulation. Social roles, in contrast, subsume only acquired behaviors and are more readily subject to alteration.

Third, personality is something that belongs exclusively to the person. The focus is on the individual and what goes on in her head, rather than her relationship with other human beings. Nevertheless, even psychologists, such as Walter Mischel, have pointed out that no one can understand what a person is doing, or why she is doing it, without understanding the social context in which her behavior is exhibited. They have observed that some people lie, not because they have a trait that automatically determines that they will lie, but because they have learned in some social circumstances to do so. People, it seems, are psychosocial creatures who have impulses that originate within themselves and also responses that are in reaction to their environment. Yet personality is a psychological, not a psychosocial construct. It implies that only the internal half of the equation counts. The social role, in contrast, is inherently psychosocial, and more faithfully encompasses the full breadth of those experiences and activities that are addressed in therapy.

Those who favor "personality" change as the object of therapeutic interventions have suggested provisos that seek to invalidate the above objections and that do, in a sense, rebut them. Yet ordinary meanings are important. Despite the technical overhauls a concept may receive, if it is in common use, it carries connotations that can ensnare even the most wary professional. Since "personality" is an everyday concept and has the implications described above, these cannot be expunged merely by declaring them null. Their presence, therefore, interferes with the use of "personality" as an adequate descriptor of the object of clinical ministrations.

Two concepts that are related to personality, namely "character" and "self," have also been used to explain the goal of psychotherapy. The notion of "character," which has lost favor in recent decades, adds little more than a moralistic patina. If the purpose of therapy is taken to be a change in a person's character, the impression that she is an unworthy human being is reinforced and no gain achieved.

The second alternative, the "self," has a much wider, and perhaps growing acceptance. It is utilized by psychoanalysts, symbolic interactionists, family therapists, self-psychologists, and many others, and seems to come closer to who a person is, and what must be altered if she is to feel better.

Yet there are problems with the concept of "self," too. When we try to pin it down, it turns out to have an elusive and abstract quality that makes it difficult to understand. The self involves such things as self-image, self-feeling, and a sense of personal consistency. Upon closer examination it is akin to concepts such as the "ego," which are acknowledged to be hypothetical constructs. Perhaps the best way to describe it is as a carrier of social roles (and hence identity) that provides the individual with a sense of continuity and a center of activity. It is having a self that makes a person more than a random assemblage of kaleidoscopically alternating role behaviors. It ensures that I am the same person today as I was five years ago, and that it is I who enact my role behaviors, rather than they that enact me. Yet this self does not change during therapy. I remain as much myself after the process as I was before. Again, it is my roles that change, not me.

## Behavioral Disturbances

Academic psychologists, in particular, have been unhappy with the notion of personality. Instead they have sought to substitute the concept of the "behavioral problem." They have quested after a concept that is concrete, observable, and scientific, and they have been anxious to avoid what they perceive as the semimystical qualities of psychoanalysis. They have further believed that a tangible object for therapy would in fact be more manipulable, and hence would enable clinicians to identify client problems more precisely so they could better target specific change techniques to correct them. The practitioner would even be enabled to invoke scientific tests to determine whether his methods were succeeding. Today this view have been widely adopted by those therapists who describe themselves as behaviorists.

Nevertheless, as with personality, there are problems with identifying behavior change as the goal of therapy. Foremost among these is that behaviorism is a reductionistic enterprise. It portrays human activities in atomistic terms, which is comparable to describing human physiology in terms of the movements of individual atoms. While such an exercise is possible, and perhaps technically correct, it is awkward and misleading. It looks at what is happening from the wrong vantage point, and fosters a Ptolemaic rather than a Copernican worldview.

Behaviorism fails to distinguish the larger patterns that give coherence to human behavior. It is especially poor at recognizing the social patterns and complex interpersonal connections that pervade this world. A person is more likely to be described by a behaviorist as having difficulty being assertive than as having a problem with authority figures. The result is that he will be taught specific ways to be assertive, rather than how to recognize and alter the way he interacts with authorities. Moreover, social relationships have a unity and consistency that an enumeration of behaviors typically ignores. They are more than mere movements of arms, legs, or voice boxes. Social roles, in contrast, are gestalts that describe something beyond individual actions. The role of "mother," for instance, consists of more than a collection of feeding or dressing activities. Even Freud was aware that "cupboard love" did not fully account for what happens between a mother and child.

Behavioral descriptions likewise fail to account adequately for the development and maintenance of complex interpersonal behaviors. Their depiction of the social negotiations in which roles arise is almost a caricature of them. They present a one-sided, nonsocial process in which reinforcements are scheduled by one person and imposed on another, rather than a world in which demands are met by counterdemands and in which people constantly make adjustments to one another. Such an approach leaves out histories, purposes, and sometimes emotions. The cruder forms of behaviorism even go so far as to ignore anything that is internal to the individual. While more recent behaviorists have implicated environmental stress in their reports of personal anguish, this considerable improvement still fails to appreciate the emotional and interpersonal complexities of human existence.

Finally, strictly behavioral accounts insist on an unnecessary specificity that often causes a misidentification of personal problems. Because they require that problem behaviors be concrete and easily observable, subtle and obscure difficulties can be overlooked. In fact, when what is troubling a person is hidden under a cloud of deception or secrecy, her overt problems may not be the ones that need to be addressed. If Freudians are correct, much of a person's sufferings are repressed and not readily observable unless special efforts are made to uncover them.

*Mental Illness*

A very different way of describing psychotherapy is as a pursuit of mental health. This strategy takes the medical aspects of therapy very seriously and either implies, or states, that people who come for psychotherapy are suffering from a physiological disorder that must be cured or controlled. Sometimes such disorders are portrayed in functional terms, but the underlying reference is to a disease entity that requires medical treatment.

If there actually are such diseases lurking beneath the complaints of therapy clients, then a medical goal is more than justified. On the other hand, if we are dealing with dysfunctional behavior patterns, a medical perspective is a dead end. What is involved here is not a matter of opinion, but of facts that in principle can be determined by empirical investigation. This volume, of course, is written in the belief that the evidence points toward role problems, not diseases—that the personal distress clients experience is the result of interpersonal behavior patterns gone wrong, not of genetic or cerebrochemical malfunctions.

*System Problems*

Many family and group therapists have taken to identifying the social systems in which their clients operate as being to blame for their problems. The goal of therapy for these therapists is the reorganization of these systems, thereby allowing their clients to lead more satisfying lives. Such an approach is dramatically different from behaviorism, in that it emphasizes the social rather than the individual. One might therefore presume that social role problems would be compatible with a system analysis, and they are; still, a systems perspective can ignore the psychological aspects of a psychosocial problem and can fail to notice the person as he attempts to negotiate his environment. This the social role does not do, for it clearly embraces both the person and those with whom he interacts.

*Problems in Living*

Critics of psychotherapy (notably Thomas Szasz) often try to demystify the process by describing its objective as the correction of "problems in living." Instead of an elusive personality or atomistic behaviors, they identify the commonplace personal difficulties we all experience as the proper focus of helping professionals. Yet straightforward and refreshing though this stance is, it does not do justice to the kinds of problems dealt with in psychotherapy. Besides being vague, the notion of a "problem in living" is not specifically social. The predicaments it might presumably include could be the discovery that one has a broken furnace on a cold winter's night or that there is a shortage of oranges at the supermarket when one is in a mood for citrus. While such circumstances are annoying and may even require the assistance of others in their resolution, they are not the sort of irritants typically addressed in therapy. Furthermore, even some social problems, such as those involving death, romance, or a snoring spouse, are not the sort for which psychotherapy was designed. They may be intractable and may benefit from interpersonal advice, but they do not require the kind of personal change that makes therapy unique.

## The Procedures of Change

It has been customary to define psychotherapy not only by its goals but by the procedures employed to effect those goals. Thus John Romano (1947) explained that therapy involves "the utilization of psychological measures in the treatment of sick people" while W. A. Neilson (1952) told us it is a "mental treatment . . . [involving] suggestion, psychoanalysis, or re-education" (cited in Reisman 1971:13). English and English (1958) related that "nearly always personal consultation is part of the technique, sometimes the whole of it" (p. 429), and the University of the State of New York (1961) called it "the use of verbal methods . . . [in] assisting . . . persons to modify attitudes and behavior" (cited in Reisman 1971:13).

Earlier Alfred Adler (1931) emphasized the relationship aspect of the procedure, noting that "psychotherapy is an exercise in cooperation." Jurgen Ruesch (1961), however, was impressed by the fact that psychotherapy is "a learning process," though he admitted that this learning requires involvement with other people. Donald Ford and Hugh Urban (1963) affirmed that it is "a procedure wherein two persons engage in a prolonged series of emotion-arousing interactions, mediated primarily by verbal exchanges, the purpose of which is to produce changes in behaviors" (p. 16). And L. Krasner (1963) described it "as a lawful influence process." Corsini (1989), in his even-handed way, sums this all up by noting that psychotherapists use "some method of treatment logically related to [their] theory . . . of [the] personality's origins, development, maintenance, and change" (p. 1).

Almost everyone seems to agree that psychotherapy involves an interpersonal relationship that is designed to help the client solve an identified problem. Usually this involves two people, the therapist and the client, but in the cases of group or family therapy there can be multiple clients and therapists. There is similar agreement about the need for communication within this relationship, but the characteristics of this communication remain at issue. Some emphasize the verbal aspects, while others believe behavioral and emotional manipulations are more important. In any event, the communication is supposed to encompass more than an exchange of information; it must create change.

We must credit Jerome Frank (1973) with our current awareness of the significance of persuasion and influence in psychotherapy. He defines therapy as "a circumscribed, more or less structured series of contacts between the healer and the sufferer, through which the healer . . . tries to produce certain [lasting] changes in the sufferer's emotional state, attitudes, and behavior" (p. 2). These changes, he explains, are the result of influence that moves primarily from the healer to the sufferer. Whether direct or indirect, whether cognitive, emotional, or behavioral, the therapist's activities are intended to persuade and to alter in an enduring manner. Because of this, factors such as the confidence of the client in the helper are apt to be more crucial in determining the extent of this influence than the rationale of the helper.

Although it is difficult to deny the ubiquity of influence processes in psychotherapy, some caveats must be offered. The first is that influence can easily spill over into coercion. What starts as persuasion can become an effort to enforce compliance. When this occurs, therapy departs. Coercively enforced behaviors rarely reduce suffering; rather, they tend to increase it. Nor are they likely to be long lasting, for coercion is resisted, if only covertly. The second caveat is that it is tantalizing to imagine influence as a one-way process. Frank specifically warns against this, but the fact is that persuasion is usually conceived of as traveling from one person to another. This, unfortunately, can be a recipe for coercion because it encourages a neglect of the subject's input.

Other practitioners have been impressed by the learning aspects of psychotherapy. They believe that clients are in distress because of things they have mislearned or failed to learn. Their prescription is to teach clients what they have missed. They believe that the changes that must be instilled result from an educational experience, not merely from persuasion.

While a learning paradigm does add a valuable element to the procedures that characterize psychotherapy, it is still incomplete and misleading. Thus, the kind of teaching suggested by learning theorists is different from the pedagogy that typically occurs within schools. It involves the acquisition of a "doing," not merely of a "knowing." Furthermore, the new behaviors that are acquired via therapy are constructed, in part, by the client, not merely appropriated from a teacher. A client puts far more of himself on the line during therapy than people do during normal educational experiences.

So far all of the processes proposed to define psychotherapy do seem relevant. Indeed, some seem essential. The difficulty is that they individually and collectively miss significant parts of the change process. In an attempt to define an enterprise as complex as psychotherapy, if the definition includes only segments of its mechanisms, it will be sterile. If it leaves out vital parts of the therapy elephant, then no matter how accurate its depiction of what it does describe, it will be of little value to those trying to implement it. Definitions of psychotherapy that are too short, and too precise, often err in being overly restrictive. Only a definition that accurately depicts the full complexity of the subject can really be useful.

In particular, most of the accepted definitions leave out social negotiations and the relinquishing of dysfunctional behavior patterns. No interpretation of psychotherapy can be adequate if it omits the fact that therapeutic change involves two interacting parties and the letting go of unsatisfying patterns of social behavior. A valid definition has to encompass the fact that new patterns develop not merely as a result of influence emanating from the therapist, but from a dialogue between the therapist and client; that is, therapy is not only a social learning experience, but a building process. Similarly, the change that occurs in therapy must be perceived not merely as an addition, but more importantly as a subtraction. Something is lost in therapy as well as gained.

### Counseling and Therapy

Before we leave the question of defining psychotherapy, it may be useful to clarify the distinction between counseling and therapy. C. H. Patterson (1986), in trying to tease out the differences between the two, concluded that the differences are often overblown. Patterson noted that one distinction commonly made "is that counseling applies to work with so-called normal individuals, whose problems are related to the development of their potential, while psychotherapy refers to work with individuals who are deficient in some respect." This, however, may be an artificial distinction. It attempts to differentiate degrees of seriousness on the basis of how close they approximate normality or "in terms of the nature of [the client's] problem . . . [where] . . . problems that are inherent in the personality of the individual ('unconscious' problems) are [considered] the province of psychotherapy." For Patterson, the bottom line is that "for practical or political reasons, . . . psychotherapy often refers to work with more seriously disturbed clients, usually in a medical setting," and he concluded that "there are no essential differences between counseling and psychotherapy in the nature of the relationship, in the process, in the methods or techniques, in the goals or outcomes, . . . or even in the kinds of clients involved" (pp. xvii–xix).

For our part, psychotherapy can be taken to refer to a frequently lengthy and intense form of treatment that deals with serious problems, albeit nonmedical ones. Although it is employed for conditions such as schizophrenia and manic-depression, even here it attempts to correct the psychosocial aspects of these disorders. Our starting point can be Freud's "talking cure." It denotes a form of interpersonal interaction in which a helper and helpee use primarily verbal exchanges to assist the helpee in overcoming some of the nonphysiological problems that are causing him distress. We thus recognize that the object of the exercise is to help a person increase his level of personal satisfaction and decrease those feelings and behaviors that cause him distress.

One necessary feature of such problems is that they are difficult to correct. A person's dysfunctional patterns of living must be such that they are hard to change, and hence that he finds himself in need of assistance in altering his life. I will suggest that this problem lies with the nature of social roles, and, specifically, that all basic, personal roles are difficult to change because they are subject to role conservation. If this observation is correct, the implication is that the problems dealt with in psychotherapy are challenging because role change is challenging. It further implies that such change is normally slow, and often traumatic, because the elements that hold roles in place are only modified with difficulty.

Therapists have often noted that they must work directly with a person's emotions. Most recognize that while the cognitive underpinnings of a client's problems are important, feelings usually become the central issue in therapy. I will further suggest that this is because emotions are the crucial mechanism in keeping social roles from changing. This means that psychotherapy can be identified, in part, by the degree of emotional turmoil it entails. It is serious, and personal, precisely because it hits people where they live, namely in their feelings.

To sum up, psychotherapy will be taken to refer to a largely verbal change technique that helps people overcome serious personal problems and that is often characterized by a lengthy, emotional period of behavioral adjustment. It is this process that needs to be explicated in its overall dimensions.

## A SOCIAL ROLE PERSPECTIVE

Though the correction of role problems has not often been recognized as the goal of psychotherapy as such, it has much to recommend it. The notion of role dysfunction goes a long way to explaining why people are in distress. Similarly, the normal mechanisms of role change can clarify why therapeutic procedures are effective. Many factors enter into making the concept of the "social role" attractive for understanding psychother- apy, not the least of which is its familiarity. "Roles" have been around for a long time, and have been found useful by both social science profession- als and laymen. Roles have an intuitive appeal that makes them more than a convenient analogy. Most people readily understand Shakespeare's assertion that

All the world's a stage,
And all the men and women merely players.

While the role concept is often treated as if it were frivolous, it deserves serious consideration. It offers a unique perspective that has developed in response to the special needs of sociology and social psychology. Because their subject matter is collective behavior, these disciplines have had to address issues psychotherapists historically have tended to discount, namely, the ways in which people interact with each other in groups both large and small. Roles are convenient for analyzing these interpersonal behaviors because they of necessity examine what is happening both between and within people.

Role theory has done a particularly good job at explaining the paradoxes of social coordination. By recognizing that there exists a division of labor in society, it has been able to inquire into the nature and development of this division. By asking who does what with whom, and why they choose to do it, it has been able to uncover explanatory patterns, and as importantly from the perspective of psychotherapy, to determine why such patterns go wrong and how they can be corrected. In order to explain group behavior, role theory must be Janus faced, simultaneously looking in opposite directions, contemplating both the person and the social structure surrounding the person. It is thus well suited to grappling with the problems of individuals participating in multiperson systems. As has been noted, roles are inherently psychosocial. They are always enacted by psychologically active performers in conjunction with complementarily active associates.

To put the matter technically, roles are complex patterns of interpersonal behavior enacted with other persons called "role partners." Together they breathe life into joint behavior patterns, thereby improving the chances of meeting their individual and joint needs. And people do have needs. These are basic to who we are and what we try to achieve. Among them are our craving for love and respect. If these are not fulfilled, life is bleak and passionless. Roles are essential because they are the central mechanism through which we implement such requirements. By providing the scaffolding for our interpersonal relationships, they allow us to work together toward urgent mutual aims. Since love and respect are only available interpersonally, they would forever be inaccessible without the linkages that roles permit.

Social roles seem so familiar because we encounter them everywhere. They accompany us all our lives and provide us with our sense of self. When asked who we are, most of us respond in terms that designate a social role. We say we are a "mother" or "father"; a "sister" or "brother"; a "husband" or "wife"; a "child" or "parent"; a "doctor," "lawyer," "worker," "artist," or "free spirit"; a "winner" or a "loser." These words illustrate the virtually endless panoply of patterns available. They tell us about the kinds of social tasks we perform, the social positions we hold, and the sorts of people we are. Moreover, such behavior patterns can be as impersonal as that of a "banker," or as basic and intimate as that of a "caretaker." Indeed, for every social task we can distinguish, there exists a corresponding behavior pattern that can be labeled a role. Basic, personal roles are especially significant in psychotherapy, for they are trans-situational behavior patterns (such as "the leader," "the martyr," and "the fat one"), which, like personality traits, can be activated in many diverse situations and which, because they are acquired early in life and pervade our most intimate associations, are closely identified with who we are.

When we enact roles, we do so with recurring partners, who cue us about what is expected by them and others. We in turn provide them with cues. These indicators form reciprocal chains of demands and responses that tie roles together. Rather as in a ping-pong match, we provide each other with the information and materials we need to perform our parts. Thus teachers need students in order to teach, and students need teachers in order to learn. Their respective roles only make sense in conjunction with one another. If a teacher tried to extemporize before an empty classroom, the results would be ludicrous, and would certainly not be teaching. Interactive patterns facilitate needs fulfillment because they enable people to do things together. Without students, not only are teachers unable to engage in teaching, but they are unable to gain the admiration and affection that doing their job well is supposed to bring.

To avoid the prospect of debilitating isolation, people must learn to collaborate in their role performances. Furthermore, when they embrace particular social roles, it is not merely because they have inherited them, but because they have collaborated in erecting them. Sociologists commonly describe roles as "negotiated products" (R. H. Turner, 1985), which are not just taught or learned, but constructed through the joint efforts of particular role partners. It is in the ordinary give and take of life that roles make their appearance. Fights about who will feed the baby, or take out the garbage, are the venue in which the details of being a "husband" or "wife" are worked out. Likewise, it is in conversations about the family budget, or about who will be promoted at work, that fundamental undertakings take shape. It is in these interactions that we as the parties agree or fail to agree about what we will or will not do, and it is in these interactions that we as individuals decide which interpersonal behavior patterns we will accept as our own and which we will reject.

To sum up, roles are mechanisms for accomplishing essential personal and interpersonal tasks. They are performative, in that they are a "doing," not just a "being." They are also transformational, in that we all have extensive repertoires we can play simultaneously or in sequence. By putting roles on or taking them off, we vary what we do and with whom we do it. Yet roles are not epiphenomena, standing somehow apart from our real selves. Basic, personal roles form the core of our identities and are not merely play acted. Indeed, roles that are learned early in life and underlie many divergent activities are essential to our self-understanding.

They are maintained with a tenacity that makes them almost impossible to relinquish, even if it is discovered that they fail to meet needs.

Moreover, roles have a coherence and spontaneity that give life meaning. They are purposeful patterns, with an inner logic embedded in role scripts. The specifics of any given role derive from a dialogue between a person's biological inheritance and his social environment, but the result of this interaction has an inner truth that resonates with the ordinary man, because he knows that it makes sense of his life. When such an important part of a person causes him difficulties, it becomes imperative to do something about it, even to seek help in making changes if that is necessary.

### Role Problems

If psychotherapy deals with role problems, it is essential to inquire into the nature of these problems. What is there that goes wrong with social roles and causes so much pain that people need help in overcoming it? Role problems are manifested at two significant junctures: (1) when people are trapped in painful roles that do not meet needs and (2) when they engage in unsuccessful attempts to replace these unfavorable roles. In other words, defective roles cause distress when they fail in their crucial task of satisfying individual needs, and they also cause suffering when people try to correct them and discover to their chagrin that the change process is itself disquieting.

Unsatisfying roles are usually imposed upon people in coercive role negotiations, often in their earliest socialization experiences. Since all roles are developed in collaboration with role partners, when these act unfairly, they have the potential for inaugurating flawed roles. Partners who are more powerful than an individual, and who are not concerned with his welfare, can enforce the adoption of behaviors that are not in his interest. The victim may protest, but will not have the strength to resist. During coercive negotiations, the partner's demands can be so compelling that they shape the victim's thoughts, feelings, and plans in directions that cause him to act in ways not satisfying to himself. These internalized patterns, which we are calling role scripts, perpetuate unhappiness even when the partner ceases his coercive demands.

Once unfavorable roles are set in train, distorted scripts prevent them from changing easily; that is, internal scripts dysfunctionally maintain the roles. Even in the cases of felicitous roles, role scripts are conservative. Their purpose is to stabilize behavior patterns by making them predictable and dependable. When, however, what is being perpetuated is onerous, these mechanisms become onerous. Role change is always difficult, but it is transformed into a therapeutic problem when it seriously impedes attempts at developing effective patterns of living. In sum, the pain of change, which even under ordinary circumstances is quite substantial, becomes unsupportable when it interferes with the development of the basic roles needed to promote happiness.

## Defective Roles

Role problems don't usually announce themselves as such. People are rarely transfixed in the middle of their day by the sudden realization that their unhappiness derives from coercively imposed roles that are being dysfunctionally maintained. Nor are they struck by an insight that their needs are not being met and that attempts at change are causing them further pain. Rather, what strikes them is that they are unhappy. They may have difficulty specifying the nature or derivation of this distress, but will be in little doubt that they are in its thrall.

Role problems can be experienced in many ways. One of these is through uncomfortable emotions. A person may be gripped by intense fear, torn by uncontrollable rage, or victimized by a deep depression or an obsessive guilt. Even frequent embarrassment or unrequited love can be difficult to bear. Such emotions seem to have a life of their own, and when they become potent they can head in dangerous directions. Intense fears intimate that they will end in death, and rages gone out of control portend murder. Extreme emotions are nothing to fool with, and so when they come unbidden or are unmanageable, they cause unease.

Another way in which role problems advertise themselves is in relationship problems. When a person is having irreconcilable conflicts with a spouse or friends, her discomfort may be palpable. Likewise, if she is feeling socially isolated or is having difficulty establishing intimacy, she may sense that something is very wrong. Similarly, child-rearing difficulties, frictions on the job, and discomfort with authority figures are experienced as problems. A person may find herself too assertive or not assertive enough, may be the victim of aggression or the aggressor herself, may be quietly resistive under the transgressions of others or loudly unhappy about their unfairness. In each of these cases, her relationships will not be on the smooth course she envisaged, and she will be dissatisfied.

Also, personal confusions are a powerful source of distress. Someone who is uncertain about his values or has difficulty in choosing a life direction may express these confusions in pessimism about the future or in feelings of weakness and inadequacy. Someone with a deep religious commitment may develop a pervasive sense of sin. In most cases, demoralization will occur and the confused person will feel that there is nothing he can do to control his destiny. For someone who is trapped in a defective role there often seems to be no way out, and his ineffectual struggles intensify his confusion. This cognizance of futility is disorienting, particularly when the person is exerting every effort to correct a problem.

Lastly, a person may realize she is trapped. She will not merely be confused by her lack of success but frustrated at its continuation. Such a person will know she is having difficulty changing her life because she will find herself repeating the same old mistakes. Perhaps she vowed she would never repeat the blunders of her parents, then discovers herself reprising them with her husband and children. This experience of being imprisoned within her own life can be devastating. Despite the energies brought to bear, she will feel powerless to effect changes and will thrash about looking for a way out of her dilemma.

The above may all be signs of being trapped in disabling roles, but we need further specifics. We have to see how particular stable, interpersonal behavior patterns can militate against a person's success in meeting needs. Love and respect, especially, are easily lost and difficult to replace. We human beings have other needs, such as for food, oxygen, and sex, but in contemporary society these seem less problematic. Few people are deprived of them if they don't want to be. Love and respect, however, are easily frustrated. Although most people desperately pursue them, they often meet with limited results. They want other people to care about them and/or treat them as important, but instead they must live with rejection and disparagement. It is the ache of this absence that makes so many roles unendurable.

Roles, we must also note, can go wrong in two ways. They can be aborted during the role negotiations that inaugurate them, or they can fail after a period of successful performance. With an aborted role, a person can struggle for a respected place in his family only to find that whatever he does is wrong. He may, for example, seek the role of "family hero," but find it denied him. In his frustration, he will then strike back at his role partners, who will seem to be his tormenters. When this fighting stabilizes into a persistent pattern, it can constitute the basis of a "rebel" role. Such a role will be evidence that another role has died aborning, for although it has a life of its own, it is generally not enacted for its own sake.

Thus when our person discovered that a hero role was impossible, his stymied role negotiations themselves came to epitomize his identity. He may even have clung to them for the attention they brought. Nevertheless, his rebel role was not a comfortable one. It arose in strife and was perpetuated by it. Should it continue for long periods, it must be at a terrible personal cost. To remain a rebel means that one's negativity makes it difficult for others ever to come close enough to give the love or respect one craves. It is a stop-gap defense, which may have saved the person as a child, but it is a painful salvation, for in maintaining it, he prolongs futile battles long after they should be over.

Failed roles are a little different. They start out providing more tangible satisfactions. One such role is that of the "family genius." The child who grows up being made to feel she is special because she is very bright may revel in the extra attention lavished on her. Yet if she does not have the intelligence attributed to her, she will be in for a rude awakening. As an adult she may anticipate automatic respect from her colleagues but find herself no longer lionized. When she discovers that this is because she isn't as smart as she had been led to believe, the realization may be shattering. Instead of her genius status being a source of gratification, it becomes a mortifying sign of failure, which has to be replaced by something more substantial if she is ever to recover her pride.

Some roles, of course, can both abort and fail; that is, they can both be inadequate when they develop and become less satisfying at a later point in life. An especially widespread example of this is the "caretaker" role. In this pattern a person, often but not always a woman, is enlisted to care for others. This becomes her primary responsibility, and she is virtually asked to parent her parents. Instead of pursuing her own need for love and respect, these are submerged in her zeal to protect others. Because their welfare is the focus of her attention, her own is badly neglected. This pattern will, however, provide some satisfactions, because performing it makes her important to these others.

When such a person becomes an adult, her tendency toward self-sacrifice may even make her an attractive role partner for self-centered people. Indeed, they will be prepared to take whatever she is willing to offer. But in perpetually giving, she loses more than ever. Because such a person may not be able to imagine herself as having any worth apart from her services, she zealously clings to her caretaker role, all the while feeling more trapped by it. Her role is thus partly aborted, because it limited her satisfactions in childhood, and partly failed, because these limitations intensify in adulthood.

Even roles that are ordinarily neutral—or positive—can abort or fail. One such is that of "poet." In a case of the author's acquaintance, a young girl grew up in very literary-minded surroundings. There was a great deal of unexpressed emotionality within her family, which had as one of its few outlets the poetry its members shared. For composing these, each member received abundant praise and acceptance. Indeed, both the girl and her older brother became accomplished poets, who as young adults used their writing as a source of solace.

However, when the brother's career suddenly fell apart and he committed suicide, the girl became distraught. She too had had difficulties at school, and hoped that her poetry would save her. Now she worried that if it could not rescue him, it might not work for her either. This led to an examination of what was happening in her life and to the realization that, satisfying though her poetry was, it could not substitute for the emotional communication that was absent from her relationships. She further realized that she would not even be allowed to make poetry a career, for this would make her too formidable a competitor to her mother, also a frustrated poet. Should she become successful, her mother might be forced to recognize her own failures and perhaps, like her son, kill herself. This the girl could not accept, and so she was miserably ambivalent. For her, the poet role was not neutral; it had aborted, in that it had always been a substitute for close relationships, and it had failed, because its limitations became increasingly evident as she pursued independence.

### The Pain of Change

Many people trapped by defective roles choose not to alter them, because deep within themselves they sense that the change process may be more traumatic than the unsatisfying role. Their problem lies not only with their unsatisfying behavior pattern, but in the dilemma of not being able to correct it without feeling worse. It is as if a pain barrier separates them from their goal of a fulfilling life. In response, they hold back and feel terrible for having done so.

As has been indicated, the process of replacing an unsatisfying role is inherently uncomfortable. The details of this process will be dealt with in the next chapter, but some indication of why it is so painful will be given here. The reasons can be classed under three headings. The first is the discomfort of reexperiencing a defective role; the second, the pain of actually letting go of it; and the third, the lingering misery when role change does not end successfully. A person hoping for a better life may be victimized by all three factors, each of which can be terribly distressing, and which in concert can be overwhelming.

As we shall soon discover, if a failed role is to be altered, it must first be reexperienced. But this often means calling into awareness circumstances and emotions that are exquisitely painful. One of the reasons few people recognize unfavorable roles as a precipitant of their unhappiness is that their pain was forcibly excluded from consciousness at its point of origin. When a person is trapped in a role he hates but can't change, not thinking about, or feeling, it can be the only respite. Consequently, reexperiencing it will not be recognized as an avenue of escape, but as a renewed invitation to pain. No wonder then that this aspect of change is problematic.

Once entered upon, a person will find that role change is like an intense mourning process. It, of necessity, includes the protests and sadness that are the hallmark of meaningful grief. Moreover, the sorrow and loss that accompany the relinquishing of an unsatisfying role are proportional to the significance of the failed role. The more that is at stake, the more painful is the letting go. Thus, the less love and respect a defective role provides, and the fewer alternatives to it a person perceives, the deeper and more profound his grief will be. Paradoxical as it may seem, the less one has, the more tightly one holds on and the more traumatic is the process of prying one's fingers loose.

But if one holds on, the lingering misery of the unsolved problem remains. Successfully resisting change only perpetuates a lower level of misery. One's unhappiness becomes like a low-grade fever that refuses to dissipate. It may be worrisome, but it will seem less dangerous than the critically high fever that one fears will end in death. One then chooses to remain a long-term invalid, interminably hovering somewhere between a promising new life and the dreadful old one.

## The Role Change Paradigm

Role change is a process unto itself. It is the mechanism through which people relinquish defective roles and move on to more satisfying ones. It encapsulates the essence of therapy and epitomizes what most psychotherapies have in common. When a clinician offers to help solve someone's personal problems, what is being tendered is the facilitation of role change. Whatever the explicit rationale for the intervention, role change is its actual destination.

Some behavioral scientists have imagined that role change is a simpler process than it actually is. They have conceived of it as "role transfer," that is, as involving merely a switch in allegiance from one role to another. If this were possible for basic roles, it would mean that all one would have to do to correct them would be to recognize their deficiencies. One could then consciously adopt an improved role and be done with it. But this hardly ever happens. Caretakers tend to remain caretakers, and rebels stay rebels. If we merely explain things to them, the explanations usually fall on deaf ears and leave us would-be helpers feeling betrayed by a client who seeks advice, then fails to heed it. This tendency to obdurately continue in an unproductive path has given people with role problems a bad name. So far do they resist role transfer that they frequently appear crazy. Their persistence in painful behaviors seems to make no sense at all.

Such behaviors would, of course, be senseless if role transfer worked as advertised. But the fact that it doesn't has led other observers to postulate a change process based upon external sanctions. In their view, roles are created and maintained by the reinforcements imposed by role partners. What these others choose to reward or punish determines what a person will do. Thus, if someone is trapped in an unfavorable role, all she needs to do is change her socially determined reinforcement schedule. Current role partners must be induced to alter their sanctions or be replaced with others who will. The person will then respond to this refashioned environment and begin living a different life.

While there is a great deal of truth to this hypothesis, and it is an improvement over the role transfer idea, it does not go far enough. People certainly are responsive to the demands of role partners, and if these are acting unfairly, persuading them to change their ways can be salutary. Nevertheless, even when different social demands are made, caretakers tend to continue in the role of caretaker. The only plausible explanation of this circumstance is that they are responding to motives originating within themselves. Their role partners' demands may be an aspect of their external role scripts, but apparently they also have internal scripts. Indeed, a person's own thoughts, feelings, and plans provide a mechanism for perpetuating roles, and these too must be modified before dysfunctional role behavior can change.

The technical term for role change is "resocialization." This concept extends well beyond that of socialization. "Socialization" refers to the process through which social roles are initiated. It includes the various negotiations and learning processes that are necessary to convert potentially social creatures into socially integrated human beings. Resocialization is a method of correcting socialization gone wrong. It entails not merely new socialization, but rectification of previous errors. More than reeducation is involved; the relinquishing of that which has failed and the constructing of a more worthy replacement must also occur.

If unsatisfying social roles are allowed to remain intact, and are not replaced by superior ones, they tend to remain operative. When least expected and least desired, they intrude into a person's life and sabotage his efforts. Merely covering over a bad role with a better one does not solve this problem. The newer role will not completely supplant the older one merely because it is superior. Long-established patterns of behavior are on automatic pilot; they swing into action when the right environmental buttons are pushed despite a person's conscious desire not to follow them. Thus, a caretaker may vow to be more assertive and less unselfish, but when a role partner says she is being unfair, she will be assailed by an internal guilt that forces her to be ingratiating. When her groveling is pointed out, she will probably hate it and renew her vow to be a changed person, but when another person pricks her guilt, she will respond as usual. As long as her caretaker role is not expunged, or at least drastically modified, it will lurk just beneath the surface ready to be exploited by the unscrupulous. Unless it is deactivated by a role change process, it is a land mine ready to go off whenever it is jostled.

# 2

# *The Role Change Process*

## LEVELS OF INTERVENTION

When people seek the services of helping professionals, they do not always desire, or need, psychotherapy. Some of the difficulties from which they suffer are not caused by role problems, and even role problems are not always best handled by the radical techniques implied by psychotherapy. Sometimes less dramatic interventions are more appropriate. It must be recognized that there exist different levels of potential intervention, of which psychotherapy is but one.

Some of the problems people face are, in fact, medical. Mental illness is no myth. Conditions such as schizophrenia and the bipolar disorders have physiological precursors that typically require medical intervention. Pharmacotherapy, which controls hallucinations and/or mania, is often essential. Trying to replace it with exclusively psychotherapeutic treatments would be misguided. Although talk therapies can correct the role problems that develop in consequence of a mental illness, they have little impact on genetic vulnerabilities or neurotransmitter imbalances. It would thus be as much of an error to conclude that role problems account for all of a mentally ill person's difficulties as to assume that the totality of his distress is caused by physiological illness.

Moreover, other personal problems, while not physiological, are still not role related. Many people suffer from environmental difficulties. Simple misfortune—being in the wrong place at the wrong time—can make life a trial. Take the challenge of poverty. Children who are born into poor families must cope with all of the disabilities attendant upon being poor. Through no fault of their own, their parents, despite the best of intentions, do not have the funds to dress or feed them in ways that avoid the ridicule of school friends. This sort of discrimination may be utterly unfair, but it does happen. Similarly, a person can lose his job because his company has gone bankrupt, fail to receive a promotion because his boss dislikes him, or see his house destroyed because a hurricane has blown it away. All of these circumstances are extremely painful, but he cannot solve them by changing his role structure. The kinds of assistance they will respond to will involve finding another job, being promoted, or obtaining financing for a new home.

When role problems are implicated, there will still be a question of the appropriate level of intervention. How much change does one need to sponsor in order to resolve a specific problem? To what degree does a failed or aborted role have to be replaced or modified? Can a person survive with his bad role intact, or must he learn a new one? And must he relinquish his old role before the new one can be established? What about the amount of help necessary? Can a person help himself, or must someone else—a professional, for instance—take an active part in effecting change?

The degree of change required can provide a rough guide to the depth of a particular intervention, and hence to the amount of help appropriate. On the least deep level are *supportive services* that enable a person to keep going with relatively few changes in himself or his life-style. Next come those interventions that assist someone in constructing new roles without regard to the malignant ones that may be lurking beneath the surface. These are characterized by *socialization*, that is, by a process of acquiring new roles. Last, and deepest, is *resocialization*. This involves letting go of defective roles and entails the greatest journey into a person's soul. It is the level of true psychotherapy. Which of these levels is most suitable to a person's particular situation depends upon the nature of his problem, his personal and social resources, and his individual aspirations. Typically, the more significant and role related a problem, the deeper will be the desirable level; but the deeper the level, the more resources and commitment will be necessary for success.

## Social Support

Supportive interventions are most appropriate for environmental problems and for self-help. They are best suited to persons with the least ability or desire to undergo profound change. When misfortune has afflicted someone, she may simply need assistance in locating a job or in finding a place to live. If she is destitute, she may require food stamps or cash. These are real and palpable forms of assistance that bring relief from tangible difficulties. If her problem is that she is being mistreated by others, she may need physical or emotional protection. Battered wives do benefit from safe houses and court orders of protection. They also benefit from efforts at mediation that persuade abusers to desist. By acting as an advocate for such a person, perhaps by convincing a coercive role partner that fairness is in his interest, a helper can provide a real service.

Often a helper will not supply a tangible good, but merely enable a person to help herself. Facing the slings and arrows of outrageous fortune can be a harrowing experience, which an ally can make less distressing. It is frightening to realize that the world can be a heartless place in which some people derive benefit at the expense of others, and that one may not have the power to protect oneself. Fear of the unknown, or of the uncontrollably evil, lowers a person's efficiency and makes it less possible to organize a defense. At such moments there mere presence of a benign other can lift the spirits and allow one to persevere. Being with someone who has one's interests at heart, and who is not afraid, is a wonderful tonic. The helper's courage will be contagious and can give a person the strength to endure. Often the secret to surviving adversity is having the bravery to carry on.

Self-help is nothing to be sneered at. We must all engage in it from time to time. Supportive interventions that foster it are therefore by no means barren. True, the courage to survive ultimately comes from the client himself, but this does not imply that a helper furnishes nothing of value. People in distress are often difficult to care about: their pain is genuinely painful to others. This means that remaining by their side as a beneficent presence takes commitment and strength. Sadly, this is a service that the normal world rarely provides.

A last form of supportive intervention is so-called "covering" therapy. In this, the therapist's aim is not to help a person fathom the nature of his problems or to surmount them. Instead, the goal is to make these less conscious and to encourage the person simply to live with them. Often a psychiatric patient will be so fragile that asking him to experience failed roles triggers decompensation. His defenses are so weak that if he is encouraged to relive his fears, his physiologically based symptoms will be activated. For such a person (often a schizophrenic), the object is to reduce felt emotion. This can be accomplished by lessening the provocations to emotion, for example, by eliminating the experience of a dysfunctional role. Such a person may be asked to live with his problems by pretending they don't exist. In a sense, he is urged to run away from them.

Common wisdom has it that running away is always bad, but for some persons it may be the best that can be hoped. Thus, when a therapist diverts such a client's attention, he may actually be helping him to survive.

Supportive therapies protect those in pain, help them problem-solve, and permit them to cope. Role alteration is not their object; the amelioration of distress is. Therapists who apply these usually content themselves with limited ambitions, but can often take comfort in achieving the best possible results under difficult circumstances.

## Socialization

Supportive services rarely help someone develop satisfying new social roles unless the person implements them himself. The assumption is that such roles are not necessary or are beyond the competence of the subject. As a consequence, many clinicians find being supportive a frustrating enterprise. They believe they discern what is missing in their clients' lives and wish to supply it, but are forced by the situation to hold back. In many ways their position is comparable to that of the parent who wants to ease the path of his offspring, but must restrain himself while his child makes his own discoveries. Since there are many role skills therapy clients have not acquired, clinicians are often tempted to pursue socialization efforts that teach these.

No one emerges from childhood as a completed entity. All of us must develop new roles as adults or, at the very least, modify existing roles so we can meet our adult responsibilities. A process of maturation takes place during which we assume the statuses of "adult," "spouse," "parent," and "employee." Even such personal roles as "caretaker" and "tough guy" must undergo a metamorphosis if they are to preserve utility. Caretakers, for instance, must learn who to take care of and what amount of care they can provide without forfeiting their own interests. In the process of constructing, or reconstructing, roles, we craft fresh skills so that we can perform necessary tasks. It is here that socialization becomes significant, for it is our central mode of skill acquisition.

Although socialization is often confused with education, the two can readily be distinguished. In its classical manifestation, education is concerned primarily with cognitive learning. It is this stress on the accumulation of facts that for many centuries led to the identification of schooling with rote learning. Socialization, however, requires emotional and volitional learning as well. This means that it is not a passive process. The person developing role skills must be emotionally involved and must actively plan his new behavior patterns. Elements such as value commitments must be acquired, and this is not accomplished through a simple act of memorization. When therapists act as socialization agents, they usually have in mind the imparting of such skills as relaxation techniques, effective parenting, and appropriate assertiveness.

Parenting is clearly a role-related skill; it involves the relationship between a parent and child and structures this interaction. Many parents are troubled about how to parent. When frictions develop with their children, they become distressed. If Mary doesn't mind or Johnny becomes too fractious, the parents get frazzled. It is not uncommon for them to overreact and impose discipline in ways they themselves don't approve. Whether they resort to abuse or overpermissiveness, they may then recognize that something has gone wrong and seek help in correcting it.

Clinicians who accept this challenge try to impart new parenting competencies. But these will not be taught as facts. The essence of most therapeutic interventions, no matter what their level, is that they are personalized. In a classroom setting it is virtually impossible to be responsive to each student. Because there is not enough time for every question to be asked or answered, it is impossible for the teacher to be relevant to the needs of all. In contrast, during ordinary clinical encounters, the helper does cultivate a one-on-one relationship with the helpee. Her services can thus be tailored to the individual case. More specifically, they can be part of a socialization intervention designed to fill in the gaps of the role the client may be in the process of constructing. Information, if delivered only in the form of general cognitive facts, fails at this because it does not connect the client's intellect with his evolving behavior patterns. He may learn the "what" of his situation but not the "how" of it. Rather, it is through the one-on-one answer to the particular question that facts become relevant to the individual role performance.

Furthermore, in a personalized learning situation there is more emotional involvement. Because of the close relationship of the therapist and client, the latter is stimulated to participate. He will care more about what he is learning because his feelings are engaged. Moreover, these lessons are more likely to stick, because it is emotions that hold important lessons in place. When the emotions are stimulated, they increase the probability that facts will be remembered and applied.

Lessons in parenting skills, it is instructive to note, can be particularly far-reaching. They are not merely lessons about a "doing" but on the negotiation of that doing. The frictions between parents and children often develop around the coordination of their role repertoires. The protagonists literally dispute who will walk the dog or how late a date can last. When these issues are successfully resolved, they help the child learn how to be a child and the parent how to be a parent. Techniques for setting limits or making compromises are no more than methods of negotiating fairly. Yet they are so essential that when absent, they must be taught. Thus, clinicians who teach parenting skills actually impart mechanisms for the development of roles.

Other therapist-imparted skills are also role related. This is easy to recognize in the case of assertiveness, which also deals with role negotiations. As will be explained shortly, fair role negotiations depend upon role partners who firmly but flexibly assert their desires. Clients in need of assertiveness training typically are too aggressive or passive to implement this. Either they are overly intense in their demands or they make them so quietly that they are barely heard. To counter this tendency, they must be taught to stand up for themselves in a manner that is likely to elicit a sympathetic hearing. If a clinician succeeds in this, the client is positioned to be a more effective role negotiator. The therapist thus indirectly helps the client solve her role problems by teaching her to participate more effectively in her own socialization.

### Resocialization

Resocialization, as I have already pointed out, involves the most profound sort of role change. It goes beyond social support or socialization, but usually incorporates aspects of both. Because role change is traumatic, a therapist must at least provide the same kind of encouragement as does the supportive clinician. And because a role changer usually lacks many skills, these too must be taught, especially role negotiation skills.

Since resocialization involves modifying and/or replacing dysfunctional roles, not merely covering them over or sidestepping them, it must reach far back into a person's past and deep down into his emotional being. As the most penetrating and profound form of therapeutic intervention, it delves into the blackest of a person's secrets and most urgent of his hopes. While social support and socialization may bypass awkward aspects of life, resocialization can afford to ignore none of these. Any truths it disregards may prevent change from unfolding. Indeed, it is usual for the more uncomfortable factors in a person's life to be the ones that most interfere with role replacement.

Resocialization is frequently the level of intervention last sought by clients because it is the most difficult. The more disturbing someone's role problem, the more likely he is to balk at confronting it. Since the pain of role change is real and unsettling, it can seem both interminable and unbearable to the one who must endure it. It is for this very reason that resocialization requires the kind of professional treatment associated with psychotherapy.

## THE RESOCIALIZATION PROCESS

The resocialization process follows a typical course. It is therefore startling that its true nature has rarely been discerned. The mechanisms of role change are so extended through time, and so transfixing in their particulars, that they are rarely recognized as part of a unitary process. More likely, they are perceived as distinct phenomena, much as the blind men of the parable perceived the elephant respectively as a snake, a tree trunk, or a piece of rope.

Yet resocialization is unitary. Before a defective role can be discarded, several things must happen, and happen in sequence. (1) The dysfunctional role must be reexperienced. Unless it is reactivated it is not accessible to change. (2) It must be relinquished. The person in its thrall must loosen his own grasp on it by undergoing a period of mourning. (3) New roles must be negotiated. Without the construction of more satisfying behavioral patterns, the letting go of what has been lost will have been in vain. (See Figure 2.1.)

The more basic a person's dysfunctional roles, the more he will be

**Figure 2.1**
**The Resocialization Process**

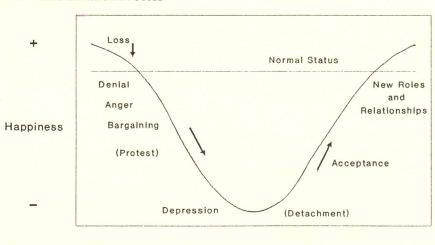

dependent upon them to meet his needs, the more unsatisfying will be his life, and the more difficult it will be for him to change. This is true despite the fact that role alteration is natural. Its apparatus was not invented by psychotherapists; the machinery for reexperiencing, relinquishing, and renegotiating roles is standard human equipment. Indeed, as people mature, they typically modify their roles through role change techniques. These, however, are usually not noticed because nothing dazzling signals their implementation. In most cases, resocialization is effected with the help of family and friends in the normal course of living and so seems unremarkable. When it works, we call it growing up; when it doesn't, we call it childishness.

But if resocialization is natural, why must professionals specialize in facilitating it? The answer seems to be that it is also capable of going awry. When it is interrupted, it often needs external help in resuming. This is comparable to what happens when an athlete goes into a slump. Hitting a baseball or throwing a strike may occur unremarked most of the time, but when something goes wrong, the person trying to rectify the situation may make it worse. Instead of allowing her normal physiological mechanisms to unfold, she may consciously try to control the bat or ball and wind up striking out or throwing the ball into the dirt. At this point a coach may have to intervene to prevent an even poorer performance. This external helper may try to reteach hitting or pitching, but will more probably be concerned with removing the mental block that disrupts the normal execution of the activity. In the fairly simple case of athletic performance, merely restoring a player's confidence, or helping her relax, can accomplish this goal. In the case of seriously disturbed roles, however, reinstating natural processes takes more doing.

Normally resocialization involves the commonplace human reactions to loss. It must be recognized that failed and aborted roles are indeed "lost" roles. This is because it is through roles that we maintain relationships with others, and it is through these relationships that we meet our deepest needs. When a role doesn't function properly, the relationships it sustains are disrupted, and the victim experiences profound dissatisfaction. This dissatisfaction marks a loss, that is, a relationship sought but ruptured.

When a person dies, those who care about him become desperately unhappy. They have lost much more than a physical entity; they have also been deprived of all those interactions with him upon which they have come to depend. It was in these interactions that the deceased person met their needs. One might almost say that when he died, he forcibly stripped his role partners of the roles they shared. Thus, when her husband dies, a woman loses her role as wife. And when a parent dies, the child becomes an orphan. Since roles can only be performed with role partners, the termination of an alliance leaves the survivor with interpersonal behavior patterns that have no outlet and no way of eventuating in satisfaction.

The case is similar with failed and aborted roles. When a role pattern ceases to be satisfying, or never has been satisfying, it is as if something has been torn out of a person's life. We human beings are not indifferent regarding the construction of viable roles. To the degree that we covet love and respect, we fight for satisfying relationships. So when role partners deny us this possibility, we lose. We have tried and been defeated. Something has been taken from us as surely as if by death. Still, though we see that a mini-death occurs when a job is lost or a marriage ends, we fail to notice that being trapped in a role such as that of "caretaker" has equivalent effects. Yet it too ensures that a part of one's life will be missing. The same is true of the roles of rebel, scapegoat, and family mascot.

Much of the loss engendered by defective roles is initiated by coercive role negotiations. A role partner who forces a person to act against her own interests, strips her of something she is desperately seeking. Normally, a person will struggle to meet vital needs, but when a more powerful adversary prevents this, she will have to find other ways to accommodate; she will have to find a way to live with her loss. Paradoxically, this may be accomplished by embracing it, and because of the existence of role maintenance mechanisms, she may continue to force herself to live in unsatisfying ways. Her loss then becomes endemic and drifts into a perpetual misery, as if a personal death is constantly being repeated.

In the ordinary event of loss by death, a person must retreat into a meaningful sadness before the deceased person can be relinquished and commonplace living resumed. It is as if he has to break the bonds with the departed before he can start forging new ones with others. With disrupted roles, the same phenomenon is encountered. Roles that don't work, or never have worked, must be given up. If they are hopeless, the person must renounce trying to make them work and accept the fact that they are dead. When this is realized there will be a sadness, in most respects identical with that of ordinary mourning. Although there may be no wake and no corpse, there will be a protracted funeral dirge. Once a role loss has sunk in, the agony of what is lost feels every bit as draining as when a role partner has died.

There is one important difference, however. When someone dies, the body cannot be denied, at least for long. When a role dies, however, there is no body and one cannot be sure there has been a death. The fact that the resocialization process has long remained unrecognized is as eloquent proof as one might wish of how difficult it is to perceive a role loss as loss. It often takes a special effort to identify what is no longer available and to realize that it must be replaced.

### Reexperiencing/Identifying

Role change begins with reexperiencing a defective role. Unless an unsatisfying role is emotionally accessible, it is not available for modification. A role that is suppressed, or only known about intellectually, is capable of causing painful disruptions in a person's life but not of being corrected. Because it is emotions that keep roles from changing easily, these must be available to experience so that they can be altered. If they are not, they will prevent change, despite the most ardent wishes of a therapist or client.

Still, an intellectual understanding of a person's role problems is not without merit. It is usually valuable for a clinician to identify the kind of defective role a person has, so the person can know what needs to be changed. Recognizing that someone is a "caretaker" makes it plain why he is unhappy. It also shows how the person's behavior patterns and relationships must change before they will be capable of satisfaction. A role does not have to be labeled as such, but its general outlines must be apprehended. For once it is identified, the helper can begin directing the client toward what needs to be accomplished.

From a role changer's perspective, reexperiencing a role can be disorienting. The role is a part of her life, not a cognitive lesson. This means that it will probably be experienced discontinuously and incompletely. The experience will not be of a whole role, but of some aspects of it, that is, of particular elements of her role scripts. It will include various emotional reactions to her role partners past and present, including her therapist, as well as cognitive and volitional reactions, some of which are integrated into her role understandings and some of which are not. She may even find herself in active relationships that recapitulate the social demands that existed when her defective role emerged. Should such an affiliation not be present, she may nevertheless imagine that archaic demands are still being made and may react accordingly.

Let us take the case of a caretaker. It is unlikely that someone who is beginning the resocialization enterprise will realize he is a caretaker, much less allow himself to experience the role. He will be in the act of sacrificing himself to caring for others and enduring the unhappiness of not having his needs met, but will not make the connections between these circumstances. In particular, he will not experience the distress as caused by a role problem. He may feel guilty when others accuse him of not caring sufficiently for them, but this will be an isolated feeling not associated with his loneliness or emptiness. He may even feel numb, without having any awareness of guilt or of anger at being cheated.

Since a person's role is fully reexperienced only when it comes back in all its salient aspects, he will have to sense that he is sacrificing himself for the good of others; will need to understand how his guilt drives him to do this; will have to get in touch with his anger at being treated unfairly; and will need to be engulfed by sadness at not having been able to change things. He may even need to experience feelings like shame and unrequited love. At the same time, it will be necessary to have a cognitive understanding of the intellectual convictions that have helped trap him. He may, for example, come to realize that he has mistakenly believed himself unlovable. To him, this may seem a fact of nature, unfair to be sure, but a fact nevertheless. He may likewise come to recognize that he believes there is uncommon merit in giving to others, that this indeed has become a central value of his life.

Reexperiencing a defective role in the presence of appropriate role partners has a special significance, because recapitulating the kind of relationship in which a role developed can stimulate the emotions, volitions and cognitions that help sustain it. When one is paired with someone who demands caretaking behaviors, one's old guilt, self-deprecation, and desire to please all come flooding back. Freud, in observing this phenomenon, described his clients as exhibiting a "repetition compulsion." Indeed, such a compulsion would seem to be an essential component of the reexperiencing phase of resocialization. Its purpose is apparently to motivate the reenactment of failed roles in all their salient particulars, so that they become available for change. If a dysfunctional role can be made to feel real, it can then be reworked.

Should current role partners not cooperate in reenacting painful roles, a client can recruit her therapist for this purpose. Again we can cite a Freudian concept, "transference," as the model for this strategy. In this maneuver a person acts as if the present partner, typically the therapist, is making demands similar to those of previous partners. Thus, a caretaker may engage in caring for her therapist, in part because she imagines him to require such care.

The clinician can facilitate the reexperiencing of a past role by sharpening his client's awareness of her reaction. First, of course, the clinician must understand what is happening. This can be accomplished by observing and exploring his client's current behaviors and perceptions and by making inquiries into her past and present relationships, with particular emphasis on problem areas. Because the clinician is also a person and has inevitably had role problems of his own, he can use his self-understanding to delve into his client's experience. As a role player, he can engage in role taking and imagine himself in her shoes. Moreover, since emotions are of special import, he can exploit his status as a feeling being to empathize with her situation.

Once a meaningful understanding of a client's role has developed, it can be shared with the client in the hope that this will spark a reexperiencing of the role. The therapist, as it were, holds the role in front of the client's nose and hopes it will be smelled as well as seen. She may explain the role, but more probably will have to dramatize it. This will bring it to the client's attention in ways that make it more discernible to him. Dramatization might entail a technique such as role playing past or present relationships, or it might take a more subtle form, such as storytelling. Once a client does begin to reexperience his role, his perceptions of it must be validated. What he feels and believes must be acknowledged, so that he can make the experience his own. It is often only when an experience is reflected back to a person that it acquires substance, that he feels he can control and manipulate it.

### Relinquishing

After a role returns to experience, it becomes available for change. It is during this second stage of resocialization that a defective role is actually relinquished. The relinquishing of past attachments is the aspect of resocialization that most distinguishes it from social support or socialization, and is characterized by protest and grief over what has been lost. As has previously been stated, this letting go is a natural phenomenon, which does not on that account always proceed smoothly. A loss can be so profound that the process of letting go is suspended. Instead of producing a sadness that breaks a person's bonds with her past, she is trapped in a nether land of unresolved issues. Thus, one of the primary functions of a psychotherapist is to help remove the barriers that interfere with change and to set natural processes of mourning in train. (See Figure 2.2.)

Normal mourning has been effectively depicted by Elisabeth Kübler-Ross (1969). Her model of grief has several distinct stages, which may overlap or be partially eliminated, but which follow a typical sequence and, when consummated, have a typical outcome. When a person experiences a significant loss, she may first enter denial. She may simply refuse to acknowledge that a loss has occurred. Next, there will be anger at having been deprived of so important an attachment. If this doesn't reverse the

**Figure 2.2**
**Impediments to Change**

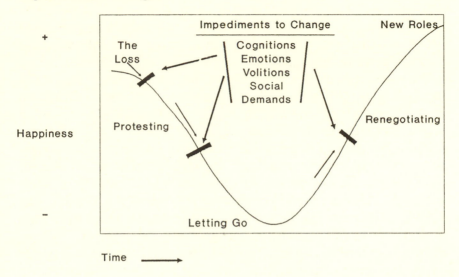

loss, she may engage in bargaining. At this point she may attempt to communicate with God, or the lost person, and try to make a deal that wipes the slate clean. These three reactions have been usefully grouped together by John Bowlby (1969, 1973, 1980) as the "protest" phase of detachment. Together they form the part of the grieving process during which a person fights against letting go. Though absolutely essential, if this protest is too vigorous, the rest of the process may never unfold.

When it is a role that has been lost, interminable protest is a frequent predicament. Because people hate being recruited into such roles as those of caretaker or scapegoat, they can be seduced into resisting them in ways that in fact make the roles more persistent. Though they have no intention of acquiescing, or of accepting the fact that these roles cannot be rectified, their attempts at self-rescue have precisely this effect. In particular, when a coercive role negotiation forces a person to be a caretaker, she does not voluntarily embrace supine submission, but tries to institute a fight against the perceived injustice. The victim genuinely wants her role partners to stop being coercive and to agree to undo the bargain. Typically, she is unwilling to concede defeat and is prepared to battle indefinitely. Yet fighting too vigorously can have tragic and paradoxical results. A determination to correct a problem can wind up perpetuating it, because it induces the person to remain engaged in a dialogue with her powerful, coercive partner. Instead of moving on to more fertile pastures, she remains in a situation where defeat is unavoidable. In short, she is trapped in a lost cause without realizing it.

The protest phase of resocialization is often the scene where such battles are recapitulated. Rather than recognize that a defective role can never work and gradually relinquish it through mourning, the person attempts to resuscitate it and make it more satisfying. Old, shopworn bargaining strategies are given renewed credibility, and letting go never begins. Since dysfunctional roles do not have the tangibility of dead bodies, it is fairly easy to deny there has been a death and to try to breathe life into the corpse.

To the person trapped in a dysfunctional role, the normal denial, anger, and bargaining inherent in the grieving process seem tailor made for rectifying the lost role. When one does not yet recognize that a loss is irreversible, it is easy to pretend that a bad role really isn't so bad, or that a newly rehabilitated role partner will now help make it better. Frustration at having lost and desperation to meet vital needs obscure what is happening and give the person the impetus to keep resisting change. She may thus try to break down walls or to cajole the devil, all without acknowledging the hopelessness of her quest.

The blockages that occur during the protest phase of mourning are fueled primarily by the emotions. Intense fear, anger, sadness, guilt, shame, and love are the engines that keep ineffective protest going. Terror of a coercive role partner persuades a person to pretend that the other has never really made unfair demands; fear of losing everything makes her determined to hang onto what she has; and anger at betrayal and abuse encourages her to be adamant in seeking restitution. If she is harboring a profound sadness, she can submerge it in an exercise regime designed to forestall the full-blown depression she fears will be tantamount to death. If she is wracked by guilt, she can force herself to continue placating others. If she is ashamed of her inadequacies, she can hide them and let the others have their way. And pursuit of an unrequited love can induce her to sacrifice her own happiness on behalf of the loved one.

These various unresolved emotional reactions perpetuate protest by reinforcing a person's efforts to deny her loss, to exact vengeance, or to seduce role partners into reversing history. Intense emotions interfere with a person's ability to think clearly, to recognize her dilemma, or to plan for the future. Thus, if an ineffectual protest is to be discontinued, these emotions will have to be disarmed or removed.

Barrier emotions can only be disarmed by lowering their intensity and helping them achieve their objectives. Emotions are not epiphenomena that decorate human lives; they have very real purposes. They are essential to our physical and social well-being because they make things happen. Their purpose is to inform us, and our role partners, about important facts and to provide us, and our role partners, with the motivation to react appropriately. Fear, for example, warns us, and those with whom we are in contact, of significant dangers, and it motivates us to neutralize or avoid these hazards. Similarly, anger helps overcome social frustrations, guilt prevents us from doing things others find objectionable, shame directs us to provide a good example for others, love reinforces our attachments to particular others, and sadness, of course, helps us relinquish lost objects. When these emotions have been properly socialized, and when they are not too intense, they function fairly well in bringing about such conditions. But when they have been learned in coercive relationships, they ordinarily become extremely intense and complicate, rather than ameliorate, our situation.

Take intense fear, for example. It can induce a person to misperceive her world and/or to run in panic from a danger she ought to face. Likewise, anger, when it escalates into uncontrollable rage, can run amok and do damage to others instead of persuading them to cooperate. If fear and anger are to eliminate danger and frustration, they must be tamed and deployed effectively. When they are, when the dangers and frustrations that precipitated them are dispelled, they subside and no longer have the energy to block the mourning process intrinsic to resocialization.

How then are intense emotions to be pacified? How can anger, fear, or guilt be managed so that they no longer fuel irrational protest? There are, in fact, several steps a person can take to accomplish this, and they are often incorporated within psychotherapy precisely because they interdict problem emotions. These steps are (1) finding a safe place, in which the intense emotion cannot cause damage; (2) incrementally developing a tolerance to it; (3) reevaluating the emotion to determine its real message and realistic goals; and (4) using the energy of the emotion to achieve these goals or, if necessary, change them. Stated in this way, these steps sound simple, though in practice they can be very difficult to realize. Incremental development of tolerance, for instance, may require a lengthy period of desensitization. Still, emotions can be tamed, and when they are, mourning can proceed.

Other barriers, however, can also impede progress. Cognitive, volitional, and social factors each independently block change. These other components of a person's role scripts also prolong the protest phase of grief by persuading a person not to let go. Mistaken understandings about himself or the world can, for instance, make it seem that change is impossible and discourage him from even trying, while wrong-headed values can induce him to decide that unsatisfying behavior patterns actually have the potential to be satisfying. Similarly, unfair role partners can persuade him not to relinquish a failed role on the grounds that it really is in his interest. Fortunately, just as with the emotional barriers, these obstacles too can be dismantled. Rational disputation can convince someone that he is not too weak to endure the rigors of role change, while moral instruction can demonstrate that caretaking is not the only way to be a good or happy person. Also, social mediation can intervene in destructive relationships and protect a person from exploitive role partners.

Once protests against role loss are worked through, they can at last eventuate in depression. This is the fourth stage in Kübler-Ross's model of grief. When a person has stopped resisting a loss, she is free to recognize that it is irreversible and can become appropriately sad at its passing. If, however, this recognition does not occur, sadness may still be present, but in a lower-level, more persistent guise.

When one enters depression full-on, one discovers that it must be handled carefully, for if it is not, it too can miscarry and frustrate change. A sadness that is too profound can have fatal consequences. Few people have the strength to endure the despondency that results from catastrophic loss. Attempting to do so can end in the cutting off of all ties to life, not merely those with the lost role. When sadness is extreme, it takes time to work through. In the case of uncomplicated bereavement, this will generally be at least a year. In that of divorce, periods of up to three years are not uncommon. For significant role loss, the duration required can be longer. It therefore behooves a role changer to allow the necessary space for adjustment. If rushed, the process will in fact be slowed.

Because of the time involved, the depression inherent in role change is usually marked by a series of low points, not by one grand splash of misery. Though these troughs can be predicted, they cannot be preprogrammed and must be allowed to unfold on their own schedule. The person engulfed by sadness may find that he needs both support and distance. Sometimes the presence of an accepting other will make his depression less frightening and allow him to cope. At other times he may need to be left alone so that he can think things through and let go of them in sequence. If both of these needs are respected, the role changer will eventually get beyond the defective role. Instead of persisting on a downward slope of unhappiness, he will find his spirits brightening. A renewed optimism will materialize, and he will begin reconnecting with the world. No longer will he be preoccupied with what has been lost, and he will be ready to consider what is to come.

## Renegotiating

Once the worst of a person's depression has been conquered and a detachment from the defective role is well on its way, the time comes for establishing substitute roles. In the fifth step of Kübler-Ross's model, one accepts one's loss and resumes life. The baton is passed to new relationships and new behavioral patterns. But these do not emerge automatically. A role changer will have to reconstruct them by employing techniques not unlike those used to negotiate her original roles. This time, however, there must be a difference. Where in the past her role negotiations were coercive and ultimately unsatisfying, now they must be fair and oriented to meeting her needs. This may necessitate not only new negotiations with fresh role partners, but more sophisticated negotiation skills better calculated to promote a desirable outcome.

After the debris of a dysfunctional role has been cleared away, there inevitably emerges a back and forth of demands with contemporary role partners. Indeed, these cross-currents are always present and provide the leitmotif of human existence. Now, however, they must lead to agreements that consider the interests of both partners. Dean Pruitt (1981) has called this the "dual-concern" model, positing that role negotiators have the option of considering (1) only their own interests, (2) only the interests of the other, (3) the interests of neither, or (4) the interests of both. In the first instance, this will lead to contending unfairly (often coercively) for one's own advantage; in the second, to yielding to the other's interests; in the third, to an inactivity in which one doesn't care what happens; and in the last, to a problem-solving orientation in which one tries to find an accommodation that maximizes the interests of both while minimizing their respective losses. In pursuing this last solution, both parties are best served by adopting an attitude of "firm-flexibility." This requires them to be assertive in pursuing their individual goals, but pragmatic in selecting the means toward their joint ends. The idea is to explore what will work and not adamantly insist upon one's first inclinations.

A dual-concern, problem-solving orientation is designed to be noncoercive and maximally productive, that is, to end with people's needs being met. It depends upon fairness and equality existing between the partners. When these are not present, it is necessary for a person to redress the balance. This can often be achieved by enlisting allies strong enough to increase one's clout or by developing one's personal powers. Thus it is that during the final phase of resocialization a therapist will often join her client in his negotiations, thereby strengthening his position. By being on his side, she makes it less likely that powerful, yet unfair, partners will take advantage. Since a person will sometimes need to negotiate independently, he can also benefit from help in attaining personal empowerment. If he can build up his personal competences, strengthen his self-image, and learn to exploit tactical advantages, he may be able to prevent injustices by himself. Furthermore, if he can increase the esteem in which he is held, others may be less inclined to resort to coercion.

An essential element in improving one's tactical advantage is knowing one's own values. If a person does not know where his interests lie, it is very difficult for him to assert them effectively. Unfortunately, most people who have been trapped in defective roles have not had the opportunity to develop their own perspective. To a large extent, their value choices have been imposed upon them by others or, at best, cobbled together in reaction to the coercive demands of others. Thus, a caretaker has usually been taught that caring for others is the highest human good to which she can aspire or has reached this conclusion independently in order to rationalize the kind of services she has been forced to render. Unless a person has adopted values that incorporate her interests too, when others make their unfair demands, she will be at a disadvantage. Since values guide the implementation of behaviors, she will not have established inner directions solid enough to counter confident external demands. She may therefore require assistance in learning to consult her inner needs before embracing personal commitments.

A dual-concern perspective, however, requires not only following one's own interests, but also understanding the interests of the other. Here again a role changer may be at a distinct disadvantage. Because his dysfunctional role originated in coercive role negotiations, these may have had the effect of blinding him to the needs of others. Not to put too fine a point on the matter, his anger at being treated unfairly may have left him more concerned with retribution than with mutual satisfaction. To rectify this situation, he needs to look past his indignation to see what makes other people tick. In the past he may have treated others like cardboard cutouts; now he will have to engage in empathetic role taking. Just as his therapist had to put herself in his shoes to understand his needs, so will he have to put himself in the shoes of his parents, spouse, children, friends, and colleagues. Only then will it be possible to discern what kinds of role bargains will meet the needs of all concerned. Otherwise the deals upon which he insists may be unfair in the opposite direction. In this case it will be his role partner who will feel abused, and the role partner who will lie in wait to redress the injury. When a deal that both partners can live with has not been effectuated, the conflict will continue.

## SIGNS AND SYMPTOMS

In Chapter 1, I described how role problems feel from the point of view of those trapped within them. We noted that these problems rarely announce themselves as such, but appear as frustrations, confusions, intense emotions, and conflicts. When examining the resocialization process, we find a similar pattern. Here, too, a person's actual situation rarely comes neatly packaged, and so its reality can be obscured. It then becomes necessary to grope through the fog of battle to perceive the underlying logic.

When role change ends happily, and without professional intervention, it may not be evident how a person's problem was resolved. Resocialization is normal, but not transparent. Because the process takes so long and has so many aspects, it is easy to get confused about the overall pattern. What is worse, the logical process I have portrayed in this chapter hardly ever unfolds in the exact sequence indicated. Instead of straightforwardly reexperiencing a lost role, then mourning it, and then negotiating an explicit role deal, one finds a confused melange of overlapping and intermingling parts, which do not officially proclaim themselves and which occur quietly amidst the normal business of living. Their arrangement is camouflaged by the messiness with which things really happen, as well as by the fact that one starts out not knowing where to look. The situation is much akin to that which existed before William Harvey discovered the circulation of blood in the human body. People had peered into the body long before Harvey arrived on the scene, but they had only witnessed a confused tangle of vessels not obviously linked in a circuit and further obscured by diverse anatomical structures equally demanding of attention. The organization of the bloodstream, which we now know was there, was not labeled or vividly colored, as it is in a medical chart. And neither are the phases of resocialization.

In actual life, the reexperiencing of defective roles is intermingled with the relinquishing and renegotiating of them. Since people suffering from failed or aborted roles are anxious to feel better, they do not politely await the official sequence of events but try to skip to the finale as soon as possible. This means that, even as they begin reexperiencing a role, they protest its loss, mourn its passing, and negotiate its replacement. Yet because adequate new roles are generally contingent upon the successful completion of previous parts of the role change process, when these have not been worked through, it becomes necessary to return and consummate them. Actual courses of resocialization are therefore much like patchwork quilts, manifesting a "back and forth and then back again" quality that can be quite disorienting. Without a pre-awareness of the resocialization paradigm, it may consequently be difficult to see how the pieces fit, or even that they fit at all.

Because of this messiness, both role changers and professional helpers are frequently diverted by a particularly salient aspect of the puzzle and take it to be the central problem needing correction. The various signs that a person is trapped in a bad role, or engaged in an unsuccessful attempt at change, are taken as symptoms of a "disorder," and it is hypothesized that in expunging them the problem will be solved. Markers of unmet needs, and unbreached barriers to change, distract attention from the larger process, and demand to be "cured." Rather than facilitating resocialization, the clinician therefore attempts to relieve the pain of intense emotions, or to correct cognitive misapprehensions, in the mistaken belief that this is all that needs to be accomplished.

## Demoralization

One of the factors that drives people to seek professional treatment is demoralization. This is the factor Frank (1973) linked most closely with the commencement of psychotherapy. It is characterized by a sense of failure, that is, by a feeling of being trapped and of having exhausted all of one's energies in a futile attempt to escape. It is the attitude a person has when his life is delimited by a defective role that he is unable to alter. Because dysfunctional roles don't meet needs, someone trapped in one feels lonely and empty. There is little love in his life, and probably less respect. And since the fulfillment of his needs is forever receding over the horizon, he may feel that life is meaningless, that no matter how hard he tries, he won't feel better. Because so many of his actions are self-defeating, he and others may even judge him to be irrational. The logic of dysfunctional role maintenance escapes them, and his actions seem senseless, perhaps crazy.

The demoralized person constantly reenacts fragments of failed roles, albeit in a kaleidoscopic, uncoordinated fashion. He thrashes around looking for a way out, but instead bangs up against the bars of his cage. Such a person becomes stalled at the reexperiencing stage of resocialization because it exacerbates his frustration through its requirement that he relive his unsatisfying role. Even though the repetition compulsion has been pushing him in this direction, it has not had sufficient force to launch change. The prospect of being in touch with all that has been denied him is simply so daunting that he throws up his hands in defeat. This surrender then becomes the cause of further demoralization, since it increases the prospect that happiness will elude him.

## Emotions

As we have seen, both bad roles and role change are permeated by intense, unresolved emotions. When a person is trapped in a role such as that of caretaker, she experiences sadness and frustration at being trapped. Unfair role partners arouse her ire, while feelings of guilt beat her into submission. In resocialization, these same feelings arise to form barriers to change. They can totally disrupt the grieving process and turn renegotiations into a folly of mutual recriminations. Because intense emotions are so transfixing, they easily exclude other factors from a person's mind.

Rage, terror, despondency, humiliation, remorse, and passion can easily seem like problems in their own right, because they are indeed problems. When anger, fear, sadness, shame, guilt, and love escalate to unbearable levels, they become dangerous and demand attention. Quite on their own, they require interventions to disarm them and make them less injurious. Nevertheless, they are only a part of the resocialization sequence. Elevating them to the status of independent disorders snatches them out of context and hinders the flow of role replacement. One may then fail to recognize that anxiety is interfering with a mourning process and, having addressed the anxiety, omit the liberating depression that should follow.

Typically, psychotherapists have been concerned with issues such as "anxiety" and "depression." These are labeled pathological and themselves become the object of therapeutic ministrations. Similarly, impulse control, shyness, and panic disorders command considerable professional attention. Yet these are all only parts of the therapeutic elephant. While real and significant, they cannot be the stopping point. If they are, much work is left undone.

## Confusions

Of course, emotions are not the only barrier to change. Faulty cognitions and volitions can have a similar effect. A person who is confused about who he is, how the world works, or what he believes, may have considerable difficulty relinquishing defective roles or negotiating alternatives. Confusion is uncomfortable in and of itself; when confronted with ambiguity or ambivalence, most of us shudder. We hate not knowing what is happening or what we want to do. An absence of answers is like a vacuum that demands filling. If unregulated, it can suck in bad answers more quickly than good ones and leave a person worse off than not knowing.

Still, obvious though a person's confusions may be, they too are not the whole picture. Merely to point out a person's mistakes about himself, or his value commitments, is to fail to understand why these mistakes have been made or what consequences they generate. Uncertainty and error will be viewed as weaknesses that deserve rectification, not as parts of a resocialization effort. Merely to castigate people for their failures—or even focus on the failures without explanation—is to designate the person, and not the role or role-change process, as defective.

## Conflicts

Social conflicts too can be removed from their context and misperceived as the essence of a person's problems. The disputes that arise between spouses, or between parents and their children, can be of monumental proportions. They can involve the worst kinds of violence and abuse and, like cognitive, volitional, and emotional difficulties, demand immediate attention. Such fights arrest the attention of everyone within earshot and understandably become an issue that precipitates therapeutic intervention.

Nevertheless, these disputes remain conflicts between role partners. They are coercive negotiations par excellence. As such, they can freeze dysfunctional roles at any stage of resocialization. This is because they are a venue in which people vainly attempt to reorganize role structures. Thus, for change to occur, conflictual relationships have to be converted into problem-solving ones or be replaced by ones that are.

# 3

# *A Multitude of Specialties*

## SPECIALIZATION

Not all forms of psychotherapy are created equal. Despite tackling essentially the same problems, they do not handle them the same way. Although role change is the common theme animating them, most do not address it as a comprehensive process. Instead there is a tendency to specialize in specific aspects of resocialization. Thus, some therapies concentrate on the reexperiencing of roles, others on the relinquishing of them, and still others on renegotiating them. Indeed, this specialization goes further, with some emphasizing the emotional barriers to change, others the cognitive barriers, yet others the volitional ones, and still others the social ones.

Since the differences between various therapies are not usually recognized for what they are, there is much confusion about which is best. Generally the various schools of therapy act like rivals, disputing precedence and legitimacy, and sound as if they are arguing over the optimum procedures for helping clients. In fact, they really dispute apples and oranges. Each, in asserting its superiority, simply directs our attention toward the areas in which it has developed an expertise. The truth is that it is possible to learn from all, for each contributes to understanding the psychotherapy elephant by expanding our comprehension of its specific parts.

Nevertheless, given the discomfort inherent in uncertainty, particular therapies continue to stake out territorial claims. This benefits each therapy individually by establishing credentials that can be used to inspire the

confidence of clients, a factor that Frank has suggested is vital to therapeutic success. Unfortunately, this propensity is also divisive. For while
it allows particular therapists to provide essential guidance to their clients
and practitioners, it interferes with the coordination of their respective
contributions. Because each speaks a discrete conceptual language, the
therapies seem to have nothing to teach one another. Indeed, it may seem
as if they are addressing different phenomena.

Most brands of therapy incorporate a model of how the human mind
works and also subscribe to an ethic indicating how life should be lived.
They weave tales about psychic structures such as the ego, id, or superego,
proffer elaborate doctrines about the individual self, or describe in intimate
detail the phenomenology of thoughts, feelings, and attitudes. Many of
these efforts are the product of sophisticated psychological investigations
and may ultimately be found to harbor considerable validity. Nevertheless,
the behavioral sciences remain in their infancy. A certitude comparable to
that of the physical sciences is now unavailable to them. So much needs
to be learned about features such as memory and emotion that a premature
confidence is foolhardy. Therefore, therapies claiming to be derived from
underlying psychological mechanisms must be approached with a degree
of skepticism.

Still, practitioners need guideposts. When one is responsible for relieving the distress of a person in pain, one must have an indication of how to
proceed. The resocialization paradigm attempts to provide this, not by
speculating about the internal mechanics of the human mind, but by
mapping the very visible pathways of role change. While these pathways
may be obscure when one doesn't know where to look, they are clearly
discernible when pointed out. The reexperiencing, relinquishing, and
renegotiation phases of resocialization are readily distinguishable when
conceptually separated from background events.

Resocialization deals with tangible entities such as behavior patterns
and intense emotions. It makes sense of them by indicating that some are
connected with others through interpersonal negotiation processes and
through the sequences in which they unfold. These feelings and behaviors,
and their connections, are not hypothetical creations, but experiential
phenomena.

### Categories of Change

If different therapies specialize in different aspects of role change, the
categories they stress must be derived from the resocialization paradigm.
Their differences must then be in the levels on which they intervene, the

phases of change upon which they concentrate, or the barriers to change they elect to remove. While no therapy has a monopoly on particular aspects of change, and none specializes exclusively in one facet, there is a tendency to develop delimited competencies. It is as if the various therapies have sought to cultivate an expertise that would make each distinctive. If this is so, many of their assertions about facts may have more to do with claiming power than with explicating reality.

In any event, some therapies have indeed emphasized one level of intervention to the disadvantage of others. Thus, some have considered therapy a manifestation of social support, while others have developed elaborate techniques for socialization, and still others have advocated resocialization as such. Since each of these levels is appropriate for some problems, it would appear that there should be no conflict among them. Their different levels of intervention may require different skills, but the validity of one should not cancel out that of the other.

Another common divider among therapies is the phase of resocialization emphasized. Although the role-change process is of a piece and includes the reexperiencing, the relinquishing, and the renegotiation of defective roles, many therapies seem to be practiced in the belief that accomplishing a particular one of these is synonymous with total success. Since the whole is not perceived, the proponents of each believe that its area of specialty is the crucial one and that the other phases are virtually automatic. Hence, if the reexperiencing of roles is the focus, it will be imagined that reliving a role is the necessary and sufficient condition for correcting it. The details of this correction will then be left to the client. Similarly, if mourning or renegotiating is stressed, the other aspects of resocialization are treated as if they were locked in a black box, beyond manipulation.

Lastly, the different barriers to change can be given different credence. Some therapies insist that it is the emotions, and the emotions alone, that trap a person in unsatisfying patterns of life, while others, with equal vehemence, assert that it is cognitive errors that prevent change. Those fixated upon the emotions may further narrow their attentions by concentrating on particular emotions. Some will become experts on fear, while other investigate anger, sadness, guilt, shame, or love. The cognitivists, in their turn, explore general facts about life or about the person. Others discount both emotions and cognitions and wax poetic about the volitional obstructions. They stress values, norms, and strategies for living and indicate that these must be altered before a person can be released from captivity. Still others become preoccupied with what is happening outside a person, namely with his social environment. They worry about the family, community, and cultural pressures bearing down on the individual. They believe that if these can be redirected, all else will fall into place.

### Doing the Translations

Anyone who practices psychotherapy has to confront an intimidating literature and must also deal with a cacophony of colleagues coming from very different backgrounds and disciplines. It is as if God had recreated the tower of Babel within the helping professions. The articles and books one reads, and the people with whom one communicates, all seem to have originated in distant lands. They purport to address the same issues, but they do so in very different terms. Within the compass of a particular clinic or professional meeting, practitioners may improvise a lingua franca, but they remain acutely aware that therapists outside their group seem to interpret the world quite differently.

Usually clinicians learn to translate between their own perspective and that of others. When reading a book from another point of view, they try to absorb its meaning through their pores, then apply it using the conceptual tools with which they are most comfortable. When in conversation with others, either the language of one or the other is adopted, or the conversation is "dumbed down." In the latter case, rather than invoke the technical jargon of one, they talk about the concrete case or introduce low-level concepts that are acceptable to both.

What follows may thus be considered an exercise in translation. Instead of depending upon the informal measures most clinicians use, it tries to make the commonalities of selected approaches explicit. The terminology embedded in particular therapies is rephrased in role-change language in the hope of clarifying its relationship to resocialization. It is expected that this will render patterns visible that would ordinarily be overlooked. Being clear about what is discussed may demonstrate that therapists often talk about the same thing without realizing it. It is only when their respective jargons are actuated that they fail to recognize that they are working on different aspects of the same phenomenon.

## LEVELS OF INTERVENTION

It is impossible to distinguish between the levels of intervention at which specific therapies specialize in absolute terms. Because authentic human problems overlap and intermingle, therapists may jump between levels when confronted with real clients. Nevertheless, some distinctions are possible. Thus, psychoanalysis and reality therapy usually operate on very different planes. The former is much more likely to be invoked for resocialization, while the latter is employed for supportive interventions. Although both claim to be psychotherapies, the sorts of changes they attempt are usually not the same.

One thing that all levels and all therapies have in common is the relationship factor. All require both trust and responsiveness in the way they relate to their clients, albeit in different combinations. Trust is uniform across interventions, because neither support, socialization, nor resocialization can operate without it. Nevertheless, the more profound the change attempted, the more trust is required. On the resocialization level, the threat to a person's identity is so acute that anxiety about the therapist can stifle any progress. Unless a therapist can diffuse this, nothing can proceed. Without profound client trust, role change is aborted. On the level of support, however, client confidence in the therapist is less critical. He may be a source of comfort and direction, but so may other role partners. It is not unusual, for instance, for clients in group therapy to find group members as supportive as the therapist. The socialization level falls somewhere between these extremes. Since it entails learning new role skills, it may be more frightening than merely coping, but less ominous than relinquishing a part of one's identity.

With responsiveness, there is even more of a difference between levels. Responsiveness is the warrant that a therapist can do what she promises. It entails possessing a skill and being ready and willing to apply it as required. But what is needed becomes more complex as the therapist penetrates deeper into a person's role problems. To offer effective support, a practitioner has to understand what is troubling her client and how best to communicate reassurance or advice. To be a competent socializer, however, requires something further. It is still essential to know what a person is ready to accept, but specific skills are also necessary. For a helper to teach a helpee, she needs proficiency in what she professes to impart. The therapist's possession of an academic understanding of assertiveness, for instance, is scarcely reassuring for a client who rejects speaking up for himself as too overbearing. Only when the helper has confidence in her own assertiveness can she persuasively model it for another, who must see it to believe it.

Effective resocialization requires still greater responsiveness. Since resocialization has so many aspects, timing takes on added significance. It would hardly do to encourage renegotiation of a role that a client has not yet reexperienced. The level of expertise required of the therapist is therefore also of a different order. Not only do fresh skills need to be socialized, but intricate roles have to be understood, menacing emotions disarmed, and efficacious new roles mediated. Each of these requires a relevant competence. It is no good for a clinician to initiate the reexperience of defective roles if he is an incompetent role taker and cannot properly identify his client's role. It would be equally inept to encourage a confrontation with frightening emotions if he doesn't know how to protect himself and his client, or to advocate the construction of new roles if he himself is an inept role bargainer. A capable therapist possesses these skills as part of his being, not merely as a list of instructions lifted from a textbook; otherwise they cannot be shared effectively, or as needed.

## Social Support

Let us consider some specific supportive therapies, that is, therapies that specialize in supportive interventions. (See Table 3.1.) Carl Rogers's client-centered therapy often falls within this category. With its emphasis on the relationship between therapist and client, and on the therapist's relationship skills, it offers real insights into what makes for trust and responsiveness. In advocating unconditional positive regard, accurate empathy, warmth, and genuineness, it highlights the skills a clinician needs to embody in implementing a supportive relationship. True, these skills are also necessary for socialization and resocialization, but these require additional skills that Rogerians sometimes neglect. Client-centered ap-

**Table 3.1**
**Levels of Intervention**

| Social Support | Socialization | Resocialization |
| --- | --- | --- |
| Client-Centered Therapy | Behaviorism | Psychoanalysis |
| Reality Therapy | Cognitivism | Culturalism |
| Medical Treatment | RET | Existentialism |
| Alcoholism Counseling (AA) | Rehabilitation | Primal Therapy |
| Group Therapy | Family Therapy | Gestalt Therapy |
| Community Psychiatry | Temperamental Fit | Jungian Analysis |
| Stress Reduction | Sociotherapy | Adler |
| Social Reform | Desensitization | Object-Relations Therapy |
| Gestalt Therapy | Beck | ACOA |
| TA | TA | TA |
| | Adler | RET |
| | Reality Therapy | Strategic Therapy |
| | Assertiveness | Self-in-System Therapy |
| | Community Psychiatry | Client-Centered Therapy |
| | | Beck |
| | | Group Therapy |

proaches tend to be problem solving, that is, they try to solve the client's here-and-now problems as they are presented. Their concern is with helping a person cope with her current reality.

Some therapies, such as William Glasser's reality therapy, are also supportive. By underscoring current life problems and deemphasizing historical events, they steer clients away from reexperiencing or relinquishing defective roles. Though some role change may occur under their tutelage, it is not usually recognized as such. In the name of realism, they can (in contrast with client-centered modes) be very directive and may virtually forbid depth issues from emerging. Some alcohol therapies are also of this sort. Thus, some Alcoholics Anonymous groups, while intent upon creating a supportive environment for their members, are uncomfortable with efforts to go "too deep." They assume that stopping drinking is all an alcoholic needs to achieve, and so their members are encouraged to describe and renounce their past transgressions, not plumb their origins. The emotional whys and wherefores of the person's behavior are less important to them than enforcing abstinence.

Stress reduction approaches, too, can be explicitly supportive. When it is assumed that a person's problems originate only in current stressors, it is reasonable to propose eliminating them. Generally, this is accomplished by using relaxation techniques or biofeedback, but these stressors can also be reduced as a by-product of a therapeutic relationship. Though behaviorally oriented therapists often discount this factor, it seems to be a decisive element in many of their successes.

Community psychiatry may also be mentioned here. While this approach is not specifically a therapy, much less a supportive one, it can function as the equivalent of one. Community interventions often attempt to lower the stress impinging upon individuals by manipulating social variables. Their objective is to decrease the coercion in people's lives by influencing their role partners and/or larger social structures. To some extent, this approach tries to renegotiate people's roles, but it does so indirectly through improving the atmosphere in which they occur.

Medical interventions also seem to concentrate on supportive factors. Physicians, especially those with a biological orientation, tend to eschew the reorganization of client roles in favor of removing symptoms. Instead of trying to change the ways in which people interrelate, they aim at reducing anxieties or lifting depressions. Often this is accomplished physiologically by the prescription of psychotropic medications. An anxiolytic or antidepressant is introduced to make the patient feel better, not to eliminate her underlying source of distress. The patient is thereby enabled to carry on without having to endure the rigors of socialization or resocialization.

Historically, when sociologists and psychologists have explored personal distress, they have been critical of medical approaches. These modalities have been reproached for exacerbating problems rather than correcting them. It has been argued that medical diagnoses label people and therefore act as stigmata that make their lot even more difficult. Labeling is held accountable for secondary deviance, which it is assumed can be dissolved by the expedient of not labeling. This would presumably remove environmental burdens and make it easier for people to bear unpleasant reality factors.

## Socialization

Among the more socialization-oriented therapies are behavioral interventions, cognitive therapies, rational-emotive therapy, vocational rehabilitation, some family therapies, transactional analysis, and temperamental-fit approaches. This diverse set of techniques varies dramatically in the extent of change attempted; what its members have in common is that they are all education oriented. Each believes that a person must absorb certain skills and/or information in order to function effectively. Skills or information are presumed to be the missing ingredient in the person's role, the addition of which will enable him to live more comfortably.

Behavioral interventions encompass a range of techniques. They are usually grouped together because of their origin, rather than their methodology. Most are an outgrowth of academic psychology. They include behavior modification, assertiveness training, and desensitization. The first, behavior modification, is derived from research on classical and operant conditioning. These historically important learning theories, despite their recent eclipse by cognitively oriented theories, continue to be applied by psychologists on an ad hoc basis. Techniques such as behavior shaping, token economies, and aversion therapy fall within their compass. By judiciously applying rewards and punishments, they attempt to steer subjects in desired behavioral directions. These so-called reinforcers are manipulated to achieve objectives decided upon by the therapist and/or client. When they work as projected, the person acts in a safer and more civilized manner, for example, by giving up smoking or becoming less violent. She will have learned new ways of living and new methods of implementing her roles.

Likewise, assertiveness training strives to apply social learning methodology and to impart useful interaction strategies. It proposes that people can be passive, assertive, or aggressive in their relationships, but insists that only the middle tactic pays off with personal satisfaction. In consequence, clients are explicitly diagnosed according to their typical pattern and, when necessary, taught how to relate differently. By doing homework or practicing in groups, they learn to negotiate in a manner unlike the one they have traditionally used.

Desensitization purports to eliminate unwanted emotional reactions by teaching a person to replace them with a competing response. Thus, someone who is being crippled by anxiety is instructed to arrange a hierarchy of fears and confront each systematically. When properly implemented, this procedure is supposed to end with the subject less frightened and more able to function. Instead of hiding out at home with agoraphobia, he should be able to perform roles that entail interactions outside of the house, for example, as a shopper or airline passenger. If it is anxiety that is blocking resocialization, desensitization can restart the process, but this is not the outcome explicitly envisioned by most behavioral therapists. They are usually content to unblock only the role behaviors already present in a person's repertoire.

Cognitive therapies too have had a recent vogue. Since, like behavioral interventions, they had their origin in academic psychology, they have had to contend with the half-century predominance of behaviorism within their discipline. In the hope of making psychology more scientific, many academics had denied the usefulness, and even existence, of mental events. For them, it was only observable behavior, and not hidden thoughts and feelings, that had substance. Cognitivists needed courage to challenge this conviction. They pioneered ways of studying what is in a person's head in an effort to prove the validity of thought. When progress was made in this endeavor, they utilized what had been discovered to allay the personal distress of individuals. Figures such as Aaron Beck postulated that if a person's thoughts can perpetuate unhappiness, learning to think differently should make him feel better. In consequence, cognitive therapists have aimed at altering the intracranial conversations that theoretically sustain client misery.

This sort of pedagogical approach to personal thinking was, in fact, presaged by Albert Ellis. His rational-emotive therapy (RET) has always been oriented more toward the rational than the emotive. He has long conjectured that the latter follows from the former. Since the 1940s Ellis has argued, with power and panache, that it is "irrational" thoughts that get people in trouble. Ideas, such as a belief that one must be loved by everyone in order to be happy, have been described by him as impossible of fruition. He therefore engages in rational disputation with his clients, deliberately trying to persuade them that they are wrong. Ellis has claimed that once cognitive errors are acknowledged, people are free to live more rationally. His method falls within the purview of socialization because it attempts to reform thinking and encourage new roles, not to promote the relinquishing of failed roles. The assumption is that letting go of the past is an automatic consequence of understanding that it is irrational.

Vocational rehabilitation, another socialization approach, may strike many as not a form of therapy, and in this they would probably have the concurrence of most rehabilitation professionals. These latter think of themselves more as educators than therapists. They openly coach clients about the vocations available to them and on how to develop the abilities necessary for functioning in these. But jobs are roles, and so whatever their self-image, rehabilitation counselors are socialization agents. When they inculcate job skills, they simultaneously instill role skills.

Family therapies are almost always considered therapeutic, but they often seem unsure in their direction. Some pioneers in the field, such as Nathan Ackerman, wanted to extricate children from roles like that of the family "scapegoat," but more recent innovators have been influenced by general systems theory. They see themselves as rearranging the boundaries within family groups and as liberating people from triangulations and overly close identifications. But given the nature of their task, such therapists can scarcely refrain from manipulating roles. Some even talk in terms of them; for example, counselors concerned with alcoholic families recognize "family heros" and "lost children." In any event, family therapists frequently try to reformulate family roles so that a mother can act out a more satisfying version of her mother role and the father a more satisfactory father role. Usually, however, this is not accomplished through relinquishing defective roles. Since family therapists are obviously present during therapy sessions, these clinicians often try to redirect the role negotiations of the participants. They thus concentrate on instilling mechanisms for role development, rather than on effecting role replacement.

Transactional analysis (TA) is a popularized version of Freudian therapy. Like the family therapies, it is very concerned with the interactions between people. According to its tenets, people can be in various ego states, such as those of the "child," "adult," or "parent," and these states can take various forms, such as the "critical parent," the "happy child" or the "rebellious child." Though not labeled as such, each of these is obviously a specific role. Persons occupying them are described by TA practitioners as having transactions with others that can be either open or blocked. When blocked, the person's problem is said to remain unresolved, and it is predicted that he will be unhappy. Therefore, transactional analysts attempt to teach people how to identify the ego states and transactions that cause them grief in the hope that this will be a first step toward making them more open. What is desired is an "I'm okay, you're okay" exchange in which both partners win. But this, of course, is another variation of role negotiation training. It socializes role negotiation skills even though it does not use role problem language.

One last socialization-type therapy I should mention is Stella Chess and Alexander Thomas's temperamental-fit strategy, which introduces the notion that infants are born with temperamental differences that may or may not match the socialization tactics of their parents. They assert that a lack of fit can produce a conflict that has tremendous import as a child matures. How she feels about herself, and what kinds of roles she allows herself to develop, may result from what has transpired between her and her parent. Thus, if a "slow to warm up" child is not handled patiently, her vulnerabilities are exacerbated, and instead of growing into a friendly, confident adult, she retreats into an anxious and wary misanthropy. Preventing this sort of predicament can be accomplished by teaching parents and/or children improved relationship skills—for example, by making a parent more responsive to a child's temperament. The parents and children will then be able to construct more viable role patterns between themselves.

### Resocialization

As we move further down the scale of therapeutic interventions, we of course come to resocialization. This sort of intervention is explicit in its desire to facilitate the dramatic reorganization of the person's life. Often it is conceived of as altering someone's personality and/or character. By all accounts, resocialization is the most far reaching and disorienting form of change. Among the therapies that specialize in it are psychoanalysis, the culturally oriented therapies, existentialist therapy, and primal scream therapy.

Psychoanalysis is probably the most comprehensive of all contemporary psychotherapies, though not always the most cogent or effective. Freudian therapy has been around a long time (almost a century), and its practitioners have had an opportunity to explore and hypothesize about a great many dysfunctional situations. Psychoanalysis has always attempted radical personal change. While Freud was pessimistic about the degree of control a person could exercise over his life, he nevertheless tried to do as much as possible. This led to long-term interventions that investigated the farthest reaches of the unconscious. Both cognitive and emotional factors were examined, with the intention of reorganizing both. If necessary, problems were scrutinized time and again from many different perspectives so that they might be "worked through." Defective roles were emotionally reenacted on the analytic couch, emotional barriers to change dismantled, and new roles reworked, both in therapy and in the client's own life. Although this process has not been labeled resocialization, or role change, it has been understood that a personal metamorphosis is the objective and that this may be difficult.

Far-reaching though psychoanalysis has been, it still has its blind spots. Indeed, many of its frustrated adherents have defected to establish alternative therapies of their own. They too, for the most part, have attempted resocialization. While accepting Freud's goal of radical personal change, they have disagreed about how this is best achieved. In general, the heirs to Freud have emphasized the social factors he neglected. Although Freud was himself interested in anthropology, his medical origins biased him toward biological hypotheses. These could be so restricting that some of his disciples sought to remedy this predilection even at the risk of being expelled from the psychoanalytic movement. Figures such as Adler, Karen Horney, and Harry Stack Sullivan advocated long-term interventions conducted very much in the Freudian manner, but hypothesized a significantly different etiology and change process. In particular, they explored the interpersonal origins of personal dysfunctions and advocated relationship-based forms of change. These cultural therapists differed among themselves about what was wrong, or needed to be altered, but concurred on the centrality of social factors.

Another far-reaching form of therapy, namely the existentialist, has had a very different derivation. It took its inspiration from philosophy and especially from the search for personal meaning. The rootlessness of twentieth-century mass society and the trauma of war and economic depression have prompted existentialists to speculate about life's purposes. They describe human beings as lonely searchers rummaging through the wreckage of their existence for something to believe in, as creatures very much in need of support and guidance. To accomplish this end, existential therapists have attempted to help people reorganize their lives, using techniques not unlike those used by the Freudians. They too delve deeply into the secret pains of their clients in the hope of facilitating basic changes in their ways of relating.

One more sort of therapy with a resocialization orientation is primal scream therapy. While it is not one of the mainstream therapies, it can serve as a useful example of resocialization because it so aggressively courts radical change. It assumes that barriers to change originate in early childhood, and so seeks to institute radical surgery to remove them. By encouraging an intense reexperiencing of excruciating early ordeals, it hopes to excise their scars and free the person to proceed with life. Implicit in this is the notion that role change is possible, but, of necessity, painful.

## PHASES OF CHANGE

While particular brands of psychotherapy can be distinguished by the levels of intervention they emphasize, they can also be differentiated by the phases of resocialization they accentuate. Some therapies, which do not conceive of themselves as fostering resocialization, nevertheless expedite specific aspects of the role change process. This varies with what they think most problematic, namely the reexperiencing, the relinquishing, or the renegotiating phase of change. Different practitioners have been struck by the importance of one or another of these, and hence have developed expertise in one area rather than another.

It must not, however, be assumed that these specializations are absolute, for some therapies have multiple foci. As can be seen in Table 3.2, psychoanalysis tries to cover the full spectrum; some alcohol therapies figure prominently in both the reexperiencing and relinquishing of lost roles; while gestalt therapies emphasize the reexperiencing and renegoti-

**Table 3.2**
**Phases of Change**

| Reexperiencing | Relinquishing | Renegotiating |
|---|---|---|
| Psychoanalysis | Psychoanalysis | Psychoanalysis |
| Client-Centered Therapy | Object-Relations Therapy | Family Therapy |
| Gestalt Therapy | Klerman (IPT) | Horney |
| Psychodrama | ACOA | Assertiveness Therapy |
| Primal Therapy | Strategic Therapy | Gestalt Therapy |
| Group Therapy | Alcoholism Counseling (AA) | TA |
| | Desensitization | Adler |
| | Beck | Existentialism |
| | | Rehabilitation |
| | | Sociotherapy |
| | | RET |
| | | Strategic Therapy |
| | | Self-in-System Therapy |
| | | Reality Therapy |
| | | Beck |
| | | Group Therapy |
| | | Behaviorism |
| | | Object-Relations Therapy |

ation phases. Moreover, the foci of individual therapies and therapists sometimes shift. They can, and do, attempt different sorts of things, at different times, with different sorts of clients.

### Reexperiencing

One of the more enduring images that has emerged from psychoanalysis is that of the client reclining on the therapeutic couch, free-associating to his therapist. Early in his career Freud encouraged patients to renounce internal censorship and allow themselves to feel and express whatever came to mind. He observed that when people allowed their minds to wander unimpeded, sooner or later they alighted on crucial materials. In Freudian terms, their problems percolated up from their unconscious and became accessible to the conscious mind. In essence, otherwise unavailable role scripts were reactivated. Clients then felt and thought things they had previously suppressed.

In some of his earlier endeavors, Freud emphasized the cognitive aspects of this reexperiencing. He wanted his clients to understand what had happened to them in their childhoods and promoted this by offering interpretations of their revelations. Later Freudians, notably Franz Alexander, shifted the focus to emotional reexperience. They tried to cultivate circumstances in which a client could have a "corrective emotional experience." It was their observation that unless someone felt his problem, substantial change was circumvented. They therefore sought a safe therapeutic environment in which a person might feel free to experience emotions such as fear and rage. Ultimately, they hoped for a "therapeutic transference." This occurred when a client felt sufficiently confident to recruit the therapist as a role partner with whom he could almost literally reenact unfulfilled roles.

Rogers, with his client-centered therapy, has been even more fixated upon the reexperiencing phase of change. Rogers sometimes seems to suggest that all a person must do to solve a problem is to experience it. He hypothesizes that people have an innate drive toward problem solving, which is activated once they understand the nature of their difficulties. To this end, client-centered therapists try to sharpen their clients' self awareness by directing it toward what they think and feel. This technique is often described as "reflecting" the client's problem back upon him. By expedients such as repeating, paraphrasing, or summarizing a client's words, she is encouraged to delve more insightfully into her situation.

Gestalt therapists too try to intensify a client's experience. Indeed, Frederick (Fritz) Perls gained fame by popularizing exercises that introduced people to themselves. Most of these involved role playing. His clients were encouraged to have conversations with different aspects of themselves and/or with role partners who were not physically present. These rehearsals were often very involving. They dramatically recapitulated lost roles and triggered a reexperiencing of the thoughts and emotions embodied in them. Very much in the same tradition has been Moreno's psychodrama. It too entails explicit role playing that reanimates suppressed experiences. Likewise, transactional analysis dramatizes role problems by encouraging role playing. Its insistence upon identifying ego states draws attention to what a client is thinking and feeling, and how he is interacting with his role partners.

As has been indicated, primal scream therapy tries to reactivate the earliest of childhood traumas. Its clients are stimulated to relive the agonies of specific punishments or separations, and success in this modality tends to be measured by the decibel level. The client who writhes upon the floor, screaming and thrashing to free herself from an invisible assailant, is judged the most successful. Her obvious discomfort is taken as proof of her being genuinely in touch with her feelings.

Some of the alcohol therapies also try to reanimate lost roles, but they are less dramatic in their approach. When people join Alcoholics Anonymous, they are expected to be honest in relating their past vices, but not to roll on the floor in torment. Their object is to movingly testify to past indiscretions. If they fail to do so, others will accuse them of "BS-ing." Only when a person successfully shares a meaningful personal experience is he rewarded by praise and acceptance. But in expressing genuine emotion, he is usually forced into experiencing past failures in more vivid detail than he had anticipated. In some drug therapies, calling people on the carpet has almost become an art form. If a person declines to be honest, he may be given a "haircut," in which other members of his group flail him until he comes clean. It is not unusual for such exercises to end with a person crying as he is made to relive excruciating incidents from his past.

## Relinquishing

The reexperiencing of defective roles is not, however, the whole of resocialization. It is only the opening salvo of a lengthy process that will remain stymied unless consummated by the letting go of what is lost. Whether they realize it or not, therapists who do not explicitly recognize the relinquishing stage of role change depend upon it to unfold naturally. Since this often does happen, concentrating on the initiation of change can eventuate in the reorganization of personal roles. Nevertheless, there are cases where nature is frustrated and obstinate barriers to change prevent success. In these instances, therapies that unblock the mourning process generally prove necessary.

Once more psychoanalysis offers a model for such an intervention. One of the reasons this form of therapy is so protracted is that it seeks to "work through" the traps into which its clients fall. Therapists trained in Freudian methodology learn that merely interpreting a client's problems rarely results in a reorganized life. They are taught that difficulties usually recur unless repeatedly discussed, albeit with slight variations in their content at each iteration. Although Freudians do not identify this as a mechanism for relinquishing lost roles, this is what it is. By constantly rehashing problems, clients are really being given an opportunity to run through the protest phase of mourning. Their working things through allows them to engage in denials of fact, in anger at obtuse role partners, and in endless quibbles about inadequate role bargains. When these are exhausted, they then obtain support for enduring the pain of sadness over what has been lost.

Gerald Klerman's interpersonal psychotherapy (IPT) includes an even more clear-cut attempt to foster the relinquishing of what is lost. It emphasizes the social origins of depression and posits the necessity of a social intervention to remove it. It explicitly seeks to promote normal grief as a mechanism for change and attempts to remove barriers to its successful completion. Among other things, it tries to resolve the interpersonal role disputes upon which change may be hung up. It also strives to facilitate role transitions and to compensate for those personal deficits that may exacerbate a person's fear of change. In short, it attempts to identify and eliminate personal and social impediments to change and to prepare the ground for the development of more fulfilling roles.

Alcoholism counseling too may try to help a person let go of what is lost. Many practitioners in this field attempt to extricate their clients from role relationships that deter them from change and to reorient them toward attachments with supportive others who encourage nonalcoholic life styles. Perhaps as importantly, Alcoholics Anonymous has stressed the need for people to seek control over only those things that are within their discretion. Its members are asked to put themselves in the hands of a "higher power" and allow things to unfold in their own way. This is tantamount to encouraging them to let go of what is lost, that is, to cease fighting against what can't be helped. When a person does this, she thereby abandons her protests and permits herself to enter the sadness of mourning. Relying on a higher power to guide one's destiny thus translates into allowing defective role patterns to lapse. Instead of maintaining efforts to restore them, one admits one's limitations and suffers change to proceed.

Those who advocate behaviorist interventions do not relate the abandonment of lost roles to a letting go of what is lost, but do recognize barriers to change. Often they wish to extinguish specific behaviors believed especially troublesome. By changing the reward and punishment schedules associated with particular behaviors, they hope to help their clients eliminate patterns that do not meet their needs. In this, they believe themselves to be grasping the nettle rather than fostering indirect interventions, such as those of psychoanalysis. Of course, some behaviorists, such as Joseph Wolpe, attempt to remove obstructive emotions rather than behaviors per se. Usually, though, these emotions are viewed as the problem, rather than as barriers to the relinquishing of something else.

Perhaps because cognitive therapies, like behaviorism, have their roots in academic psychology, they too are concerned with the bottom line. They seek to delimit a person's problem and then scientifically extirpate it. Since cognitivists identify problems not with behaviors but with illogical thought, it is this that they attempt to alter. They try to educate clients about their mistakes in logic and to implant a rational inner voice that directs them toward more satisfying behavior patterns.

One last type of intervention that should be mentioned under this rubric is strategic therapy. While this kind of technique comes close to not being a therapy, it is usually practiced by people who consider themselves therapists and who do try to foster personal change. Nevertheless, they assume a pessimistic stance toward the willingness, and/or ability, of clients to participate consciously in meaningful change, and therefore manipulate them in directions they, the professionals, judge suitable. Little attention is paid to helping clients reexperience or rework a role, because their ability to do either is doubted. Instead, a kind of reverse psychology is used to turn the client's protests against himself. He is maneuvered into doing the opposite of what the therapist seems to want, and thereby renouncing what is in fact lost. While this is not perceived as expediting a mourning process, when successful it has this effect.

## Renegotiating

The last of the three phases of resocialization is renegotiation. This is the stage during which new roles are negotiated to replace those that have been relinquished. Sooner or later replacement roles must be constructed or a person is left with a void in his life. Indeed, many people would like to jump to this stage without undergoing the turmoil of reexperiencing or relinquishing. Quite naturally, they want things to be better right away. Given this press toward a more satisfying life, it is not surprising that many psychotherapies make renegotiating their focal point. They recognize that a person needs new roles and attempt to accelerate the process by implementing role negotiations first, often without even a nod to what must be lost. Some therapies, however, do integrate renegotiating into a larger context and truly make it part of resocialization.

Psychoanalysis is among those methodologies with an integrated approach. It builds renegotiating into the larger process called "working through." Many texts on analytic technique devote considerable space to the termination phase of therapy. Clients are not simply dropped when they have identified their problems or when they have endured the pain of letting them go; stress is also placed on assisting them in cutting their ties to the therapist and in shifting their loyalties to other role partners. This usually entails developing a more independent status vis-à-vis the therapist and talking through the practical problems of learning to control one's own destiny. Since such control is dependent upon being able to deal competently with role partners, clients in psychoanalysis usually receive help in becoming more proficient role negotiators.

Transactional analysis, a derivative of psychoanalysis, has underscored the negotiation processes implicit in its progenitor. The very name "transactional" demonstrates its stress on interpersonal relationships. As previously indicated, it contrasts open, productive interactions with those that go awry and tries to discourage the latter while promoting the former. Clients are taught about "blocked" and "ulterior" transactions, and how to avoid both. Indeed, Eric Berne, the founder of transactional analysis, achieved celebrity with a book entitled *The Games People Play* (1964), which purported to expose a species of ulterior transactions, namely "games." In another celebrated work, *I'm OK, You're OK* (1969), Thomas Harris, a Berne disciple, discusses "life positions" and the negotiating dispositions that derive from these. He endorses an "I'm OK; you're OK" stance, in which one expresses confidence in oneself and trust in others. This attitude in its operation is not unlike Pruitt's dual concern model, in that it fosters fair negotiations.

Cultural therapy, another offshoot of Freudianism, also stresses positive relationships. Horney, for example, discusses attempts at conflict resolution that involve moving toward, moving away from, and moving against other people. These too seem to be variations on the dual-concern theme. They are concerned with the way one asserts one's interests during negotiations, that is, the degree to which one contends, yields, or is inactive. It is, of course, the problem-solving stance that is recommended by Horney.

A fairly obvious form of role negotiations is fostered by family therapists. Since they identify personal problems with disruptions in family role structures, they openly manipulate these arrangements toward more favorable patterns. Family therapists not only talk about who is doing what with whom, they attempt to initiate family communications that lead to problem solving. Success is often measured by the degree to which therapist-mediated negotiations prosper. When family members learn to treat each other as worthwhile individuals who must make shared adjustments to meet their individual and joint needs, they build a common structure that shelters all. In this edifice, each will have negotiated a role configuration that works for him without interfering with those of the others.

Existentialist therapists, as we shall shortly see, tend to be concerned with values. Since values help people determine their goals, they are critical to determining their interests, and hence are critical to role negotiations. If a dual-concern negotiating posture is to succeed, each party, including the role changer, must understand and assert her interests. It is for this reason that existentialism may be considered as specializing in renegotiations. By enabling clients to identify what they want from life, it helps them develop satisfying roles when they enter negotiations with role partners. They then become able to function as confident, goal-directed negotiators who can have a positive impact on outcomes that affect them.

RET, Albert Ellis's version of cognitive therapy, is also concerned with final results. While his method tends to be disputatious, and argues people out of their mistakes, it is also designed to cajole them into more productive patterns. Ellis, a man of firm opinions who has never been bashful about informing people how to live, has promulgated rules about illogical ideas, which when examined closely are found to incorporate firm value judgments about life. Most of these are the sort one can readily endorse because they are calculated to strengthen satisfying role behaviors. In essence, they function like the values of the existentialists; that is, they promote fair-minded assertiveness during role negotiations. Thus, whether intended or not, they support the successful renegotiation of defective roles.

At first blush, behavior modification seems not to focus on role negotiations, in part because it seems to ignore the interpersonal element. Indeed, sometimes its practitioners act as if they were manipulating laboratory animals, not human beings engaged in complex interactions with other human beings. But this interpretation leaves out the role of the clinician herself. Through her manipulations, she directly negotiates role behaviors with her clients.

Indeed, behavior modifiers tend to slight the reexperiencing and relinquishing of defective roles and move straight through to the final stage of resocialization. As the behavior modifiers might express it, they are more interested in solving present-day problems than lingering over historic events. Yet this entails negotiating improved roles whether or not past ones have been surrendered. Behaviorists also tend to be explicit about the sanctions they use in their negotiations. Usually they advocate positive reinforcement as the mechanism of negotiation (although they are not above aversive interventions). Because these sanctions are described in stimulus-response terms, they are usually conceived as one-sided rather than negotiational. Nevertheless, clients do have an input in these interactions. Adjustments must be made to accommodate them whether the practitioner likes it or not.

Some categories of behaviorists are more overtly attuned to client inputs. One sort even offers assertiveness training to clients. Being appropriately assertive, as opposed to passive or aggressive, is, of course, just what is needed for productive negotiations. The person who is not able to articulate his interests is unlikely to have them heeded. It is when he learns to communicate his desires effectively that others can be recruited into shared problem solving.

Finally, vocational rehabilitation is much interested in the establishment of successful occupational roles. Its proponents hardly ever discuss the negotiation of behaviors, but in their operations function through them. Rehabilitation usually occurs in programs planned to impart new roles. These may be conceived only as educational, but because clients must struggle to adapt learned skills to their life situations, more than simple knowledge is acquired. To be successful, the clients have to construct an occupational niche for themselves in which they interact with other human beings and make adjustments as needed. This, of course, is role renegotiation.

## BARRIERS TO CHANGE

During any phase of resocialization, but especially during the relinquishing stage, the various elements of a person's defective role scripts can interfere with change. If his emotions, cognitions, volitions, or social relationships are themselves defective, they can freeze him in his unsatisfying behavior patterns. If these script elements are misguided in their direction, or too intense in their implementation, they form barriers to change. They then appear to be difficulties in themselves and may be fixed upon by individual psychotherapies that identify them as the critical

**Table 3.3**
**Barriers to Change**

| | |
|---|---|
| Cognitive | Cognitive Therapy, Vocational Rehabilitation, Rational-Emotive Therapy (RET), Adler, Family Communications, Labeling Theory, Jung, Dollard and Miller, H. S. Sullivan, Psychoanalysis, Transactional Analysis (TA) |
| Volitional | Cognitive Therapy, RET, Existentialism, Reality Therapy, Psychoanalysis, Adler, Horney, Gestalt Therapy, H. S. Sullivan |
| Social | Object-Relations Therapy, Psychoanalysis, Labeling, Horney, H. S. Sullivan, Family Therapy, Adler, Community Psychiatry, Assertiveness Training, Strategic Therapy, Social Reform |
| Emotional (generalist) | Gestalt Therapy, Client-Centered Therapy, Psychoanalysis, Family Therapy, Psychodrama, Group Therapy |
| Fear (anxiety) | Desensitization (Wolpe), Primal-Scream Therapy, Horney, H. S. Sullivan, Stress Reduction, Psychoanalysis, Dollard and Miller (Behavioral) |
| Anger | Assertiveness Training, Adler, Stress Reduction, Primal-Scream Therapy |
| Sadness (depression) | Klerman (IPT), Object-Relations Therapy, Psychoanalysis, Existentialism |
| Guilt | Existentialism, Psychoanalysis |
| Shame | Rational-Emotive Therapy (RET), Alcoholism Counseling (AA) |

problem to be solved. (See Table 3.3.) Usually these obstructions must be lifted for progress to occur, but sometimes practitioners are so convinced that only one element is responsible that they neglect the others.

Unfortunately, limited space does not allow for a full explication of the way script elements become misguided or overly intense. (For more details the reader is directed to the author's book *Role Change: A Resocialization Perspective*, 1990.) Here we will briefly survey how specific therapies try to disarm intense emotions, others to correct faulty intellectual understandings, yet others to reconstruct value systems, and still others to intervene directly in coercive relationships.

### Emotions

Because a person can be trapped by any role component, it is misleading to assert that only one component causes difficulties; nevertheless, the emotions are easily the most disruptive factor. When they are intense or misguided, they are very difficult to correct. After all, it is the function of strong emotions to stabilize roles by perpetuating them in the forms in which they arose. This role conservation can be a good thing when it is positive roles that are safeguarded, but becomes negative when the roles conserved are negative. Consequently, many therapists insist that an emotional reworking is essential for change. Although this recognition is critical to the facilitation of far-reaching improvements, when focused upon too exclusively, it can give short shrift to other important script elements.

Among the emotions that serve as barriers to change are fear, anger, sadness, guilt, shame, and unrequited love. These are the primary colors of what is in reality a complex emotional palette. Indeed, the emotions upon which therapists concentrate are often identified in more refined hues, such as anxiety, panic, or hostility. Moreover, some therapies are generalist and attempt to unblock any variety of intense or misdirected emotions, while others are more restrictive in their attentions. They specialize in fear, anger, or sadness on the assumption that their choice is the most problematic one.

Among the generalist psychotherapies are gestalt and client-centered therapy. In their efforts to intensify the experience of dysfunctional roles, both of these intensify the experience of any salient emotion. Both types of therapy direct client attention toward what is being felt. Thus, when a Rogerian tells a client that she seems to be feeling fear, this effort at reflection gives her fear a prominence it might not otherwise have. Similarly, when a gestalt therapist arranges an imaginary confrontation with a repressive parent, the anger aroused by past injustice flashes back to life. Since both of these therapies value an honest representation of what the client feels, no one emotion is encouraged over another. Whatever it is that the client is feeling is what is wanted.

Generalist therapies often treat emotions as if their mere expression had curative power. Though they urge clients to feel what they are feeling, they are less likely to offer mechanisms for disarming a feeling or moving forward in the resocialization process. Nevertheless, when a person is helped to experience intense/misguided emotions, this can initiate a process of coming to terms with them. For example, when a terrifying fear is made real, it can gradually be tolerated, then reexamined to determine whether it actually betokens danger. When properly assessed, it also provides the impetus for neutralizing whatever dangers do exist. If these sequelae to experiencing the emotion occur, it will be disarmed and lose its ability to prevent change.

Family therapies have generalist tendencies and may spotlight any emotional conflict that materializes within a therapy session. Since passionate anger is frequently present when family members dispute their roles, a venue that brings these currents to the surface is in a position to restructure them. One of the functions of the family therapist is often to serve as a referee who encourages fighting fairly. Communication of even nasty emotions is fomented in the belief that they can thereby be resolved. On a more individual level, family therapists often confront emotions that hold one family member in the thrall of another. This may mean uncovering the guilt or shame that ties someone in injurious bondage. She may then be encouraged to free herself from these feelings and extricate herself from the debilitating relationship.

On a more particularist level are therapies, like assertiveness training, that focus on one part of a person's experience. In the case of assertiveness training, the spotlight is on anger. Its object is to help people who are either too free in their expression of anger, or not free enough. Both aggressiveness and passivity are proscribed, and clients are taught to modulate their passion. The dangers of excess in either direction are explained, and practice in more effective emotional expression provided.

Also particularist are the behaviorist strategies of Wolpe, who concentrates on helping people reduce the intensity of their irrational fears. Using emotional desensitization, either in the clinic or in vivo, he induces clients to confront their anxieties in measured doses so that eventually they lose their sting.

Klerman's interpersonal psychotherapy obviously specializes in sadness. It was designed for this specific purpose, and emphasizes the centrality of depression to many personal problems. The unresolved sadness it addresses is socially widespread, precisely because so many people are trapped in roles they cannot relinquish. One of the merits of Klerman's system is that it urges clients to accept the normality of grief and to develop ways of coping with it. Too many other therapies encourage clients to bury their sorrow in diversionary activities without ever finding ways to supersede it.

When properly implemented, primal therapy can serve a similar purpose for rage and terror. By providing circumstances that foster emotional regression, its clients are steered toward heroic expressions of their inner pain. When they writhe on the floor, kicking and screaming, it is because they have been given permission to hate openly the people who have hurt them. Years of impotent frustration are washed away, and they may be better able to make peace with their coercive role partners. That, at least, is the theory. Usually the results are less dramatic, for it takes time to rework destructive emotions.

Until recently shame has not received much attention from therapists, but this is changing. Lately several books have come out on the subject, but a debt is owed to Albert Ellis, who pioneered in this area. Although RET allegedly corrects irrational thinking, it has done more to rectify distorted values. Ellis has aggressively motivated people to stand up for themselves and not be embarrassed to defy conventional standards. By putting clients on the spot and forcing them to defend their personal choices, he has helped them expunge misplaced shame.

### Cognitions

Cognitive therapies were originally formulated as an alternative to rigidly behavioristic approaches. Once academic psychologists demonstrated that people had thoughts, they contrasted these with practices that sought only to manipulate measurable external events. More recently, cognitive techniques have been pitted against emotionally oriented methods. Some cognitivists (e.g., Beck) have explicitly argued that thoughts appear prior to emotions and that therefore if one is to diminish inappropriate anxiety or depression, one must first correct the fallacious ideas that stimulate them. By objectively examining the facts and his own logical processes, a person can uproot the egregious mistakes that lead to debilitating emotions. He can recognize the inner voice that urges him toward error and substitute a more reasonable set of directives.

Cognitivists usually speak of this as correcting one's "thought" processes, but the beliefs they seek to remedy often involve values. When clients are instructed that it is not logical to try to be loved by everyone, they are in part being told a fact about the world, namely that it is virtually impossible to be loved by everyone, but they are also being cautioned not to pursue universal love. The philosopher David Hume warned that a "should" can never be derived from an "is," but this is a transformation that cognitivists regularly perform. It is standard practice for them to dismiss those client values they perceive as extreme or self-defeating. In this surmise they are probably accurate, but it ought to be acknowledged that they are going beyond the facts and indulging in value judgments.

When cognitivists try to rectify distorted self-images, they are on firmer theoretical ground. The ideas a person has about himself are more strictly cognitive. When someone's role partners have poisoned his mind so that he believes himself to be incompetent or unworthy, these are mistaken facts that can be rectified. Also, because a person's beliefs are stabilized by being validated by others, verification of the true, and disqualification of the false, can be a pivotal therapeutic service. It can unblock change by dislodging beliefs that mistakenly persuade a person that change is not possible and give him the courage to attempt what is admittedly difficult.

While it is not usually grouped with the cognitive therapies, vocational rehabilitation similarly addresses thought processes. One tip-off to this is that it is often described as "counseling" and is associated with advice giving. This advice is usually considered an educational intervention and aims at teaching a person what is feasible given the limitations imposed by his disability. This knowledge may include an understanding of himself, of the job market, and of the skills necessary to perform a particular job. The client should then be better situated to implement viable occupational efforts.

## Volitions

As has been explained, many so-called cognitive therapies really specialize in removing volitional barriers to change. The volitional component of role scripts encompasses those factors specifically having to do with decision making. While cognitions refer to an understanding of facts, volitions convert ideas and emotions into actions. They include the values and norms that guide personal decisions. Since it is rarely obvious what actions will fulfill particular needs, people need rules that increase their probability of success. Thus, seeking love from everybody is a strategy for bolstering one's stock of love, but it is an incompetent one because it rarely works. Learning to accept love from those who are willing to give it is much more realistic. This maneuver does not alter one's need for love, but adjusts one's moral outlook so that one seeks love in more reasonable places.

RET has been especially productive in challenging inappropriate "shoulds." It rightly alerts people against pursuing perfection or engaging in excessive competition. Acting upon the belief that one must always be competent sets a standard that no one can meet, while always competing at full throttle interferes with the recruitment of potential allies. These strategies are thus calculated to leave one alone and frustrated. In consequence, if a person can be persuaded to alter his commitments and make action decisions more in line with the possible, eventually more satisfying roles will emerge.

Also, as previously indicated, existentialist therapy specializes in values, and so does reality therapy. When existentialists explore the meaning of life, they are helping people choose directions to which they can commit themselves. They emphasize the necessity of personal responsibility and encourage clients to examine their lives to decide what they truly believe. Reality therapists, likewise, are concerned with personal choices, but are far more directive in their methods. They contend that unhappy people make mistakes in pursuing basic needs because they lack responsibility, and they take it upon themselves to teach them how to acquire it.

### Social Demands

Finally, there are therapies that concentrate on social barriers to change. Most defective roles are inaugurated in coercive role negotiations, but this coercion may not end once a role has been established. Role partners may continue to be unfair and to demand that a person enact behaviors that leave him unhappy. Unless these others can be persuaded to desist in their demands, the person will remain trapped in his misery. Psychotherapists who venture out from the protective cocoons of their offices and meet the role partners of their clients are often impressed by the sheer malignity of many client environments. Not surprisingly, some have devoted themselves to amending this wrong. Instead of blaming faulty client instincts or cognitive errors, they see their clients' pain as something imposed upon them, not something perversely embraced.

From the first, psychoanalysts have worried about how their clients were raised, but it wasn't until the emergence of cultural therapy that social considerations assumed paramount significance. Sullivan and Horney were particularly instrumental in focusing attention on relationship difficulties. Because they understood client distress as emanating from conflict-ridden partnerships, they urged that these be rectified. Beginning in the early 1950s, another movement, namely object relations, has developed out of psychoanalysis. It too stresses the negative developmental effects of distorted primary relationships, and it has promoted responsive parenting to intercept these problems before they arise.

At its outset, psychoanalysis objected to direct interactions between the therapist and his client's family. It was thought that these would contaminate the work of the analytic session. The presence of family members within the clinical sanctuary was virtually banned. It was supposed to destroy the trust upon which the therapeutic alliance was founded. Not until innovators like Nathan Ackerman broke this taboo was family therapy considered possible. But once it became conceivable, the obvious next step was to try to reorganize destructive relationships. When some family members were visibly being unfair to others, and the therapist was also present, it seemed almost unethical not to try to make their interactions more just.

In the course of time even this came to seem inadequate. Family therapists who worked with whole families had difficulty identifying one person as the wrongdoer. The better one understood a family, the more it seemed that everyone was a victim. The blame was then moved up a notch, and society was censured. It began to make sense to try to correct social iniquities. There was thus born a community psychiatry movement that had social reform as its objective. The notion was that dysfunctional societies force people to enact dysfunctional roles, and that if their exploitative institutions can be reorganized, much distress will be alleviated.

Although sociologists have been tangential to most psychotherapeutic concerns, the reform of social institutions was a formative element in their discipline. It was thus natural that they should examine the role of psychotherapy as an institution. Subsequently they developed a theory that suggested much of the pain endured by mental patients was inflicted by the therapeutic interventions themselves, that client anguish was essentially iatrogenic. This so-called "labeling" theory posited that diagnosing people as suffering from a psychiatric disorder inadvertently subjected them to stigmatization. This secondary deviance then became the primary problem, because it coerced its victims into a subordinate social position. The prescription therefore was to stop labeling; if people were not treated as if they were different, they would not be different. They would be freed from unfair social blame and able to establish more satisfying patterns.

Those who have assigned social pressures a central position in causing personal happiness have had mixed success in establishing their empirical claims. Sometimes their purported villains have proved less than villainous, so in the act of allocating blame, they have themselves been unfair. Nevertheless, coercive stereotyping can interfere with resocialization. When it is properly weighted, its removal can be a valuable constituent of psychotherapy. As is often the case, however, taking account of the whole usually produces more desirable results than launching an all-out assault on a part. It is when labeling alone is considered the problem that attacking it is counterproductive.

# 4

# *Psychoanalysis*

## FREUD

Of the most prevalent forms of psychotherapy, Freud's psychoanalysis remains one of the broadest and deepest. A specialist in resocialization, it addresses all three phases of role change and all four barriers to change. Although by now psychoanalysis has become an old-fashioned method of intervention, it retains a relevance that belies its antiquity. Its staying power is no accident and goes back to the origins of the technique. Both named and invented by Sigmund Freud, psychoanalysis is rooted in his history and evolving discoveries. To understand why many of its tenets retain their validity, it is useful to review the path that Freud traversed. To appreciate what he achieved one must comprehend what he sought to accomplish and the obstacles he had to overcome.

Freud began his work over a century ago, in a world of bustles, high-button shoes, and fin-de-siècle monarchies. That his writings still strike sparks is eloquent testimony to the universality of his concerns. Although he was a patriotic citizen of the Austro-Hungarian empire, he was much more an inhabitant of the human condition and was able to turn his own preoccupations into observations that resonate today.

Nevertheless, the rootedness of Freud in his own life and times limited his vision. The concepts he chose reflected the enemies he fought and the tools he had at his disposal. Like all of us, he had to begin at his starting point, and his accomplishments must be measured against this standard. He did not have the benefit of a hundred years of social science behind him. As we shall see, much of what he uncovered fits nicely into a role change perspective, but this perspective was not available when he worked. He therefore wrote in terms of the categories with which he was familiar, and because he was a physician, many of these categories were medical.

As a gifted, ambitious Jew in nineteenth-century Vienna, Freud sought a profession in which merit could lead to success. As a consequence, he gravitated toward medicine and ultimately neurology. Indeed, much of his early work was in the laboratory, staining nerve cells to make them more visible during microscopic examinations. He hoped for an academic career, but given the realities of the university system, found that he could only support himself and his family by hanging out a shingle.

Freud, the neurologist, quite naturally attempted to address the complaints of potential patients. Since "neurosis" and "hysteria" were hot topics, he sought to become expert in them. But he pursued his investigations with a difference. As an outsider, who also wanted to be a conqueror, he delved into forbidden realms. Where more establishment figures like Josef Breuer drew back, he forged ahead. He inquired courageously into the histories of his patients and chanced upon the dirty secrets of middle-class Victorian society. Many of these turned out to be sexual and violent, and they ultimately proved too explosive for him or his society.

Originally Freud postulated that hysterical patients had been victimized by traumatic sexual incidents in their childhoods and that these might be relieved through catharsis. Yet accusing proper Victorian parents of abusing their offspring went against the grain. Neither Freud nor his medical colleagues were prepared to accept such a conclusion. The so-called seduction theory was therefore relegated to the scrap heap and replaced by a psychologized theory that relied on the wayward instincts and confused interpretations of the patients themselves. Thus, instead of pursuing a role explanation that traced disruptions in a person's functioning to early socialization processes, biology and isolated pathology were made to do heavier duty than they were equipped to handle.

In this instance, as in so many others, Freud pointed straight to an area of difficulty, then flinched by biologizing and/or psychologizing his findings. Because he was dealing with taboos, he had to utilize a socially acceptable mode of expression. Here his medical/scientific credentials proved serviceable. They enabled him to publicize conclusions that would otherwise have been inadmissible. Yet language can put constraints upon thought. The fact that his vocabulary was medical and psychological prevented a full appreciation of the social relations nature of his discoveries.

Still Freud persisted. When forced to retract the seduction theory, he did not renounce his explorations. Indeed, he intensified them by turning inward. He began a self-analysis that led to the development of the therapeutic techniques we have come to think of as central to psychoanalysis. Dream analysis and free association were products of this period. Having been forced to use his personal conflicts as a source of information, he was also compelled to devise methods of penetrating his own internal secrets, and these methods were to prove useful in delving into the secrets of others.

Once more, however, the conceptual scaffolding for these advances was inspired by biology and psychology. Freud believed, for instance, that he had discovered how infantile sexuality, and more particularly fixations within normal psychosexual development, eventuated in neurosis. Formulations such as the Oedipus complex became central to his thinking and were conceived as following the vicissitudes of biological energy (christened the libido). Likewise, reflections of brain physiology were embedded in such concepts as the "unconscious." These made visible aspects of human problems not previously recognized, but continued to minimize their social origins.

It was not until his later years that Freud became explicitly social in his thinking. Even then he did not have a role theory, but apparently World War I shook him into an awareness of larger social forces. It was after this upheaval that he was able to write about the superego, group psychology, and the discontents of civilization. By this time, however, his earlier biology and psychology had been enshrined in the rapidly formalizing psychoanalytic movement. The fact that this was dominated by physicians made biology attractive and reduced the influence of his insights on the clash between the individual and his social environment. Most psychoanalysts remained more concerned with how the libido had been fixated than with how interpersonal conflicts resulted in dysfunctional behavior patterns.

Nonetheless, Freud and the psychoanalytic movement he inaugurated deserve credit for establishing the parameters of a resocialization perspective. Despite numerous mistakes in emphasis and theoretical formulation, the main outlines of a role change theory are clearly visible within his thinking. When the proper translations are made and some of the more egregious biologisms eliminated, many of the insights of resocialization are plainly to be found. We must now proceed with these translations and determine the level of change with which psychoanalysis is concerned, the phases of change in which it specializes, and the barriers to change it emphasizes. With this task accomplished, it should be evident how psychosocial and role oriented Freudianism really is.

## LEVEL OF INTERVENTION

Psychoanalysis has always been conceived as facilitating radical change. It was not meant to solve petty problems in living or even to teach more effective methods of coping. Freud clearly meant to extricate his clients from painful styles of life and to enable them to construct more satisfying patterns of living. He wished to proceed deep into their psyches and initiate a radical reorganization of the way they thought, felt, and behaved.

Indeed, the putative depth of psychoanalysis has often been contrasted with generic psychotherapy, to the latter's disadvantage. Analysts talk about the "pure gold" (Fine, 1979) of their method, implying that alternative procedures are somehow adulterated. Only analysis, it is asserted, is capable of penetrating to the heart of a person's problem or initiating meaningful change. Other methods are deemed incapable of neutralizing a person's defenses or uncovering what needs to be changed. It therefore follows that only psychoanalysis can reach the deepest level of intervention, or what we have called resocialization.

### Role Problems

Were modern psychoanalysts to be asked what they are trying to change, most would probably answer: the client's personality, character, or self. On first sight this seems far removed from role change, but it is surprisingly close. The aspects of the personality that are being altered turn out to resemble the role scripts of basic personal roles. Certainly some aspects of personality, such as temperament, are not touched by psychoanalysis. Nor do analysts even claim to impact factors such as cognitive style or level of energy. Rather, it is emotional sticking points or cognitive errors that are analyzed and modified. Moreover, it is when the client is able to establish effective ways of loving and working that success is solidified.

Observing Freud's original clientele reveals his clear interest in role problems. He began, it will be recalled, by treating women diagnosed as suffering from hysteria. Though his contemporaries medicalized this disorder, he first sought its origin in childhood sexual traumas. Freud explained the dramatic behaviors of these clients as defenses against unresolved pain. A resocialization perspective would take a similar viewpoint. It would describe dysfunctional patterns as having been established in childhood and remaining unchanged because painful mechanisms hold them in place. It might not even challenge the idea that these patterns are part of someone's personality, merely insisting on their social origin and social reconstruction. In these terms psychoanalysis is but a variant of resocialization that has not fully appreciated the social element in the formation and alteration of dysfunctional interpersonal behavior patterns.

To recognize the role-problem nature of the cases Freud treated, one has only to glance at some of his most famous cases. We may begin with Anna O., who although not Freud's patient (she was Breuer's) was a focal point in his study of hysteria. When Bertha Pappenheim, the real Anna O., came to see Breuer, she was 21 years old and had been caring for her physically ill father. She was described as very intelligent, given to daydreaming, and possessing a "sympathetic kindness" (Breuer and Freud, 1957). Despite her gifts, she was also said to be living a monotonous life, with her sexuality "astonishingly underdeveloped." There subsequently evolved a series of "symptoms" that were taken as defining her "manifest illness." These included paraphasia, disturbances of vision, paralyses, and later somnambulism. Most of these conditions lifted within a year after her father's death.

Breuer treated Pappenheim first with hypnosis, then with a "talking cure" that was virtually invented by her. Since both Breuer and Freud were medical men, called in to minister to a medical disorder, her physical manifestations received considerable attention from them. Freud, however, went beyond these to speculate that Breuer's patient was trying to cope with a sexualized trauma involving her father and derived from early childhood. From our perspective, her situation might also be interpreted in social role terms. If Pappenheim is seen as having developed a "caretaker" role vis-à-vis her father (one is almost tempted to describe her relationship as "enmeshed"), her struggle can be perceived as an attempt to assert independence. Her symptoms make sense if they are understood as manifestations of an internalized role conflict not yet resolved.

From what we know of Pappenheim's subsequent life, the notion that she had adopted a caretaker role becomes more persuasive. Breuer's description of her as gifted was indeed correct, for she went on to become one of the founders of Germany's social work movement. Any conflicts she may have had regarding her sexual role seem, however, to have remained unresolved, for she never married. Ironically, Freud's gifted daughter, Anna, seems to have been caught in a similar dilemma. She too spent much of her energy in caring for a dynamic but physically ill father, and she too never married.

Another of the cases that interested Freud, namely that of Dora, can similarly be depicted in social-role terms. Writing about her, he presents a young woman diagnosed with hysteria and having sexualized difficulties. In heavy-handed and insensitive language, he describes her as resisting his well-meant, psychosexual interpretations. A disinterested reader becomes aware of a vulnerable adolescent trapped in horrendously conflicting roles, being harassed by an older man who seems intent on blaming her for her own troubles. Dora, we discover, was contending with overlapping sexual triangles that included her father's liaison with a woman other than his wife and attempts by his mistress's husband to seduce Dora. In this complex soap opera, Dora's loyalties were severely tested and, not surprisingly, she was unsure where her duties as a loving daughter and a chaste young woman lay. While Freud did try to help her out of this dilemma, his psychosexual speculations were aimed in the wrong direction and she subsequently refused treatment. Had he more explicitly viewed her misfortune as a role problem, and less as a matter of sexual instincts, the outcome might have been different.

If we turn to Freud himself, we see that he too was suffering from role difficulties and was heroically trying to extricate himself from them. His famous self-analysis can be interpreted as an attempt to solve role conflicts involving both his parents and his Viennese surroundings. Freud was the eldest son of his father's young second wife. He had elder brothers for whom he might almost have been a son, yet to his mother he was a precious gift who was expected to accomplish great things. Moreover, as the son of a Jewish father trying to be successful in an Austria ambivalent about Jews, he inherited a mantle of ambivalence, himself hoping to be both a good Jew and a good Austrian.

In his effort to cope with these conflicts, Freud sought to create a role he himself described as that of a "conqueror." Looking back from a century's distance, we can perceive that he was remarkably successful in this, but from his own perspective the issue was very much in doubt. Throughout his life, he oscillated between tremendous self-confidence and enormous apprehension. Yet he persevered and allowed himself to achieve success. He became the great man his mother expected him to be and the father of a social movement, capable of supplanting his own father. Regarding his role as the Jewish outsider, he also found a resolution of sorts. His later writings make it clear that he was skeptical of all religion, but he never renounced his Jewishness or his Austrianness. Almost to the end he remained in Austria, a well-known Jew, despite the depredations of Hitler's Anschluss. His solution was to become a world-famous, secular, Austro-Jewish psychoanalyst, who was above labels and was entitled to acceptance as a scientist and man of letters.

## Etiology

When we turn to Freud's explanations of the role problems that so attracted him, we find a developmental perspective at work. He essentially attempted to convert his biomedical roots into a biologized psychology that explained the derivation of personal problems. Because he needed places for supposed psychosexual traumas to attach themselves, he postulated that early childhood passes through distinct, sexualized, developmental periods. These include the oral, the anal, and the phallic. (Later childhood was said to contain latency and genital stages as well.) Such a perspective placed its emphasis on the particular tasks a child had to achieve during each period, tasks that, if unresolved thanks to some traumatic event, must eventually be completed lest a neurosis ensue. Freud understood his stages as tracing the development of the libido, that is, as documenting how sexual energy first adheres to the mouth area, then the anus, then the phallus. Today, few except the most orthodox Freudians are impressed by the libido theory, but many still cleave to a developmental sequence that places the locus of difficulty within the person and his biological maturation.

Obviously, as a child grows, his biology, cognitive equipment, and emotional resilience all evolve. But something else, equally important, also changes, namely his social relationships. Both his role negotiations and his skills as a negotiator metamorphose, and this evolution has enormous implications for the nature of his role problems and their potential remediation. Since roles are negotiated products, how they arise affects what they are and how they can be altered. Thus, another way to interpret the evidence for a developmental sequence is as affirmation of changing role negotiations.

If social roles are negotiated, it is to be expected that the interchanges in which they are created also develop as a child gets older. During different periods of his life, a growing child will engage in varying activities with a multitude of role partners. He will, in turn, be enmeshed with parents, siblings, peers, and strangers, and out of these encounters will emerge his roles. It is when these go awry that dysfunctional roles are launched.

To understand how this works, we can examine the oral stage. This is a time when the activity of sucking is extremely important to a child. It is also the period during which social negotiations are first established. While it was once thought that infants were passive receptors of external ministrations, today we know that interactions between a baby and her mother begin at birth. From the start there is a mutual exchange of smiles, gurgles, vocalizations, and touches. The two develop a reciprocity that gradually carries the child into the social world. These exchanges can be thought of as negotiations in which the influence flows both ways, with the parent and child reinforcing each other's offerings.

This same mutuality extends to the feeding process. It is not merely a matter of a mother delivering food to a baby who passively receives it. While it is true that a mother teaches her child how to eat, it is equally true that the child teaches her mother how she wants to be fed. During the early part of this century, when children were still viewed as docile bundles of protoplasm begging to be molded by their parents, scheduled feeding was in vogue. A bottle was to be delivered to the child at the scientifically correct moment and she was expected to consume a specified volume of liquid regardless of how she was feeling. Nowadays it is understood that demand feeding is more appropriate and that a child's input is relevant and essential. Indeed, the child is now allowed to indicate what she likes, as well as when she wants to eat. She thus becomes a party to the process. Today, even mothers of neonates recognize that their infants will inform them of the most commodious feeding position, if so allowed.

When reciprocity exists between a parent and child, each learns to be responsive to the other. If effected with sensitivity and love, these primitive negotiations set a healthy precedent for succeeding negotiations; if not, they lay the groundwork for future disruptions. Early interactions, grounded in coercion, destroy the bases of social trust and make it difficult for a child to engage in smooth negotiations later on. They form a kind of template for later controversies. It is through this mechanism that the so-called oral stage has its greatest impact.

When we move to the anal period, a different form of social negotiation arises. Even at the oral stage, children try to assert themselves as distinctive role partners, but at the anal stage this becomes their raison d'être. If a fair bargain is to be achieved, each party to it has to have a say in the final decision. But for this to occur, each must have a separate point of view that is separately asserted. Indeed, to become an individual is to have such a viewpoint and to be able to propound it with energy.

The anal period is notorious for being the era of the "terrible twos." It is the period during which a child learns to say no, and to say it with gusto. Parents of toddlers discover to their grief that their children refuse to do things just for the pleasure of refusing. The simple act of claiming one's personhood becomes a source of gratification and may be repeated with endless variations. One of these, of course, occurs over the issue of toilet training. During more repressive ages, when parents felt it their duty to break a child's spirit, learning to use the bathroom was a scene of interminable battles. In an effort to fight back a child would use the feeble weapons at her command—for instance, refusing to evacuate her bowels; similarly, she might choose to reward her parents by defecating on command. Either way she was using the negotiating tactics within her control, in the first case punishing her parents by denying them what was wanted, and in the second by using the same mechanism as a reward.

If the above analysis is correct, then the anal stage is in reality a milestone in the development of assertiveness as a negotiation tool. A 2- or 3-year-old is far less vulnerable than a neonate and far more capable of being disruptive. Learning to use this new-found power in interaction with parents thus also contributes to the creation of templates for future role negotiations. But given recent changes in parenting styles, the "anal" appellation has become a misnomer and the stage might better be characterized by improved mobility and communication skills. These, after all, are the areas in which most conflicts arise and in which the powers of the child, and the patience of the parent, are most sorely tested.

The phallic stage also reveals an evolution in the child's social negotiation skills. If we pass over Freud's emphasis on the male sexual organ, attributing it to the chauvinism of his time, we can instead concentrate on the Oedipus complex, supposedly the most important landmark of the period. Indeed, Freud believed that oedipal difficulties were the source of most childhood fixations. He firmly asserted that no psychoanalysis could be successful unless oedipal entanglements were successfully resolved.

But what is this Oedipus complex? Is it primarily concerned with the little boy protecting his sexual organ from attack by his father, or with the little girl trying to compensate for a presumed injury to hers by her mother? In Freud's version, the boy wishes to wrest his mother away from his father, but because he is not strong enough, and because he fears his father will attack his vulnerable parts, he relinquishes his claim and identifies with his father. Similarly, the young girl mourns the loss of a once-present penis, blames her mother for this deficiency, and wishes to gain her father and his penis, but because of the mother's competition she cannot achieve this, and like her brother has to settle for an identification with the same-sex parent. Unless the child, boy or girl, makes this final identification, the complex remains in force. In consequence, the goal of analysis is to consummate the proper identification.

It should, of course, be noticed that the identification of the child is with the sex role of the same-sex parent. The boy wants to be like his father and the girl like her mother. In sum, the social negotiations of this era decide what sexual status the child will later assume. While the boy gives up a desire to have his mother, he does not give up his desire to have someone like his mother, and in future negotiations as a young adult he may even obtain one. In his subsequent negotiations, his having accepted a male style of relating will therefore be an asset. Similarly, the young girl will prepare to become a woman who can get a man of her own, likewise with the help of her new-found femininity.

Recent research has shown that gender identifications originate as early as the second year, and perhaps earlier, but Freud's description of the "family romance" still rings true in many particulars. Penis envy and fears of castration may not be as prevalent as he supposed, but little boys do fall in love with their mothers and little girls do want to marry their fathers. Moreover, these desires cause disruptions in the family that must be calmed. Indeed such conflicting ambitions and their resolution are the stuff of social negotiations, and their denouement generates enduring role bargains.

The major negotiational advance that must be made during the oedipal phase is discovering how to conduct multiperson negotiations. As children mature, they are capable of handling greater and greater complications. For instance, they must learn to cope with two parents who themselves have conflicting interests. To achieve this, they have to develop a relationship with one parent that is acceptable to the other parent. A stable gender identity can help realize this, so it occupies a featured place in the oedipal drama. Work within other cultures suggests that this sort of resolution evolves even when there is no nuclear family, as was the case with Bronislaw Malinowski's Trobriand Islanders. There the little boy interacted with his uncle rather than his father, but still learned to make appropriate identifications and to resolve potentially antagonistic arrangements.

Freud, in looking for a developmental etiology, stumbled upon the social negotiation dilemmas of childhood. While he thought he was describing the biological underpinnings of neurotic behaviors, he was as well, if not better, describing the origin of role dysfunctions. To surmount these dysfunctions people have to relinquish and re-form the negotiations that have gone wrong in childhood. And when they do, they may well feel like little children arguing with their parents about what to eat, where to walk, or what friends to play with. Psychoanalysis owes its acknowledged depth to its attempts at changing basic roles and reworking early role negotiations. It is this very fact that makes it so proficient a specialist in resocialization.

### Resocialization

From the beginning Freud was interested in going deep and effecting radical change. One of his earliest concepts was that of the unconscious. In introducing it, he asserted that individuals do not have complete control over their destiny, that many of their motives are buried beyond their awareness and operate independently of their conscious decisions. Changing the person therefore necessitates piercing this hidden realm and manipulating its contents. Dream analysis was one tool for achieving this. Freud considered it the royal road to the unconscious and hoped it would illuminate the secret wellsprings of individual behavior.

In digging deep, Freud anticipated an arduous task. Indeed, his original methodology included daily one-hour sessions that could last years. The defenses of the unconscious were assumed to be formidable and not ready to yield to anything less than a determined assault. In this, he certainly foreshadowed the difficulty that resocialization theory assigns to changing basic personal roles. While Freud thought that he was reworking fixations of the libido that were not understood for what they were, from a resocialization perspective it is dysfunctionally maintained roles that are similarly misinterpreted. The unconscious thus proves a very useful concept in highlighting the inaccessibility of what needs to be changed before a person can implement satisfying actions. It is this very inaccessibility that makes it necessary to obtain outside help in replacing dysfunctional roles.

But what was it Freud thought he was changing? Not social roles, but fixations of the "id." Sexual energy was thought to be trapped at specific developmental checkpoints; by liberating it via cognitive understanding and emotional catharsis a person would be enabled to proceed with mature living. This notion of being freed to get on with life is very like the resocialization belief that only when a dysfunctional role is relinquished can more functional ones emerge. Instead of imagining that a fluid-like sexual energy (libido) has been trapped, resocialization-oriented therapists propose that normal mechanisms of role conservation are perverted so that they interfere with needed change.

## PHASES OF CHANGE

Compared with other forms of therapy, psychoanalysis is generalist. As much as any other form of intervention, it encourages the reexperiencing, the relinquishing, and the renegotiation phases of role change. Since psychoanalysts perceive themselves as undertaking an arduous task, they do not shrink from the extended periods of time necessary for resocialization. This allows the space needed to support all aspects of the process. While they do not understand their exertions in role-change terms, psychoanalysts do conceive of themselves as proceeding in stages. Usually these are identified as an opening phase, a working-through phase, and a termination phase. Though these do not exactly coincide with the phases of resocialization, they are roughly parallel.

Freud permitted his clients to reexperience their dysfunctional roles by activating their repetition compulsion, allowed them to relinquish their roles through an extended rehearsal of their problems, and countenanced a renegotiation of roles through a gradual return to the world at the end of therapy. In practice, these objectives tended to run together and were not identified with the task of role change. Nonetheless, when psychoanalysis was successful, all three phases were represented.

## Reexperiencing/Identifying

Although the early Freud was more cognitive than emotional in his methods, he always expected his clients to delve deeply into their past. Whether intentionally or not, he brought this past back in vivid color. As a by-product of trying to identify and interpret the kinds of problems his patients were having, he stumbled onto the "repetition compulsion." He noticed that, both in therapy and in their private spheres, clients tended to reconstruct past circumstances and form relationships similar to ones they had experienced. In part this mystified him, because it did not seem to make sense for people to deliberately reexperience painful events and relationships. Still, when they persisted in their efforts, rather than stop them, he resolved to understand and help them alter these. Freud even gave a name to this situation, labeling it the "transference neurosis."

Because Freud considered himself an archaeologist, delving into the remains left behind by his patients' earlier lives, he sought tools with which to dig. His primary instruments were free association and dream analysis. Many contemporary psychotherapists find that such excavations can be satisfactorily conducted by using questions and role taking, but Freud thought he needed more exotic implements. As a pioneer investigator of the human unconscious, he frequently did not know what he was looking for, and sometimes imagined that his quarry was better guarded than it was. For this reason he favored indirect methods of approach.

Consider free association, the chief Freudian probing instrument. This technique requires patients to say whatever comes into their heads, censoring nothing. When inspected closely, it seems a rather profligate device, designed to bring up more chaff than wheat. But Freud was certain that when given a chance, unconscious tidbits would percolate to the surface, where they could be tracked down in a logical sequence. Similarly, dream analysis, his "royal road to the unconscious," was intended to dredge up even more deeply hidden gems, which could then be fit together by the therapist to form a good portrait of the client's problem.

In practice, these explorations are more coherent and focused than the theoretically unguided processes of free association and dream analysis might seem to allow. First, Freudian clients are always more aware of what their therapist wants than a "say whatever comes to mind" declaration would suggest. The pieces of information an analyst follows up, and the interpretations given, function like questions to focus attention on specific areas. Nor are orthodox Freudians undisciplined in their observations. Because they seek wheat, it is wheat they generally find.

Second, because psychoanalysts are very concerned about the phenomena of transference and countertransference, they provide themselves with an opportunity for considerable role taking. While they theoretically try to be a blank slate upon which clients can write, analysts usually are active interpreters with whom their clients can, and do, interact. This certainly was true of Freud, whose own patients reported him to have been a more active participant in their therapy than his writings indicated.

Because the analyst is a human being, he is someone with whom a client can recapitulate dysfunctional roles. This act of "regression" allows the analyst access to the client's past. By using such internal mechanisms as empathy, he can project himself into his client's role, thereby gaining a better grasp of its particulars. He is then able to use this information to identify the client's dysfunctional behavior patterns. Whether by means of interpretations or confrontations, he puts the client in touch with herself and reinforces the experience of her role. Although historically many analytic interpretations have been cognitive in nature, they can still precipitate an emotional recapitulation of the past.

Countertransference, it must be added, is an excellent vehicle for tuning into client roles. When a therapist is able to distinguish what he adds to a therapeutic encounter, he is better situated to recognize his client's contribution. Understanding that he too recapitulates antique roles can make the present clearer for both.

## Relinquishing

Despite Freud's having perceived the connection between mourning and melancholia, psychoanalysts have not, until recently, fully appreciated the utility of grief in working through personal problems. Nevertheless, they have facilitated a letting go of the past. From the beginning they have recognized that relinquishing old patterns is difficult and have tried to find a way past this hurdle. Early on Freud spoke of "resistance" to change, and indeed, working through this resistance became the focus of most analytic sessions.

Because relinquishing dysfunctional roles begins with a protest against loss, this needs to be analyzed and resolved. Yet in attacking resistance, some Freudians have acted as if a client's protest were directed against them personally. Fortunately, most discover that the protest is a response to past coercion or fear of an unknown future. Though the client's resistance might look like perversity, making it a focal point of analysis encourages its examination and ultimate acknowledgment.

Working with resistance also allows psychoanalysts to approach client problems from many different directions. The working-through phase of analysis frequently involves repeatedly talking about the same problem, albeit each time from a slightly different vantage point. Although such repetition may seem wasteful and exasperating, in reality it facilitates the removal of obstacles to mourning. During the process of analysis, cognitive impediments to change are examined, emotional barriers disarmed, volitional errors corrected, and unhelpful social demands countered. Otto Fenichel, one of the more respected interpreters of Freud's legacy, has emphasized that problems, and especially emotional ones, must be reviewed many times before they gradually lose their power to cause mischief.

The time-consuming nature of the working-through process is itself good evidence that ties to dysfunctional roles are being severed. Protesting and mourning a loss, especially a disguised one, inevitably go slowly. The emotional changes involved need space to occur. Such transitions do not take place quickly, because they are very frightening. A therapist's reassurances, therefore, are often necessary for them to proceed. By giving a person permission to move methodically, and by being present as a security object, the therapist legitimates the relinquishing phase of resocialization and enables it to go forward.

### Renegotiating

When Freudians address themselves to the last phase of role change, they do not explicitly think of themselves as renegotiating new roles. Historically, they have been more concerned with terminating the analysis. Yet they have recognized that during therapy the client will have developed an attachment to his analyst, and that this must be weakened before he can pick up the pieces of his life. Indeed, many outsiders have been aghast at the intense dependency that can develop during the working-through phase of therapy, and have not understood it as a form of security that eventually facilitates independence.

Psychoanalysts themselves do not make this mistake. They have always been exquisitely aware that they become intensely important role partners for their clients. They have also been mindful of the fact that despite the difficulty of renouncing such attachments, the attachments themselves can interfere with the establishment of other relationships. These powerful bonds are not perceived as positive in themselves, but as an unavoidable side effect of a valuable end. A later separation is understood as absolutely necessary, and part of their task to encourage.

Because departing from analysis is difficult, much of the final phase of analysis is devoted to present-day client relationships. Freud recommended that patients postpone decisions about love and work until their therapy was almost complete. It was when nearing termination that they were invited to think about reality problems and to shift their focus from therapy to interactions with outside role partners. After all, it was with these latter that their role adjustments ultimately had to be negotiated. At this juncture, the analyst became more a coach than a participant in change. Although he might not label this process as renegotiating roles, his advice could substantially advance (or inhibit) this effort.

Theoretically, psychoanalysis is against advice giving, though Freud himself gave much counsel. Still, he recommended that the therapist be relatively silent, thereby allowing the client to make discoveries for herself. Clinician interpretations were supposed to be sparse but insightful. The objective was to avoid forcing a person in directions of the therapist's choosing. In essence, this is a strategy for preventing coercive negotiations. Unfortunately, too rigorous an attachment to silence can itself be coercive. In this case the therapist becomes an implacable interlocutor who cannot be dislodged from her position, however reasonable the importunities of the client. Instead of allowing interpretations to be talked over and modified in the light of the client's experience there is an implication that she is a sage whose wisdom must be accepted unaltered. The danger, therefore, is of a disguised form of coercion.

Termination can be a self-conscious affair. Both analyst and client know what is coming, and a shift in role partners may be explicitly decided upon by them. In Freudian terms, the "transference neurosis" is resolved and normal living resumed. Interminable therapy is not desired, though a rigid therapeutic style can make terminal negotiations very long lasting.

## BARRIERS TO CHANGE

In discussing the relinquishing phase of resocialization, we have noted that psychoanalysts typically include obstacles to letting go of the past under the rubric of resistance. It has also been remarked that they deal with cognitive, emotional, volitional, and social barriers to change. We must now get a clearer fix on how these are addressed.

### Cognitions

During his formative years, Freud believed that a cognitive understanding could itself bring release from neurotic symptoms. In substituting free association and dream analysis for hypnosis, he sought an intellectual understanding of client fixations. The object was to make the unconscious conscious, which is to say that vague impressions were to be converted into verbalized convictions. Such understandings were never thought of as completely free standing (even in the beginning they were to be a bridge to catharsis), but they often did become the goal of therapy. Freud, and many of his immediate disciples, reveled in the clever interpretations they made and were as much concerned with developing theory as relieving client anxieties.

From at least the decade of his self-analysis, Freud stressed the importance of self-understanding. He believed that it was absolutely essential to define the parameters of a client's Oedipus complex and for him (or her) to achieve a cognitive acceptance of castration fears (or penis envy). The dynamics of the client's earlier life became grist for the analytic mill, to be appreciated for what they were before progress could be made. In the public imagination, at least, the analyst was seen as browbeating his patients until they admitted the facts of infantile sexuality. Unless the therapist's interpretations were accepted, it was assumed that the client's resistance had not been breached. While most analysts never lived up to this caricature, they did hold firmly to the officially sanctioned psychosexual interpretations.

### Emotions

Despite Freud's cognitive biases, emotions have always had a prominent place in his methodology. From its origins, the "talking cure" was an emotional cure. Freud was, after all, the person who made "catharsis" a watchword for psychotherapy. His hydraulic model of the libido operationally defined catharsis as an emotional release. It was thus in the expression of anxiety and/or anger that people were to find relief. The mere manifestation of an emotion was supposed to reduce tension and eliminate the need for the symptoms that defended against its appearance.

As psychoanalysis matured, it became more sophisticated in the emotions it recognized. It was Freud who introduced the theory of "signal anxiety" and who first raised the subject of "melancholia." Many of his adherents picked up on these and were even more explicit in emphasizing the curative value of unblocking problem emotions. Fenichel, as we have seen, stressed the need for gradually reworking intense emotions, and Alexander spoke persuasively of the necessity for a "corrective emotional experience." This was in part because practicing analysts discovered that without an emotional connection, progress was not forthcoming.

If we take a closer look at psychoanalytic concepts, we see that even the id is emotionally laden. While Freud may have thought of it as a repository of irrational sexual energy, its intensity and ungovernability make it the very paradigm of what emotion should be. Freud has been roundly condemned for introducing irrationality into psychotherapy, but this was no more than a recognition of the way emotions really work. Our feelings do not submissively follow our cognitive judgments, and so in working them out, feelings must be addressed on their own terms. This insight, however indirectly it was expressed by Freud, is fundamental to the unblocking of the emotions that interrupt role change.

## Volitions

If the id is the fountainhead of emotion, the superego is Freud's repository for volitional constraints. The superego is the shadow of the internalized parental admonitions that he identified as providing us with a conscience. Such internalizations form the nucleus of a person's value system, keeping him in touch with reality or at least aiding him in making unavoidable social compromises. The superego provides us with rules for action, some of which may be helpful and others of which may not. This distinction makes it possible to identify the overly repressive superego and to extirpate unnecessary guilt. With this burden of guilt removed, another obstacle to resocialization is eliminated.

Freud advertised himself as, and was largely accepted as, a scientist. In recent decades it has become evident that he was also a moralist. Despite his honest desire to understand the human mind, he was a reformer, who wanted to leave the world a better place than he found it. For him, psychoanalysis was not merely a technique; it was a calling. Reports of conversations from his inner circle make it clear that neurosis was considered virtually immoral, and that self-awareness and mature development were deemed noble. Within the analytic movement there was (and is) no surer way of deflating an adversary than to point out that he is speaking from his own unresolved conflicts. Indeed, the fact that it is a movement, with a strictly enforced orthodoxy, is testimony to this moral commitment.

Such a moral allegiance does have its positive aspects. It enables practitioners to persevere in what has been called an "impossible profession" (Malcolm, 1982) and to bolster client efforts at resocialization. To strongly covet role change is to embrace an ethic that helps one endure the rigors of change.

## Social Demands

In his later years, Freud became occupied with the demands that society placed on the individual. The trauma of World War I caused him to reflect upon the occasional intransigence of this world. He then produced works on group psychology and the nature of civilization that emphasized the incompatibility of social requirements with individual needs. He had always been aware that the individual had to adjust to society; this was the nub of the "reality principle" described by him as the ego's main task. But now the conflict between the two became more salient.

Freud speculated about the primeval revolt of sons against their fathers, and the subsequent legacy of guilt inherited by all sons. He interpreted prevalent religious conceptions as comforting projections of an all-powerful childhood father onto the universe, and he delved into archaeological roots of monotheism. He theorized that in order to reduce social conflicts, individuals have to suppress their innermost desires. Throughout his career he had dabbled in anthropology and tried to reconcile his Jewishness with the surrounding German culture; now he put his theories in writing. Nonetheless, all of this remained abstract, having little to do with the problems his clients experienced.

Moreover, Freud insisted upon seeing clients apart from their families. While he knew that childhood socialization helped shape adult problems, he considered family participation a potential interference best controlled by exclusion. Similarly, he asked clients to postpone decisions about their careers and romances until they were close to finishing therapy. Once again social interferences were to be limited and social barriers to resocialization not directly tackled in therapy.

Many of Freud's successors rightly complained that while he might theorize about the social bases of personal problems, in practice he did not sufficiently address these. It was no accident that Adler, Horney, Sullivan, and the object relations school have all tried to fill gaps in the social aspects of psychoanalysis. Nor was it an accident that one of Freud's earliest acts in establishing psychoanalysis was jettisoning the seduction theory in favor of blaming client problems on cognitive distortions originating with the clients themselves. He was simply more comfortable working one on one with patients and trying to correct their psyches than with restructuring social environments.

## Summing Up

Interesting as are many of the specifics of Freud's theory of psychotherapy, many of them are irrelevant to the success of his therapeutic interventions. Specifically, the biopsychological machinery he invented is in no way necessary to explaining why psychoanalysis fosters resocialization. Concepts such as the libido, the psychosexual stages, the ego, the id, and the superego may illuminate the dynamics of the human mind, but contemporary psychology and neurology seem to be doing a better job without them. Likewise, specific intervention strategies, such as analyzing the Oedipus complex or encouraging free association and dream analysis, may be useful to expediting role change, but they are not essential and can be replaced by other techniques.

Though many of Freud's theories are provocative, a role interpretation explains many of the same phenomena without resort to fictional entities or unverifiable dynamics. Indeed, many of his basic concepts, like the repetition compulsion, transference, and resistance, make more sense in social-role terms. Indeed, they almost call out for such a reading. Thus, dysfunctional roles seem to be what is repeated in the "repetition compulsion"; the reactivation of these same roles with the therapist as role partner is apparently at the core of "transference"; and "resistance" to change is the expectable response to barriers in resocialization.

# 5

# *Cultural Therapies*

## REBELLION

Orthodoxy breeds rebellion. Because the insights of Sigmund Freud and his immediate followers solidified into an almost religious formalism, doubts and resentments were bound to arise. No matter how insightful their theories or efficacious their therapies, their insistence that theirs was the only right way essentially defied others to put forward alternatives. Ambitious souls with ingenious minds were sure to discover other techniques and invent new theories, and if these were suppressed, they were certain to chafe at the restraints and insist upon their own vision.

Freud and his colleagues operated within a hostile environment, against which they felt compelled to defend themselves. To achieve what they believed an essential solidarity, they enforced a virtual catechism, which if not espoused led to ejection from their ranks. Were psychoanalysis merely a science this might be difficult to understand, but given its nature as a quasi-social movement, it is less unexpected. Since it promoted a value system as well as hypotheses about facts, other orthodoxies felt threatened by Freudianism and did indeed assail it. They were not going to accede mildly to what they considered perverse ideas regarding sexuality and the unconscious.

What, then, were sympathetic skeptics to do? Those attracted to psychoanalysis, but doubtful about some of its tenets, were placed in a quandary. Should they suppress their questions, or voice them and risk excommunication? And if excommunicated, should they eschew psychotherapy completely or initiate a competing orthodoxy? Often despite themselves, they did the latter. Some therapists, including Adler, explicitly rejected the notion of establishing a countermovement, but their followers discovered that in order to retain a separate identity, a new orthodoxy was required. At the very least, they needed training facilities under their own aegis.

One of the first areas in which dissent arose concerned the relative salience of social factors in establishing and correcting the sorts of problems clients brought for therapy. Freud and his colleagues, especially in the beginning, tended to emphasize the biological underpinnings of personal distress. They insisted that it was vicissitudes of the client's own libido that caused the most difficulties. This instinctive component of the individual psyche, later to be identified as the id, was described as misdirected or overly developed, and so taming it became the objective. But this often entailed blaming the person for his own distress, even when it was instigated in childhood.

Despite the fact that most early psychoanalysts were physicians, some bridled at the notion that biology was all. Contact with clients taught them that social factors were of enormous import. They could see how families, and social institutions, fomented difficulties. Early socialization, it became clear, was of special significance in establishing later problems. They consequently concluded that correcting social influences might be as important as adjusting instincts.

Among those who brought social insights to their critique of Freud were Alfred Adler, Erich Fromm, Karen Horney, Harry Stack Sullivan, Heinz Hartmann, Ronald Fairbairn, Edith Jacobson, René Spitz, Heinz Kohut, and Margaret Mahler. For our purposes I will label these all as culturalists, though in fact this appellation is more properly reserved for Horney, Sullivan, Fromm, and perhaps Adler. This term will be used to call attention to their joint debt to the cultural and social traditions of the twentieth century. It was, after all, in this century that anthropology and sociology established the significance of cultural factors in understanding individual human beings. Figures such as Ruth Benedict, Edward Sapir, and George Herbert Mead demonstrated the importance of social interactions and the transmission of social beliefs in determining the life-styles of individual persons. They also made it clear that many of the difficulties of individuals had their origin in sociocultural mechanisms. What is more, there is ample evidence that many of their ideas directly influenced the theories and practices of those here being termed culturalists.

Adler was, of course, the first. Although he is often identified as a disciple of Freud's, he is more properly thought of as a colleague who ultimately decided to go his own way. While throughout his life he acknowledged his debt to Freud, especially regarding the significance of unconscious processes, he was never comfortable with the libido theory and early on regarded power as a more important determiner of human action than sexuality. Later figures, such as Horney, did not consider themselves Freud's peers, but rebelled against the Freudianism in which they had been trained. They asserted that social conflicts, not internal biological ones, triggered personal distress. It remained for Sullivan, an American only tangentially influenced by Freud, to codify those theoretical alternatives to psychoanalysis that had at their base a fuller appreciation of the potency of social relationships.

Meanwhile, psychoanalysis was itself evolving. Therapists, such as Hartmann, who maintained their personal allegiance to Freud also felt a need for changes in Freudian doctrine. They too were discovering that individuals are more than mere slaves to their libidos and that people exercise a significant degree of control over their destinies. They expressed this in Freudian terms by emphasizing the import of the ego, as opposed to the id. These so-called "ego psychologists" celebrated the individual's control over his life and his ability to cope with social forces. Their brethren, the "object relations" therapists, took this insight further and stressed the degree to which people react to their social world. In Freudian jargon these others are "objects," hence the name of the school. These therapists' emphasis on, and research into, the sequelae of early socialization effected a revolution in psychoanalysis that reverberates to this day.

## ALFRED ADLER

Adler may well be considered the godfather of the neo-Freudians. This Viennese psychiatrist began his explorations of alternatives to psychoanalysis at the beginning of the century. As a member of Freud's Wednesday evening meetings, he was privy to the master's seminal ideas, but he was never entirely their captive. Almost from the first he asserted the significance of social factors, especially power and hierarchy. Adler took a more commonsense approach to client problems than Freud, one that clashed with Freud's biometaphysical machinery. This eventually led to conflicts between the two, and each ultimately went his own way.

There was in Adler a strong tinge of the reformer. He was more influenced by the socialist stirrings of turn of the century Vienna than was Freud, and he more explicitly hoped to build a better society. Thus he was not only interested in individuals, but also in the institutions that might help them deal with the world. Because of this social orientation, as a psychotherapist Adler was very interested in social psychology. He focused on the social urges that motivated people rather than their presumed instincts. He perceived his clients not as sick, but as discouraged by social failure. His aim, therefore, was to aid them, either by improving their ability to cope or by altering the social milieu impinging upon them. Adler especially hoped to transform the kinds of socialization to which children were exposed. To this end, he diligently promoted the spread of child guidance clinics.

Despite his social orientation, Adler was not a role theorist. Role theories were not prominent in his surroundings, and so he evolved a perspective all his own. Like Freud, he began with biology. The physician in him was fascinated with how patients coped with organ weaknesses by developing compensatory strengths. But Adler quickly moved on to purely social weaknesses and added to our vocabulary the phrases "inferiority complex," "masculine protest," and "will to power." He was also fascinated by the "as if" quality of human thought and with the teleological nature of human activity. As a result, his therapy emphasized the need to correct "basic mistakes" by taking corrective purposive action.

### Levels of Intervention

As a colleague of Freud's, Adler was naturally influenced by the comprehensive nature of psychoanalysis. He too engaged in psychotherapy with individual clients in the hope of effecting dramatic changes in their lives. But his therapy was far more cognitive and less depth-oriented than Freud's. Much Adlerian counseling facilitated resocialization, but sometimes almost inadvertently. If taken literally, Adler's ideas accord more with a socialization than a resocialization perspective. Indeed, much of his work was geared explicitly toward socialization.

#### Socialization

As a founder of child guidance clinics and family education centers, Adler certainly believed in the value of teaching more effective forms of socialization. He was concerned with the way children are raised, and although he abhorred neglect and abuse, equally loathed what he called "pampering." He wanted children to be able to overcome the limitations they acquire in the competitive cauldron of family socialization, yet believed they should learn to assert themselves rather than be given an easy way out.

In one-on-one counseling, Adler believed in change. He stressed the fact that adults have choices available to them, but that in order to take advantage of these, they need the courage to take risks. He described people as having various life tasks to perform—including those involving society, work, and sex—and needing to devise social strategies that further these tasks. This pragmatic orientation is, of course, a socialization one. While it recognizes the difficulties inherent in change, it urges people to build new role structures, not to relinquish old ones. Adler insisted upon new thinking and new action, not letting go of past attachments.

### Resocialization

Nevertheless, Adlerians also foster resocialization, Because they seek to change styles of life, they instigate dramatic changes in their clients' lives that entail nothing less than role change. The very concept of a "style of life" is close to that of the "social role." A style of life is for Adler the principle that holds the various aspects of an individual's personality together. This, of course, is also what social roles do. Roles are complex patterns of interpersonal behavior and, more particularly, basic personal roles are congeries of personal behaviors that include the very elements of personality Adler would have included within the style of life. Examples of styles of life such as those of the "athlete" or the "intellectual" make it plain that something like a role is implied. In any event, altering such complex patterns can be a prodigious undertaking that involves more than tinkering with existing patterns.

Adler recommended that clients make choices, but for them to comply with this advice would have required that they forge more than the cognitive changes he seems to have envisaged. The changes in life purposes he encouraged necessitate the relinquishing of earlier, often tenaciously held, commitments. Thus Adler's work usually implies resocialization, albeit he does not directly advocate it. Courage, which he knew clients need, is indeed a prerequisite for confronting the risks of new behaviors, but it is of even greater utility when facing the dangers latent in a renunciation of the old.

## Phases of Change

Because Adler was not explicit about resocialization, he had little to say about the relinquishing phase of resocialization. Although he does not speak of the reexperiencing/identifying and renegotiation phases of role change either, his writings are more fertile in providing ideas on how these stages can be implemented. When they are analyzed through the filter of role theory, it becomes apparent that he wrestled with many of the difficulties inherent in facilitating role change.

## *Identifying*

Adler was concerned with uncovering the dynamics of his clients. He wanted to discover the style of life to which they were committed and the underlying goals they were trying to realize. Because he looked to early childhood socialization as the source of adult role problems, he emphasized retrieving and interpreting early memories. Adler wanted to uncover the purposes of his clients rather than Freudian-style causes for their behavior, and he thought that because basic purposes originate in childhood, exploring the past should shed light on them. He believed that it was in the relationships of childhood, namely those between parent and child and between siblings, that life goals emerge. For instance, he hypothesized that birth order influences the nature of a parent-child relationship, and hence that an eldest child might become insecure and conservative, while a second child would be more ambitious or rebellious.

To gain insights about the social environment in which a client developed his plans, the Adlerian therapist first seeks to establish a solid therapeutic relationship. Because his client is not conceived of as a dependent patient, a more equal relationship is sought than in classical psychoanalysis. Usually the client and therapist are seated face to face and speak directly to each other. Moreover, their communications tend to be direct. Instead of musing about the symbolism elicited in free association or dream analysis, the Adlerian is apt to ask direct questions and offer straightforward advice. Problem areas are then identified by the therapist, and his observations are passed along to the client in the form of interpretations. The client is not encouraged to reexperience his dysfunctional role but to understand it, and ultimately to change it.

## *Renegotiating*

Even though Adler was socially oriented, he did not conceptualize the implementation of new roles as involving their renegotiation with contemporary role partners. Rather, he encouraged cognitive change and "task setting" in order to institute new behavior patterns. This meant that the new goals clients were to seek could be established by themselves, and not in the give and take of social interaction. Nevertheless, Adler's social orientation implied much about the reality of social negotiations.

In contrast with Freud, Adler was aware of, and indeed insisted upon, the implications of social hierarchy. For him power and aggression were more salient than sexuality, and could be used to alter one's social position. All people, he contended, strive for superiority, and it is a threat to this dynamism, rather than frustrated sexuality, that causes them the greatest pain and arouses their most valiant efforts at change. It thus becomes apparent that coercive social negotiations generate social distress and that unequal and unfair renegotiations perpetuate interpersonal difficulties. This said, it must be acknowledged that Adler emphasized realistic personal "intentions" rather than fair negotiations. He seems to have believed that rational actions naturally result in fair negotiations.

## Barriers to Change

If, as has been indicated, Adler said little directly about relinquishing dysfunctional roles, it might be expected that he said little about removing the barriers to role change. In fact, however, he extensively discussed removing such barriers, except that these were thought of not as impeding the letting go of failed roles, but as interfering with the establishment of successful new ones. Of these barriers, he concentrated on the cognitive ones. Because Adler made little distinction between the cognitive and volitional dimensions, much of his cognitive orientation also includes the latter. There is also a great deal about social barriers in Adler's work, but again this is often implied. It is the emotional barriers to change—the barriers that role theory would implicate as the most detrimental to resocialization—that Adler most neglected. He did not seek corrective emotional experiences for his clients, but instead expected cognitive corrections to initiate emotional ones automatically.

### Cognitions

Adler taught that a person's beliefs can virtually determine her style of life. When these beliefs (most of which develop in childhood) are mistaken, the behavior patterns they encourage are counterproductive. Thus, before someone reorganizes her style of life, she must first tackle her "basic mistakes." It is talking clients out of these mistakes that gives Adlerian psychotherapy its cognitive cast.

Not all of the "basic mistakes" Adler identified as cognitive actually fall into this category, but some, like "overgeneralizations," obviously do. They clearly involve mistaken beliefs about the world, such as the conviction that all people are hostile. Because they paint a picture that is often untrue, they can mislead a person when he plans his interactions with others. Likewise, misconceptions about life and life's demands, or a minimization or denial of one's own self-worth, are cognitive errors of the first magnitude, which merit correction, and the rectification of which can permit the relinquishing of dysfunctional life patterns.

## Volitions

Many of Adler's "basic mistakes" are volitional rather than cognitive. They involve errors in action plans, not in understanding of the world. Among Adler's greatest contributions to psychotherapy was his stress on teleology, and it would be a shame if this were buried under a cognitive haze. Human beings have purposes, only some of which are founded on their understanding of their environment, and these too can be misleading. This is a profound truth that deserves independent recognition, for action plans and their implementation can facilitate, or obstruct, resocialization.

Adler described what has been called "fictional finalism." He noted that in their pursuit of final goals, people often act "as if" particular things were true. They project into the future and make decisions based upon what they imagine it will be. This kind of planning is an integral part of the decision making called volitional. Thus, when Adler talks about correcting basic mistakes that entail impossible goals or faulty values, he is essentially pointing out that defective action plans must be corrected. Goals and values are parts of our plans, not of our understanding of the universe. When they are remedied, one does not necessarily learn more about the nature of things; rather, one implements strategy in a more effective manner. Goals and values tell us what to aim for and often how to get there; they do not say what is, but what ought to be.

## Emotions

It is in the area of the emotions that Adler is weakest. Because he did not explicitly recognize the need to relinquish past roles, he seems not to have understood how emotionally charged the letting go process is. Adler was determined to be rational about life, and this translated into not being too emotional. As has been indicated, he seems to have believed that emotional changes follow automatically upon cognitive and volitional ones. Unfortunately, this neglects the extreme difficulty inherent in changing intense and misdirected emotions, and disregards the importance of the emotions in holding dysfunctional roles in place. Adler did, however, direct our attention toward the detrimental effects of excessive aggression and encouraged a more rational exercise of power.

## Social Demands

It is in the area of social etiology that Adler differed most from Freud. His emphasis on power and hierarchy, as opposed to sexuality, brought his worldview closer to reality than Freud's. Adler recognized that this is a competitive world, even from childhood. Sometimes his reformist aspirations made him imagine that competitive tendencies might be fairly easily countered, but he was well aware that excessive and unfair competition creates and sustains personal problems. He was especially sensitive to the way misguided parental demands can precipitate cognitive and volitional mistakes in children. He was, however, less sensitive to the ways in which ongoing social demands sustain dysfunctional patterns.

When Adler applied his theories to psychotherapy, he became action oriented. While he talked about the interpersonal "scripts" that can disrupt social negotiations, his primary concern was with what the individual did or did not do. It is ironic that someone as socially conscious as he should label his system "individual psychology," but this is symptomatic of his therapeutic strategy, namely to encourage the individual to make changes in his social tactics. Adler was aware of people's social interests and their impulse to compensate for feelings of inferiority, and he wanted to channel these in productive directions. Still, he treated their striving for superiority as an internal need for self-actualization, rather than as a contest with others for hierarchical precedence. Had he emphasized the latter, his therapy might have been more relevant to current, unfair, social demands.

## KAREN HORNEY

In many ways, Karen Horney was paradigmatic of the rebellion against Freud. Unlike Adler, she was not Freud's contemporary, and she came to his work as a student determined to learn an established discipline. Ultimately she became a star within the psychoanalytic movement and was a minor power within its ruling circles. Like Freud and Adler, she was trained as a physician, and, like them, in time she interpreted her work as less and less medical. Originally from Germany, she became a refugee to the United States, where she established a thriving private practice in psychotherapy and obtained recognition in the psychoanalytic training institutes as a charismatic teacher and controversial theorist.

It was not, however, until Horney began to write books geared toward the general public that she attained independent status and the leverage to open a training institute of her own. Until this independence was achieved, she was considered a semi-orthodox Freudian, provocative but not heretical. Yet Horney had always nourished an independent and sometimes stubborn streak. As one of the first women in Germany to obtain a medical degree, she had long fought established authority, and as a wife and mother who had come to surpass her husband professionally, she learned to tolerate the loneliness of being different.

Such a person could not long remain silent when she differed with someone, even someone as eminent as Freud. Because she was a psychotherapist who had crossed cultural boundaries, she had learned the significance of social variables and felt the need to speak up about them. Also, as a woman who had striven to assert her independent intelligence, she was offended by Freud's demeaning views on women, and she said so. As Freud's psychosexual theories became less persuasive to her, she sought a more commonsense and socially oriented explanation of her own and her clients' difficulties. Consequently, instead of an Oedipus complex, it was basic anxieties inaugurated in childhood that she placed at the center of her thinking. Rather than blame an overactive id for personal problems, she described tormenting inner conflicts that were internalizations of real external conflicts.

## Level of Intervention: Resocialization

As a traditional psychoanalyst, Horney was interested in the same radical change as Freud. From this she did not deviate; rather, it was what she wanted to alter that changed. Instead of fixations of the libido, it was neurotic defenses against basic anxiety that she was determined to eliminate. She too expected radical transformations in her clients when their internalized conflicts were resolved and they became free to adjust to adult life as it was. Horney did not discuss role change, but did try to make significant changes within the person—changes that were to lead to dramatic differences in interpersonal behaviors.

## Phases of Change

### *Reexperiencing/Identifying*

As a psychoanalyst promoting radical change, Horney had perforce to engage in all phases of resocialization. Still, it was not in all of these areas that she made significant contributions to psychotherapeutic theory. We will begin, therefore, by discussing the reexperiencing/identifying phase. It was in this phase that she differed most from Freud. Because she did not share his psychosexual theories, it was not libidinal fixations that she identified in her clients. Rather than uncover biologically based Oedipal conflicts, she delved into social conflicts stemming from their early lives.

Since she believed it was the internalization of real disputes between parents and children, and not merely cognitive distortions, that caused distress, it was these she sought to understand. It was real neglect and rejection she tried to unearth, not an overactive imagination. In particular, with regard to women, she searched not for a mythological penis envy but for actual experiences that undermined their self-confidence.

### Renegotiating

Surely Horney's most salient contribution to the renegotiation of dysfunctional roles derived from her explanation of their original development. She tells us that there are three basic orientations people can assume toward others. They can either move toward others, away from them, or against them. In the first instance, one may seek love and affiliation; in the second, isolation and independence; and in the third, power and/or retaliation. When these three orientations are moderate and balanced, people engage in productive interpersonal relationships; when they are not, their relationships become neurotic.

If Horney's scheme is compared with Pruitt's dual-concern model of negotiations, one is immediately struck by the parallels. Moving toward people can be equated with a yielding strategy in which one considers only the interests of the other and gives him whatever he wants in the hope of having benevolence returned. Moving away from people is comparable to Pruitt's inactivity. In this case, a person respects no one's interests and aspires simply to being left alone. Moving against people, of course, is a form of contending with others. In this last case, one's own interests are all that count and the other be damned. As Pruitt indicates, thus confirming Horney's insight, all three are defective. It is a problem-solving orientation, taking account of both partners' needs, that is most likely to eventuate in a satisfying outcome. Although Horney did not state this in so many words, it is implied by her scheme, which hence is of import to the renegotiation phase of resocialization.

## Barriers to Change

### Emotions

Of the many potential barriers to resocialization, Horney identified anxiety as the most potent. It was from this nameless internalized terror that she indicated people neurotically try to defend themselves. And because such defenses are both faulty and energy consuming, they do not meet real needs. Horney defined basic anxiety as

the feeling a child has of being isolated and helpless in a potentially hostile world. A wide range of adverse factors in the environment can produce this insecurity in a child: direct or indirect domination, indifference, erratic behavior, lack of respect for the child's individual needs, lack of real guidance, disparaging attitudes, too much admiration or the absence of it, lack of reliable warmth, having to take sides in parental disagreements, too much or too little responsibility, overprotection, isolation from other children, injustice, discrimination, unkept promises, hostile atmosphere, and so on and so on. (1945, p. 41)

It is evident that this anxiety is an internalized fear, the origin of which may not be known to the person, but is clearly social in nature.

### Volitions

According to Horney, in their attempt to defend against basic anxiety, people often engage in interpersonal strategies that backfire. She thus describes a series of neurotic needs designed to find solutions to the problem of disturbed human relationships. These needs are in actuality a set of goals that, when sought, fail to satisfy underlying needs. They are consequently parts of action strategies that if implemented keep a person unhappy and unable to relinquish defective patterns. These strategies, as Horney notes, tend to be enduring and hence give succor to dysfunctional roles.

Among the neurotic needs she enumerates are those for affection and approval, for a partner who will take over one's life, for a restricted life-style, for power, for the exploitation of others, for personal admiration, for prestige, for personal achievement, for self-sufficiency, and for perfection. These goals have frequently been identified as potential sources of trouble, and we will meet them again (for instance in the discussion of Albert Ellis's work). They are indeed misbegotten aims that typically increase a person's pain and anxiety. Thus, too single-minded a search for affection makes a person vulnerable to role partners who are exploitive and who subtract more happiness than they add. Being too willing to please these role partners usually does not gain their favor, but instead gives them permission to take whatever they can. It is almost a prescription for enduring misery.

### Cognitions

In the area of cognitive barriers to change, Horney has relatively little to contribute. Perhaps her most significant emphasis in this area is on the self-ideal. As she explains, the image one has of oneself can have a major impact on what one hopes to be. If, for example, a woman's confidence has been undermined, she may mistakenly believe she is incapable of independence.

### Social Demands

Given her clear specification of external conflicts as the source of internal ones, Horney knew about the adverse consequences of untoward social demands. She, however, placed more stress on their effects in childhood than adulthood. Similarly, her discussion of basic (negotiation) orientations shows an awareness of the impact of unfair negotiation strategies, but again she had little to say about adult negotiations, except by implication. Certainly, the person who as an adult is actively and single-mindedly moving toward, away from, or against other people is likely to be trapped in outworn styles of behaving.

## HARRY STACK SULLIVAN

Unlike Adler or Horney, Harry Stack Sullivan was an American by birth and training, and never a direct disciple of Sigmund Freud. Though he sought training in psychoanalysis, he was more influenced by the Americans William Alanson White and Adolph Meyer. He was also thoroughly imbued with the doctrines of the Chicago school of sociology. The ideas of George Herbert Mead, W. I. Thomas, Robert E. Park, and E. W. Burgess made a profound impression on him, and he took up much of the symbolic interactionist tradition. This made him aware of the significance of social relationships in generating personality, and of linguistic symbols in organizing the interactions among people.

Sullivan radically rejected an instinctive interpretation of human behavior and insisted upon the primacy of relationships. Although he too was a physician, he was concerned with the development, and misdevelopment, of personality, rather than with biology. For him personality consisted of "the relatively enduring patterns of recurrent interpersonal situations which characterize a human life" (Sullivan, 1953, p. 103). In this he neglected to mention the place of social roles, but his definition suggests that it was the role dimension of personality that concerned him most.

With this atypical background, it should not be strange that Sullivan's system is atypical. Because he was not a Freudian, he did not use Freudian language. As a theoretician, however, he did introduce linguistic conventions of his own. Thus he talked of "dynamisms," "personifications," "tension systems," and "prototaxic," "parataxic" and "syntaxic" modes of experience. At the time of their introduction these terms helped Sullivan draw the social relationship distinctions he wished to make, but with the passing of several decades, they seem to have made his ideas less available or influential.

### Level of Intervention: Resocialization

Sullivan worked at depth with his clients. He was especially noted for his work with schizophrenics. These individuals, whom most people find utterly inaccessible, were for him a challenge. He sought entry into their private cosmos, trying to help them find an exit. Since these worlds were far removed from ordinary experience, for these clients change was of necessity profound. It entailed digging down to the earliest years of their lives and attempting to compensate for major defects. Yet Sullivan's "interpersonal theory of psychiatry" was meant for the man on the street too. The changes it sought were transformations in personality, and this applied to everyone.

### Phases of Change: Reexperiencing/Identifying

Sullivan introduced many innovations to the art of the psychiatric interview. He had no qualms about the use of the direct interrogatory and employed indirection only when necessary. For him, interviews went through four stages that included (1) the formal inception, (2) the reconnaissance, (3) the detailed inquiry, and (4) the termination. These were carefully structured, with the interviewer acknowledging his role as an expert on interpersonal relations and striving to find out about the patient's past, present, and future.

In many ways, Sullivan perceived the clinician as a participant observer who was not only present during the interview, but an active party to it. Although specific questions were asked, there was also a reciprocal exchange of emotions between the therapist and client. To be effective, the therapist was required to use her empathetic resources to penetrate the meaning of the client's communications. This demanded that the therapist be as sensitive to the expressiveness of nonverbal messages as to verbal ones. Then, as the interview progressed, she had to make tentative hypotheses about what was happening within her client, all the while trying to remain open to information that would either confirm or disconfirm these. Only in this way could she accurately interpret her client's situation.

## Barriers to Change

### Emotions

Sullivan laid great stress on the ill effects of anxiety, rightly comparing these with the consequences of being hit over the head by a hammer. He suggested that a kind of neurotic stupidity results from excessive anxiety, and that this interferes with a person's ability to cope. Sullivan also recognized that fears, and the internalized tensions they produce, are initiated by irrational social arrangements, not by instincts gone awry. For him it was in order to manage real or imagined social threats that people engage in the security operations that make them neurotic or psychotic. Removing anxieties therefore became a major objective of his therapy.

### Cognitions

It was in his approach to the cognitive barriers to change that Sullivan was most influenced by the symbolic interactionists. They sensitized him to the fact that people understand their world, and interact with one another, through the medium of symbols, and that often what people believe is more influential in determining their actions than what is true. He therefore went to great pains to specify the ways in which cognitive skills develop. His classification of experience as prototaxic, parataxic, and syntaxic was based on the cognitive operations through which it is organized: the prototaxic coinciding with the raw experience of the infant, the parataxic with the emergence of causal thinking, and the syntaxic with the appearance of consensually validated symbolic activity.

Sullivan also stressed the "personifications" people use to understand their world. He described these picturings of the self and others as compilations of feelings, attitudes and images that guide actions. They therefore cross the lines between cognitions, volitions, and emotions. Many of these, such as "the good mother," are highly personal, but others cover categories of people and can devolve into stereotypes. One way of interpreting personifications is as mental images of particular roles.

### Volitions

Another of Sullivan's unique concepts is the "dynamism." It is defined as "a relatively enduring pattern of energy transformations" (Sullivan, 1953). These energy transformations are conceived of as patterns of behavior, almost as small packages of activity. But they are packages with a difference. As energy transformations, they translate needs into actions, and are therefore not very different from what is meant by volitions.

Though they still confuse behavior with what motivates that behavior, they take a giant step beyond pure behavior. Unfortunately, the very intellectual quality of this concept makes it difficult to convert into therapeutic interventions.

### Social Demands

Because Sullivan's social sensitivities went further than Freud's, his understanding of the development of the person took on a more socially oriented cast. He too spoke of stages, but his were not based upon a presumed psychosexual evolution. Rather they reflected the social relationships through which a child passes. These stages began with infancy, moved through childhood, entered the juvenile period, then preadolescence, early adolescence, and finally late adolescence. Thus infancy was dominated by the vicissitudes of nursing and the beginnings of social learning. The next stage, childhood, it is significant to notice, was marked by the emergence of interpersonal speech, not by anal or phallic stirrings. The juvenile area was characterized by a need for play groups involving other children, and preadolescence by a need for "chums." This social mind-set is underlined by Sullivan's "dramatizations." These as-if performances are none other than the kind of role plays all of us use to learn role behavior. As adults, we tend to forget how important playing house, or cowboys and Indians, can be.

The social learning of childhood is, as Sullivan indicated, a venue in which social demands can further, or impede, role development. He has less to say, however, about how excessive social demands interfere with adult resocialization. One can nevertheless infer that he was aware of this possibility from the attention he lavishes on the interview process. His emphasis on the need for gentle but firm direction contrasts sharply with the coercive manipulations many of his clients experienced from other role partners.

## OBJECT RELATIONS

It must not be supposed that while the various critics of psychoanalysis were making their case for a more social understanding of personal problems that those who retained their allegiance to Freud were sitting still. Nowadays few therapists are Freudians in the sense that Freud's contemporaries were. The libido theory, in particular, has fallen upon hard times. Even those who have tried to salvage it have been sure to interpret it in ways that include social reality.

This shift toward the social has been gradual and cannot be attributed to any one person. Nevertheless it has been dramatic. Freud was a comprehensive theorist, but his lineal descendents have expanded rather than contracted his views. Over the years there has been ongoing internecine warfare within his tribe, and many attempts to enforce a rigid orthodoxy, but as their surrounding world has changed, these combatants have been forced to do so also, and today Freudians are more inclusive and less rigid than ever.

The first major shift we must note was that toward ego psychology. During the 1930s figures such as Heinz Hartmann and Anna Freud helped move psychoanalysis away from its fixation on the instincts. While they perceived themselves as clarifying Freud's views, they nudged them toward a greater acceptance of social inputs. Thus, Hartmann emphasized concepts such as "adaptation" and "ego autonomy." He recognized the need for an adjustment between the individual and his social environment and proposed that this could be achieved by the conscious (or preconscious) part of the person, namely the ego. Hartmann resurrected Freud's reality principle, but enlarged the area of control the individual could exercise in his contest with the social world.

Anna Freud, Sigmund's daughter, believed that she was elaborating upon her father's ideas when she wrote about the defenses the ego uses in protecting itself from both internal and external threats. Much of this danger and displeasure was social, and Anna Freud recognized that it could be defended against, both cognitively and affectively. Some of the mechanisms she described, such as identification with the aggressor, are clearly a reaction to social threats. They try to mask an awareness of the danger, to escape from it, or to appease the transgressor.

Someone less directly connected with psychoanalysis, but whose ideas evolved from Freud's, was Erik Erikson. His nonsexual reworking of Freud's developmental sequence probably saved it from the scrap heap. Erikson started with Freud's stages, but retooled and extended them. While he recognized validity in an oral, anal, and phallic classification, he stripped it from its moorings and reinterpreted it using social relationship milestones. Thus, the significance of the oral stage shifted to the development of basic trust. This trust in human beings (first and foremost in one's mother) was contrasted with a mistrust that could dissuade an infant from attempting meaningful social attachments. The second stage, Freud's anal period, was for Erikson a time for developing autonomy, or risking being lost in a sea of shame and doubt. The terrible twos hence became a locale for becoming a separate individual, able to assert one's own needs vis-à-vis others. The third stage, Freud's era of the Oedipus complex, became one in which a child developed initiative or became paralyzed with guilt. It was still a time for the Oedipal triangle, but the triangle was now reconceptualized as a further assertion of the child's ability to act within an increasingly complex social environment.

Of particular significance from a role perspective is Erikson's way of describing adolescence. This he explicitly characterized as a period of identity formation or role confusion. He perceived it as a time for adult role formation and acknowledged that this might be achieved in opposition to one's parents and/or in conjunction with peers. The further stages of adulthood and maturity Erikson viewed as enlarging upon the roles initiated in adolescence. The roles of marriage, parenthood, and even grandparenthood came within his compass, and their successful construction was viewed as a necessary task for personal gratification.

Other more orthodox Freudians, such as Edith Jacobson and Margaret Mahler, sought to adjust Erikson's ideas more closely to Freud's. Thus Mahler explored the earliest periods of a child's life and described them in more Freudian terminology. She theorized about the initial symbiosis of a mother and child, and the later development of separation and individuation. In this she openly acknowledged the need for a child to develop a separate social identity.

Which brings us to Ronald Fairbairn. To this British psychoanalyst we probably owe the term "object relations." Some have characterized recent developments in psychoanalysis as a shift to interpersonal theory, but the phrase "object relations," which pays homage to Freud's language, has gained a general acceptance and has therefore been chosen to represent this section. This phrase has been appropriated by many recent theorists and cannot be taken to specify a particular viewpoint. Instead it is here being used to mark a trend toward the recognition of social failure as a precipitant of personal dysfunction.

Fairbairn postulated that a child's ego is present from birth, that the libido is a function of the ego, that the earliest form of anxiety is separation anxiety, and that the internalization of an object (read "person") is a defensive measure a child adopts to deal with an unsatisfactory object. The internal vicissitudes of the ego are thus a reflection of the vicissitudes of its relationships with significant others. Of critical interest to us is Fairbairn's stress on separation anxiety, which begins to point the way toward a full-blown concept of resocialization.

The outstanding name in the next stage of this evolution is that of John Bowlby. His fascination with the concept of good mothering led him to explore the many aspects of "attachment behavior." In monographs that are a cross between psychoanalysis and ethology, he notes the ill effects upon young children of separation from their parents during crucial periods of their early development. He argued that, contrary to some previous observers, these children become extremely sad when separated against their will. Indeed, he explained that they experienced a sequence of mourning that began with a protest phase, moved on to depression, and eventuated in emotional detachment. This progression, which is remarkably close the Kübler-Ross's work on adult grieving, forms a basis for the way anyone deals with loss.

Once the significance of childhood loss had been demonstrated, therapists were quick to see its relevance to other forms of loss. Losses due to parental death, personal maturation, marital separation, and changes in one's social status were recognized as causing pain that can only be relieved via a process of mourning. The connection with role loss, however, was not made. Though the value of mourning as a therapeutic tool was greatly enhanced, its merit as a template for the extended process of psychotherapy was not fully appreciated. The orientation of most therapists to internal psychological events apparently was too strong to allow them to realize the sweeping range of role loss.

## Level of Intervention: Resocialization

The newer forms of psychoanalysis are every bit as comprehensive as the original Freudian version. They too specialize in extensive personal change and, whether they recognize it or not, in role change. Object relations therapists deal with the same sorts of clients as did Freud, and complain of the same difficulties he faced. If anything, an increased acceptance of the social aspects of personal problems has made contemporary analysts more effective in promoting change. Since they no longer force their clients to admit psychosexual crises they didn't experience, they can more candidly explore the social impasses that actually interfere with personal development.

### Phases of Change

*Reexperiencing/Identifying*

The loosening of old Freudian verities has enabled object relations therapists to treat clients more humanely. Almost gone are the old analytic couch and the silent therapist. The widespread acceptance of socially initiated difficulties has made it easier to talk about them without using the timeworn jargon. Instead of tying themselves to dream analysis or free association, the analysts of this new breed are able to appropriate techniques from many sources. Their object has become identifying what has really happened to the client, rather than forcing him into a prearranged script.

Moreover, some analysts, notably Heinz Kohut, have pushed back the frontiers of internal experience that they feel free to explore. In his self-psychology, Kohut has theorized about the stresses to which very young children are subject. He, in consequence, claims an ability to treat conditions, such as narcissism, that necessitate the restoration of a person's damaged early self. This sort of therapy requires a special sensitivity on the part of the therapist, something quite akin to Sullivan's special empathy.

### Relinquishing

It is in the area of relinquishing dysfunctional roles that the object relations school has made its most spectacular advances. The working through of clients' problems has become less vague and more conversant with the need people have to let go of their losses. Thanks to Bowlby and his successors, it is now well established that mourning may be a necessary step toward personal growth. Even though the relationship between role loss and psychotherapy has not been completely realized, when individual clients are confronted with loss, contemporary psychoanalysts know what to do. They can allow their clients to go through the anger and denial that usually signal the advent of a loss, and do not automatically interfere with the depression and detachment through which grief completes its mission. In short, they can allow mourning to occur without treating it as a symptom to be removed.

### Renegotiation

Because ego psychology has accepted the need of the ego to adjust to social realities, it is easier for contemporary psychoanalysts to help clients renegotiate dysfunctional roles. Questions about what works socially are no longer deemed irrelevant. Ego autonomy supposes that there is an external social world that can be coped with. This means that the demands of contemporary role partners can be validated and that role bargains accounting for the needs of both partners can be strategized. Thus, the termination phase of therapy can be devoted to accommodating the world as it is.

## Barriers to Change

### Emotions

Although Freud was very aware of the significance of the emotions, his successors have become more so. Both Jacobson and Anna Freud have made contributions to understanding emotions and protecting against their dangers. For our purposes, however, we will concentrate on the advances made in understanding the emotion of sadness. Freud himself may have linked the concepts of mourning and melancholia, but detailed investigations of the nature of grief have awaited the contemporary era.

More specifically, Bowlby's investigations have made it apparent that sadness is not merely a marker of loss, but that it is an integral part of the process of letting go. Until depression was linked with the process of separation (as opposed to Freud's concept of internally directed anger), the necessity of experiencing it was not fully appreciated. Because failing to experience sadness can cause it to be perpetuated indefinitely, when an intense sadness blocks the release of a dysfunctional roles, this sadness must be endured before the role can be dropped. It is this insight that has allowed role loss depressions to be more appropriately treated.

Gerald Klerman's interpersonal psychotherapy (IPT) for depression relies upon this insight too. Conceptualizing clinical depression as caused by incomplete loss, he tries to promote grief through nonjudgmental explorations and an elicitation of feelings. Also used are reassurance, the reconstruction of the relationship with the lost person, and development of a more accurate awareness of one's situation. If a loss involves unresolved role disputes, IPT diagnoses the nature of these disputes and seeks their resolution, often via a modification of maladaptive communication patterns. If a role transition is at fault, the client's ability to cope may be enhanced by increasing his social supports or expanding his repertoire of social skills. The object here is to make it possible to relinquish what is lost by making it less threatening to do so.

## Social Demands

Because objects relations therapists engage in individual therapy, they are sometimes weak on determining, or thwarting, unfair demands emanating from contemporary role partners. While they recognize the social origins of many personal problems, they sometimes act as if their clients were isolated from their present surroundings. Nevertheless, because their therapy places the client within a sheltered relationship, it can be protective. The therapist, by setting an example of a fair role partner, provides a model for fair role negotiations and can implicitly give the client permission to resist unfair others.

# 6

# *Ecological Therapies*

Although the cultural therapists introduced a greater sensitivity to social factors, many practitioners felt they did not go far enough. They were impressed with the degree to which social pressures can influence an individual, and consequently, in their therapeutic interventions they have gravitated more toward social manipulation. They believe that modifications to a person's social environment can have more of an impact on correcting her problems than working directly with her. The person is viewed almost as a helpless pawn, tossed about by social forces beyond her control.

Those we will be calling "ecological" therapists have specialized in influencing the social negotiations of their clients. They have been so enamored of the power of social causation that they have tried to alter the mechanisms through which society exercises control over the individual. Nevertheless, most have not perceived these as role negotiations and so have not thought of themselves as altering social roles. Instead, one finds a plethora of competing theories, many of which do not openly acknowledge their social leanings.

Ecological therapies come in many shapes. They include family therapies, group therapies, social milieu techniques, social labeling, social reform, and parent training. These subsume a loosely integrated professional community, the members of which have their roots in different disciplines and may or may not acknowledge each other's existence. They are here being grouped together, not because they share a consciousness of community, but because they partake of a common predilection for here-and-now social influence strategies.

In part this common orientation emerged in reaction to psychoanalysis. The dominance of Freudianism in the first half of this century, together with Freud's distrust of his clients' families, combined to discourage psychotherapeutic interventions with anyone other than the identified client. Other human beings were considered distractions to be contained, rather than opportunities for further therapeutic work. Those who wished to more directly counter the negative influences of the social environment had, therefore, to battle the reigning Freudian orthodoxy. Otherwise their activities would simply have been labeled therapeutic errors.

It was imperative for those who wished to pursue social interventions to procure an alternative source of legitimacy. They needed a theoretical formulation that would be separate from the existing disciplines but flexible enough to allow them practice as they thought necessary. This doctrine might have been found in role theory, but was in fact found in systems and communication theories. Because much of it was imported from the nonsocial disciplines of physics and biology, practitioners could simultaneously co-opt the scientific prestige of these disciplines while steering clear of the political entanglements of the more established helping professions. Thus they could allude to energy transformations, open systems, and feedback loops rather than family relationships, role negotiations, or personality change. In this, they followed the time-honored scientific tradition of borrowing the successful paradigmatic innovations of other scientists.

More recently, social workers have sought to combine a systems orientation with ego psychology. They call this an ecological approach and try to place the person in the context of his environment. They note that individuals are immersed in family, economic, political, educational, and religious institutions, all of which help determine solutions to inevitable problems of living. This approach is explicitly action oriented, for its architects worry that intellectualized systems theories are sometimes far removed from the actual problems of people.

## FAMILY THERAPY

Obviously, the social system in which family therapists seek to intervene is the family. By influencing its dynamics, they hope to correct the individual difficulties of its members. Indeed, it has often been observed that these difficulties are merely symptomatic of system problems. That is, not only do systems have a reality of their own, but this reality takes precedence over the individual's reality. It is believed by many that changing family relationships automatically changes the individual and corrects any unhappiness of which he may complain.

Family therapies can operate at any level of intervention, but seem to specialize in socialization. Although work with a family can provide support for its members or lead them to undergo resocialization, it is overwhelmingly employed to alter the roles currently being enacted within the family. Since much family practice is oriented toward correcting the problems of children, and since the family is the chief venue in which children are socialized, changing the way roles are negotiated within it can have a profound impact on the kinds of roles children adopt. If family negotiation patterns are unfair, rectifying them can facilitate the emergence of fair bargains that better meet needs.

The other major orientation of family therapy, namely couples counseling, deals with the negotiation practices of marital (or premarital) pairs. If these are coercive, it is difficult for a mutually satisfying partnership to materialize. The construction of more functional roles can thus be expedited by teaching fair fighting, correcting confused communication patterns, or helping a pair understand their individual and joint goals. This form of adult socialization, when erected upon a foundation of reasonably well functioning adult roles, can be very successful. The secondary benefit of improved negotiation skills is, of course, that it generalizes to other relationships, including those with children.

Family therapists have been less successful in sponsoring role change. Because most have a here-and-now orientation, they have been less than appreciative of the fact that people are trapped by internalized role scripts, not just the coercive demands of external role partners. While unfair negotiations do form a barrier to the relinquishing of dysfunctional roles, there are also cognitive, emotional, and volitional barriers. Yet family therapy is not inherently incapable of facilitating resocialization. Some recent practitioners have cogently argued that it is possible to consider the self within the system, thereby enabling more profound personal change to occur. These practitioners are frustrated by system interventions that fail to modify persistent patterns of interaction, and they rightly suppose that looking for sticking points within the individual members can free them collectively.

## Nathan Ackerman

Nathan Ackerman was an American psychiatrist trained in the psycho-analytic tradition. Experience working with unemployed Pennsylvania coal miners and in child guidance clinics convinced him that treating families as a nuisance (in the manner of his mentors) was a mistake. Instead, he found that the control the family exercises over the so-called "identified patient" is formidable, and that if it can be tapped, this control may be directed into more productive channels. Gradually it became families with which he worked, and he tried to reorganize the way they transacted their business.

Although he was trained in Freudianism, Ackerman's pioneering writings were relatively nonpsychoanalytic. They were also relatively non-theoretical and concentrated on the dynamics of dysfunctional families. Nevertheless, there was a conscious social-role bias to his efforts. He indicated that personality evolves within the context of the family and that it is through family interactions that individual roles emerge. Through identifications with her parents, or reactions against them, the child constructs her specific role repertoire. This meant that the way family members fill their roles, and the behavior patterns they demand of the child, will markedly influence the final result.

It was especially the role of the "scapegoat" that captured Ackerman's attention. He recognized that often an identified patient is singled out and bullied by his family. It is as if all of the family's problems converge on him, and it is his task to relieve the others' tensions by accepting their projections. Moreover, he noticed that children who took up the role of scapegoat often seemed to do so willingly. They apparently felt they had no choice, and that the punishments visited on them were deserved. In other words, the scapegoat role became their own. Reversing this situation required changing the child's perspective and, as importantly, reducing parental punitiveness. Without the latter, the child would only be forced back into the same role once therapy ended.

Despite Ackerman's explicitness about the social-role aspects of family problems, his lead has not been universally followed. Psychoanalysts have felt that their master's concepts were not being sufficiently respected, while systems theorists have marched off in a direction all their own. Because Ackerman did not provide a sufficient theoretic grounding for his role perspective, it tended to be dismissed. What might have resulted in a conscious effort at determining how roles are forged within families, and altered by manipulating them in ensemble, has lain fallow.

## Murray Bowen

Murray Bowen, another psychiatrist, who began by treating psychotic children, like Ackerman was influenced by psychoanalysis; indeed, both trained at the Menninger Clinic in Topeka, Kansas. It was during the course of research on the families of schizophrenic children that Bowen switched to family therapy. He began to emphasize the functional significance of individual behaviors for the family system and to stress interpersonal causal factors. He interpreted systems theory as an alternate way of conceptualizing individual problems, one that promised superior therapeutic outcomes.

In Bowen's system, the concern is with the balance of forces (especially emotions) among interacting individuals. There is also concern with the corresponding tension between a person's need for individuality and her desire for togetherness. Too much of the former can result in isolation, too much of the latter in a fused relationship. What is wanted is an emotional complementarity among individuals. Still, this can be difficult to sustain. It should be noticed that this balancing of opposing forces is none other than a social negotiation process. While Bowen does not stress the negotiation of social roles per se, his observations offer many insights into how this can be achieved.

One particular form of negotiation that he has highlighted is what he calls "triangulation." This expands the negotiation process from a two-person system to a triad. According to Bowen, the dyad is basically unstable, and under stress another person will be brought in to balance it. Thus, to solve the problems of too much fusion, another person is invited to act as a kind of safety valve. But this often results in a situation in which there are two insiders and one outsider. The end product is a new form of tension. Bowen's perceptions about triangles have proved especially fruitful for understanding the socialization of children. Where there is tension between the parents, a child may be designated as an ally of one or the other, or treated as a scapegoat by both. In either event, this distorts the negotiation of the child's roles and saddles her with behavioral patterns that may function within her family of origin, but prove woefully inadequate in subsequent relationships.

In light of the above, the Bowenian tradition is oriented toward the renegotiation of family relationships. Questions of marital conflict, emotional distance, and sibling position become paramount. In fact, Bowen has become interested in the multigenerational transmission of family difficulties. He has helped to pioneer multiple-family therapy and has sought to correct the negotiation processes that extend beyond the nuclear family.

### Family Communications Theories

Family communications theory is most closely associated with the so-called Palo Alto group. This assemblage of specialists, which began its work at Palo Alto, California, in the early 1950s, included Gregory Bateson, Jay Haley, John Weakland, Don Jackson, and Virginia Satir. Eventually all of these went their own ways, but the synergy of interacting disciplines they created, embracing anthropology, psychology, medicine, communications theory, and social work, produced a burst of innovation the impact of which is still reverberating.

Bateson headed a research project at the Menlo Park veterans' hospital, the aim of which was to study the strange communications and nonsensical language patterns of schizophrenic patients. There he gradually came under the influence of Jackson's notion of family homeostasis. Applying ideas derived from Jerome Weiner and Ludwig von Bertalanffy, together they explored the positive and negative feedback between psychiatric patients and their families. They looked for things like circular causality and patterned rules used to define family interactions. More particularly, they examined the patterns of communication through which these mechanisms operated.

Out of these studies came the notions of metacommunication and the double bind. While looking for the symmetry, complementarity, and competition thought to exist in communications, they noticed that some communications made comments on others, and that these modifiers sometimes contradicted the original intent. Thus, a child confronted with a double bind simultaneously receives two incompatible messages. The child may, for instance, be told by his mother that he is being bad for not taking care of her, but when he tries to help will be criticized for not doing it properly. In this situation the child can't win. His well has been poisoned, and whatever he does is wrong.

Such confusions, it was hypothesized, disturb a child's internal equilibrium. He might, in consequence, become schizophrenic (i.e., confused in his internal and external communications) precisely because he is confused and trapped by parental communications. This, of course, suggests a therapeutic strategy of correcting the communications to which he is subject. It therefore did not take long for the Palo Alto group to take the next step of trying to reorganize the communication patterns of disturbed families.

One of the techniques to which this led was "reframing." In this clearly cognitive manipulation, the language in which a client's problems are couched is altered to make change seem more feasible. Thus an adolescent "misbehavior" may be reconceptualized as a "striving for independence," in the hope that this will make it more acceptable to his parents. The notion is that linguistic maneuvers can dispel cognitive barriers to cooperative role negotiations and that clients will not perceive these new words as distortions of what they really meant.

Among the first of the Palo Alto associates to go public with these theories was Satir. One of the ideas she promoted was that communications patterns adopted under stress can cause dysfunction. She indicated that in their relations with others people can become (1) placaters, (2) blamers, (3) super-reasonable, or (4) irrelevant. Instead of engaging in the congruent communications that solve problems, in their anxiety they create further ones. These stances, it should be recognized, are similar to those that emerge from Pruitt's dual-concern model. Here the placater is remarkably like the yielder, for both abdicate their interests in favor of the role partner's. The blamer likewise compares closely with the excessively contentious negotiator in that each assumes that her needs are paramount and tries to force others into submission. The irrelevant person, that is, the one who says whatever comes to mind even if it is unrelated to the dispute at hand, engages in inaction by acting in an irrelevant way. The super-reasonable person might seem to be a problem solver, but he really engages in a form of intellectual inaction. Because what he says is also irrelevant, he is really concerned with neither his own interests nor the other person's. In addition there may be an element of coerciveness in his efforts—for instance, if he surreptitiously tries to manipulate the other into complying with his wishes.

It should be evident that communications theorists are deeply interested in the social negotiations that occur within families. These theorists highlight dysfunctional relationships, and more particularly the communications that make these relationships dysfunctional. In this, they tend to discount the social role and fail to recognize that it may trap individuals in behaviors that are inimical to their interests even when external pressures are relieved. Therapeutically, this approach emphasizes socialization interventions in which new roles are negotiated regardless of the status of previously negotiated ones. Nevertheless, family therapy of this sort can promote resocialization by removing social barriers to change. The relinquishing of dysfunctional roles then becomes a by-product of the new negotiations because the emergence of improved roles is fostered by the changes that occur in the person's emotional, cognitive, volitional, and social role scripts. Changing these, in fact, allows painful old roles to be mourned and abandoned.

### Structural Family Therapy

Another influential family therapist has been Salvador Minuchin. This psychiatrist, who did much of his early work with disadvantaged and often aggressive boys at the Wiltwyck School in New York, also moved from working with children to working with families. He too was influenced by systems theory, but instead of dealing with communications per se, he stressed the interaction of the components of a family system. He contemplated the ways various roles develop within a family and specifically how they divide by age, sex, and power. These roles, he indicated, emerge from the routines that evolve within a family. Moreover, because of the normal changes that occur during the family life cycle, these roles must continually be altered to meet new circumstances.

By family structure, Minuchin meant the transactional patterns through which family roles are negotiated. The question was: Who is allowed to negotiate with whom, and following what rules? Such behavioral rules were judged to form the linkages between the family members' roles and to shape their particular outlines. For families under stress, the boundaries of these interactions could become confused or misaligned, in which case rigidities or misalliances would result in the development of routines that were not in the interests of one or more of the parties.

Once more we have an instance of a family therapy concentrating on the negotiation aspect of personal problems. Minuchin is especially concerned with "enmeshed" or "disengaged" relationships. In the first of these there is too much closeness between the negotiating partners, so much so that the two are not able to distinguish their respective interests. A child in this situation may not even recognize those areas that are his responsibility, and so not be motivated to assert his needs. In contrast with enmeshment, disengagement is exemplified by an overt renunciation of parental responsibility, where the adult exercises almost no appropriate control. Because the child is given excessive freedom, he doesn't have a negotiating foil against whom to establish his identity and so may have difficulty determining who he is. Thus, both too much interference and too little will disrupt social bargaining and produce uneven exchanges.

Minuchin's therapy actively tries to correct these problems. He is not afraid to sculpt a family so that its boundaries favor productive negotiations. If this means acting as an ally to one family member in opposition to another, Minuchin will do it. He intends thereby to correct imbalances and promote fairness. The consequence is supposed to be improved intrafamily socialization, and, secondarily, resocialization that results from the removal of social, cognitive, and emotional barriers to change.

## The Self in the System

In recent years a new trend has been developing, of which Michael Nichols may be taken as an exemplar. In his book *The Self in the System* (1987), Nichols explains that focusing exclusively on the family system can serve as a straitjacket. He notes that when working with a family, one is also working with individuals. While not denying the power of social influence, he describes clients who are resistant to it and who do not change when family negotiation patterns change. His solution is to recognize the validity of the person, too. He contends that while family therapists have been right to insist on the reality of social truths, they cannot afford to lose track of the individual. They must therefore be on guard against being seduced into subscribing to a systems dogmatism.

In consequence, Nichols recommends a greater emphasis on empathy within family therapy. He stresses the importance of listening and role taking as one interacts with a family. Without utilizing such techniques, one disregards the reality of the individuals present, making it impossible to identify what's really bothering them and preventing them from openly expressing themselves in the presence of their domestic enemies. The view one then hears is biased and, if mistaken for the complete truth, can lead to seriously flawed change strategies.

Indeed, Nichols recommends that ego psychology, self-psychology, and object relations be applied within the context of family therapy. The therapist, operating almost as he might in individual therapy, tries to identify the role transactions of the individuals and then explain and interpret these to them. He should also recognize that, to the extent they are trapped in difficult problems, they will resist change, and that this resistance may have to be addressed using transference and countertransference techniques. The modifications that Nichols champions would therefore bring the resocialization tools of individual psychotherapy to bear within the family setting.

Another voice, ostensibly making a similar plea, has been that of Charles Fishman. A disciple of Minuchin, he too has been dissatisfied with the incomplete change promoted by family therapy and believes that both the system and the individual interact to create the individual's deficits. He describes these deficits as "isomorphic behavior patterns" and claims they show up unaltered in many different circumstances. Upon closer inspection these isomorphisms turn out to be no more than enduring behavioral structures, such as derive from the Oedipus complex. They are, in short, dysfunctional roles. The sad implication of this is that therapists schooled in systems theory may utterly neglect role theory. Because they are accustomed to their own idiosyncratic language, they find more comfort in convoluted phrases such as "isomorphic behavior pattern" than in the more familiar "social role." The shame is that what could prove a fruitful collaboration between systems and role theorists may be aborted for want of a common linguistic turf.

## GROUP THERAPY

Families are naturally occurring groups that provide therapists with a ready-made opportunity to manipulate role negotiations. When, however, a person in distress is not part of a cooperative family unit, it is logical to construct an artificial group in which similar manipulations can be performed. The establishment of such groups is what group therapy is about. These are usually composed of persons who have comparable problems and wish to collaborate on their solution. Sometimes these groups have been advocated as a cheaper alternative to individual psychotherapy, but in recent decades they have been described as having advantages of their own.

Nowadays all sorts of problems are treated via groups. Some of these are role related, but many are not. The long list of purposes served by groups includes brainstorming, assertiveness training, stress management, controlling chemical dependency, problem solving, values clarification, grief management, weight control, correction of eating disorders, time management, psychotherapy, control of spousal abuse, parent training, friendship, relationship development, and support for those with physical and emotional illnesses. It seems that the number of these functions grows almost daily.

The type of people deemed suitable for groups by some practitioners also spans considerable territory. They belong to all ages (except the very youngest), both sexes, all sexual orientations, the mentally ill, and the normal. They have motivation levels ranging from very high to very low; have virtually any degree of social or psychological sophistication; almost any level of intelligence, from genius to profoundly retarded; and almost any degree of problem severity. These groupings may also be homogeneous or heterogeneous.

Likewise, most psychotherapeutic systems have reckoned their theoretical orientation applicable to group therapy. Thus there are psychoanalytic, general systems, Adlerian, gestalt, transactional, existential, behavior modification, cognitive, and encounter groups of every stripe.

The length and settings of the group meetings are also variable. Some are limited to a specified number of sessions, while others continue long enough for their members virtually to become family. Most formally organized groups have one- to one-and-a-half-hour sessions, but some last a whole evening, and marathons go on for days. Many of the techniques used are gentle and supportive, while others (such as those dealing with chemical dependency) are highly confrontive and manipulative. Most groups are voluntary, but many are imposed by institutions, including courts, prisons, and mental hospitals.

Because groups are both inexpensive and easy to organize, they have proliferated widely. They are conducted by professionals, semiprofessionals, and nonprofessionals. Indeed, there now seem to be informal support groups for everything from serious illness and ethnic group solidarity to coping with trauma and separation. Many people have come to believe that any problem with an emotional component can be addressed by them, and they are convinced that the mere act of getting together and talking about something has curative power.

Here we will deal with some of the commonalities of the more therapeutically oriented efforts. We will primarily be concerned with those groups that deal with role problems. These usually have a defined purpose and attempt to alter members' lives through the medium of talk. Some, however, are more active, and encourage participants to engage in collective exercises and role plays. All typically foster interaction between members and enforce specific norms of interaction. The goal of dramatic change, however, is not universal. Many groups merely help members cope with role difficulties, rather than aiding them with role change.

## Social Support

Support groups naturally specialize in social support. Whether dealing with serious illness or emotional separation, these frequently non- or semi-professional efforts explicitly promise to help their participants cope with the consequences of particular social conditions. They do not presume to change the problems themselves, only to make them easier to manage. Thus, it is not the disease of cancer that cancer support groups try to eliminate, but the social disabilities that come with having cancer. Even here support groups do not try to reorganize society; rather they foster personal adjustments to it. Similarly, groups helping Navy wives to cope with their husbands' long sea duty do not try to change the role of seaman or wife, but to make both easier to accept.

There are many mechanisms that enable groups to provide this service. First and foremost is the phenomenon of social solidarity. When people cleave together in a face-to-face effort to which they are jointly committed, bonds form that make each feel stronger than she would independently. For the same reason that most people are uncomfortable eating in restaurants alone, they feel uneasy when confronting serious problems on their own. The physical and emotional presence of a known other somehow cuts problems down to size and makes them appear more manageable. One feels more secure and more powerful, not unlike the child who feels safe enough to go to sleep once his parent comes into the room to comfort him.

Social solidarity provides both hope and an illusion of competence. As long as there is sufficient cohesion between group members, they can feel part of a shared effort, even if each must individually solve his own problems. For such cohesion to emerge, the members must want to belong to the group and feel they are accepted by it. Because of this there is often a period of testing when a group first forms. In what amounts to a rite of passage, members make demands of each other and enforce stringent organizational norms in an effort to determine who has sufficient allegiance to the collective and who doesn't. Those who find these requirements too demanding, or too irrelevant, are expelled, and only those who are committed remain.

The group members can then get down to business and begin providing services for one another. Among these are (1) imparting information, (2) giving feedback for reality testing, (3) being altruistic, (4) demonstrating the universality of particular problems, and (5) permitting ventilation. When coping with momentous problems, people almost always lack bits of information. Therefore, the advice and experience of others can prove useful in broadening their perspective and helping them make more knowledgeable decisions. Likewise, given the breadth and complexity of the world, it is difficult to be sure that one's perceptions are accurate. This is especially so when the shifting sands of social norms are at issue. We then depend upon consensual validation to confirm our views and assure us that we are not crazy. Since people with role problems usually have role partners who are telling them they are mistaken in their views and actions, more disinterested peers can help them test the truth and act accordingly.

One striking feature of most groups is the degree to which their members genuinely attempt to help one another. The mere act of inaugurating an assemblage dedicated to mutual assistance seems to bring out altruistic impulses. Moreover, groups establish norms of reciprocity in which help offered requires that help be returned. This assistance may be crude and inexpert, but its presence is a warrant of hope that can work miracles. Also, the stories that group members tell about themselves make it apparent that many sorts of problems are widely distributed and not unique to the individual. It may even occur to a person that if others share his difficulties, and they can solve their problems, then perhaps so can he. Exposing the universality of some reactions, especially emotional ones, makes one feel less like a freak to whom special laws of nature apply.

Lastly, the process of telling one's problems to others allows for ventilation and catharsis. Group members will listen to one's woes when other role partners will not, and this relieves many inner tensions. One may have had to carry one's burden alone, but now others know about it and have not ostracized one because of it. Exposing one's situation and feelings brings no automatic solution, but it can make the situation and feelings less oppressive and easier to tolerate. The fact that others accept them also allows a degree of desensitization, which expedites a more competent, and less panic-driven, management of problems. Ventilating in safety is thus a wonderful deterrent to hysteria.

## Socialization

The normative pressures that exist within cohesive groups are a powerful inducement toward socialization. Groups of interacting individuals not only support one another; they influence each other. In a group, people don't merely listen, agree, and help; they direct. They tell each other what to do. And because members are committed to their shared enterprise, these directions have force. They can even be coercive when a majority tries to impose its will on a recalcitrant minority.

Socialization, namely the inculcation of social roles and their associated skills, is often a matter of demand rather than invitation. The social negotiations through which roles emerge are not always fair, and sometimes they are downright menacing. Groups, because of their pressures toward conformity, can therefore be both used and abused. They run the gamut from brainwashing to voluntary friendship. Often those who run groups do not think of them as manipulative, yet don't hesitate to manipulate group opinion in directions they consider beneficial. Even establishing a norm as benign as turn taking contains a coercive element when it is introduced outside the awareness of group members. Indeed, in some groups coercion is celebrated. Many chemical dependency programs revel in giving uncooperative members "haircuts," during which they are forced to admit their most embarrassing weaknesses and humbly solicit absolution.

One of the precursors of modern group therapy was Kurt Lewin's T-group. In this arrangement group leaders renounce overt interference and theoretically allow social interactions between group members to develop as they will. Even here, however, group pressures develop, with leaders, followers, and group norms all emerging. Such pressures are simply a normal concomitant of group activity. Consequently a role assigned by a group is difficult to resist.

Among the ways in which groups impart role skills are sharing information and encouraging interpersonal learning. Groups are good forums for both teaching and learning. Much of this can be via explicit lessons in which one person proffers information to another. Perhaps even more knowledge comes through an imitation of the behaviors and thought processes of others. Because much role behavior is acquired by observing and identifying with role models, a structure that facilitates modeling—like a group—can expedite the acquisition of roles. Moreover, groups can motivate such learning with their ever-present threat of social sanctions for failure. The prospect of looking stupid and being ostracized works wonderfully to focus attention and encourage compliance. Most people will learn almost anything rather than appear the fool.

Given the enormous power of social sanctions, there is little wonder that therapists have employed groups to teach lessons believed imperative. Thus parenting skills, assertiveness, and relaxation techniques have all been taught within the context of groups. Even rules about proper eating or the management of grief have been imparted this way. When more than intellectual learning is advisable, when it is essential that there be some emotional growth too, socialization groups can be just the ticket.

### Resocialization

Groups have also been used for the equivalent of individual psychotherapy, but in this they are a less than perfect instrument. It is with good reason that support and socialization organizations have proliferated, while resocialization efforts have had more modest success. Groups that aim at role change tend to offer a shallower and less far-reaching version of what is available in individual therapy. While cheaper and more accessible, they are less well equipped to facilitate the letting go of dysfunctional roles. More than social solidarity or normative pressure is needed to expedite the relinquishing of failed rules.

Nevertheless, because group therapy can be less threatening than individual interventions, it is a good point of entry to psychotherapy. Those who are frightened by their inner turmoil can use a group's support and encouragement to gain a glimpse of their problem without having to immerse themselves fully in it. Because they will be one of several, attention will rarely be directed entirely on them, and so they can escape taking too hard a look at what is troubling them. Nor are other group members likely to ratify a plunge into emotional depths they themselves are uncomfortable with. Indeed, they are more likely to offer diversions when issues surface for which they are neither cognitively nor emotionally prepared. In this, they protect the person from himself, though in so doing they slow any resocialization that may be in the offing.

It may even be that resocialization is dangerous in a group whose members are not ready for it. When people are threatened, the defenses they raise can inflict unintended injury. If someone's own terrors are activated, his thinking is colored by a need for protection, not for the other person's growth. Members of therapy groups tend to be instinctively aware of this and rightly shy away from too much depth.

### Reexperiencing/Identifying

Nevertheless, groups excel in the identification and reexperiencing of problem roles. Because a group can recapitulate a person's family experience, it provides an unrivaled opportunity to rehearse and become aware of historic role behaviors. Also, its multiperson character allows for a division of labor and hence a differentiation of role performances. This greatly facilitates role playing, for it allows a person to recruit others to take the parts of previous role partners. Thus, someone who was oppressed by an overbearing father can coach another group member on how to reenact the demands once made of him.

The advantage of faithful role reenactments is that they bring the past to life. Merely thinking about what once was cannot elicit the vibrancy of feeling that is engendered in a spirited role performance. It is when important emotions are rekindled that a person recognizes the reality of his past difficulties. There is nothing like the spontaneous anger or fear of a role play to convince someone that his problem is real, and not a figment of his, or anyone else's, imagination. It is this realization that can be the opening wedge to psychotherapy.

A particularly notable variation on the theme of group therapy is Jacob L. Moreno's psychodrama, sometimes referred to as role-playing therapy. Moreno was one of the pioneers in role theory and firmly believed that it offered significant advantages for therapy. The concept of the social role, he noted, is simple to understand and can be grasped intuitively by most people. He hypothesized that by consciously playacting a part, a person could establish the psychological distance needed to consider alternatives and to realign the social expectations through which his roles are maintained. It would thus be possible to socialize him within the context of the group and expand his role repertoire to incorporate viable new roles.

In psychodrama, a person's former family arrangements are consciously recapitulated, with the therapist taking the part of the stage director and the other participants assuming actual roles from the hero's past. In so doing, they make the person's former relationships more concrete than mere talk ever could. Consciously trying to reenact scenes from long ago has the effect of enormously heightening their impact. Kinesthetic cues, nonverbal communication, and emotional contagion all serve to dramatize the action, which then becomes very emotionally salient to the characters. Indeed, actors in psychodrama have been known to dissolve in tears or tremble uncontrollably in fear. Moreno's technique specializes in a form of emotional catharsis. It makes it fairly easy to identify roles that have gone wrong and makes evident the fact of their being reexperienced.

### Renegotiations

Just as with families, groups are an excellent vehicle for role negotiations. Here too people are engaged in the actual give and take of life, and hence are open to the alteration of specific negotiations and the learning of improved negotiation skills. Nevertheless, role renegotiations depend upon the successful completion of a relinquishing process that may not be fostered by group therapy. As with family treatments, it is the addition of new roles that is most probable. Members of therapy groups often work to develop different ways of interacting with others (e.g., being more assertive), but because these new techniques are often grafted onto existing dysfunctional commitments, their new skills and resolutions are often overtaken by the press of events, and they find themselves trapped in relationships they vowed never to repeat.

Still, the negotiations that take place within groups can be useful, and if barriers to change are somehow overcome, they can promote lasting effects. Professional group therapists, it should be noted, can be quite expert in teaching fair negotiations. By being models of equity themselves, and by acting as referees between overexuberant group members, they discourage injury and cultivate the evolution of mutually satisfying bargains.

### Barriers to Change

Even though groups may not specialize in resocialization, they do remove many barriers to change. By encouraging the expression of emotions, they can make them less threatening. In particular, group solidarity can tamp down personal fears, and group pressure can force a person to use his anger in a more mature fashion. Similarly, cognitive distortions can be corrected through the reality testing that takes place in groups. Other group members can point out errors and forcefully advocate that they be recanted. Also, because groups are a caldron of normative pressures, they can decisively influence volitional choices. Almost all groups have value commitments (allegiance to which they make a condition for membership), and if these commitments are rational, they can bolster personal growth. Lastly, unfair social demands can be countered by group members who urge a person to stand up to those persecuting him. The shared courage of the group can be used to resist even intimate others.

## ALCOHOLISM COUNSELING

A special case of group influence is to be found in alcoholism counseling. Alcoholics Anonymous (AA) and its progeny are widely regarded as possessing a distinctive expertise in dealing with the problems of alcoholics and their children. Whereas some therapists have avoided working with the chemically dependent, fearing that their potential success would be limited, AA-style organizations assert that they are particularly competent at helping those entangled in addiction problems.

The primary mechanisms through which AA has always functioned are the group meeting and the personal sponsor. In the former case, the addicted person joins the company of others with comparable problems and together they ventilate their difficulties. These meetings often have a confessional quality, in which a speaker openly declares his alcoholism and gives a detailed recitation of his misdeeds. Others give him support and advice, and in the end he is supposed to find it easier to remain sober.

The specific sequence through which sobriety is to be achieved is the "twelve-step" process. In this the person honestly admits his powerlessness over alcohol, commits himself to the care of a higher power, asks to have his shortcomings removed, and makes amends to those he has harmed. The individual himself must implement these steps, although he may benefit from the moral support of a voluntary sponsor who has already traversed this territory. To many members of AA, the higher power to which they commit is God, but the organization affirms that no specific religious belief is necessary for success.

Historically AA has been most concerned with keeping individuals sober, believing that once this is achieved other problems resolve themselves. Recently, an Adult Children of Alcoholics (ACOA) movement has changed all this. When it was recognized that the children of alcoholic parents suffered even if they didn't become heavy drinkers, it became apparent that stopping drinking might not be enough. Borrowing from other approaches, most notably family therapy, alcoholism professionals began looking for ways to correct the role problems of those harmed by alcoholic upbringings. They began worrying about "codependents" and "family heros" and sought ways to help people relinquish these roles.

### Levels of Intervention

#### Social Support

The traditional AA meeting specializes in social support. Individual confession and group acceptance create strong bonds among those who regularly attend (a minority of all alcoholics). The availability of sponsorship, advice, and role models enhances this effect. Moreover, strong social pressures promote the development of norms that solidify group cohesion and that are applicable to the individual's life. ACOA meetings have attempted to follow this pattern, including the promulgation of a belief that faithful group participation is essential to personal salvation.

#### Resocialization

In its pristine form, AA is concerned with helping the addict cope with his alcoholism. It is committed to assisting her in relinquishing the alcoholic role, yet less desirous of developing new sets of roles. Often AA has not been supportive of its members' need to renounce other dysfunctional roles. Indeed, there was a period when its culture was positively hostile to exploration of the family causes of personal distress, most of its members being convinced that digging up old grievances only diverted them from the central task of remaining sober.

With the advent of the ACOA movement, much of this has changed. The concern of nonalcoholic sufferers with the socialization patterns that cause their unhappiness has promoted a desire to be rid of the behavioral complexes that sustain pain. The object of ACOA is for a person to cease being a codependent or family scapegoat. This is conceived of as either healing the child within or setting one's adult self free. In essence, the concern is with undergoing role change and escaping relationships instituted by emotionally abusive parents.

## Phases of Change

### *Reexperiencing/Identifying*

Both AA and ACOA groups are adamant about identifying defective personal roles. Whether this translates into admitting that one is an alcoholic or recognizing the signs of codependency, it is fervently believed that without such an admission no change is possible. Extracting this confession is often given primacy over everything else, including the ventilation of personal pain. Although confession can be accompanied by the reliving of old hurts, the reexperiencing of dysfunctional patterns is often viewed as a danger to be avoided. After all, reliving alcoholism presents many of the same hazards as actually being alcoholic.

Much of the recent literature on self-help in alcoholism (and it is truly voluminous) lays out in detail the signs of particular problem roles. Codependence, for instance, can be compared to the caretaker role. The person who remains in a destructive relationship with an alcoholic is said to be engaging in self-defeating, learned behaviors that prevent satisfying relationships. Due to a prolonged exposure to oppressive family rules, she seeks out and remains committed to a partner who perpetuates her oppression. The role of "family hero," also related to the role of the codependent, is often occupied by a first child, who devotes himself to rescuing family members from the degradation of alcoholism. His caretaking takes the form of being so good, and so responsible, that he more than compensates for the problems of the others. The fact is, however, that neither he nor the codependent is strong enough to save the alcoholic or even to persist in these efforts in the face of fierce role-partner resistance. Such roles fail because they are beyond human capacity, and a recognition of this limitation may allow a person to contemplate changing.

### *Relinquishing*

Alcoholism programs have become far more active in the area of relinquishing past roles. Though it is not often acknowledged, even the twelve-step process fosters a letting go of the past. A strategy of admitting one's powerlessness and placing oneself in the hands of a higher power is the equivalent of permitting a mourning process to unfold. In mourning too, one is powerless to compel change; one simply allows it to happen. There may be no higher power effecting this change, but acting as if there is can give a person the courage to let go and see what takes place, even when considerable pain is involved.

In the ACOA setting there is an insistence on personal responsibility and on setting oneself free from the past. One is supposed to move beyond old family involvements and carve out a life of one's own. While mourning may not be the prescribed method of making this happen, in practice it is difficult to avoid.

### Barriers to Change

Alcoholism approaches have relatively little to add regarding the removal of barriers to change. Like many other therapies, they often recommend that people feel their feelings, and thus they too are advocates of catharsis. In fact, the dysfunction in alcoholic families is frequently so severe that the anger, fear, guilt, or sadness unleashed is ferocious. Also, in consequence of the strong negative bonds that exist in many alcoholic families, the social supports integrated into alcoholism groups can be essential to neutralizing the demands of role partners who benefit from continued drinking or codependency. Lastly, the unique value commitments of the alcoholism field deserve special notice. Energetic norms favoring sobriety and personal responsibility can have a powerful impact on an individual's choices.

## SOCIOLOGICAL APPROACHES

Sociologists have rarely provided direct services for clients. This they have relegated to social workers, psychologists, and other counselors. There have been abortive attempts to establish a clinical sociology (see, for instance, the writings of Louis Wirth and John Glass), but for the most part sociologists have been content to be critics of the enterprise. They have, for example, been profoundly concerned with censuring therapeutic techniques that blame the victim for his distress or that coercively induce change. Such influence on practice as they have exercised has come primarily through cultural therapists such as Sullivan, whom they have made more sensitive to relationship variables.

Nevertheless, sociologists have advocated social changes that if implemented would profoundly influence the negotiation of social roles. In essence, they adopt the strategy of family and group therapists, but at another level. Instead of trying to alter role negotiations by manipulating the groups in which they occur, they hope to manipulate the social institutions in which they arise. The goal is to change the social practices that create or maintain unfair roles. Because they are very aware of the difficulty individuals have in resisting large-scale social forces, such as social class arrangements, they propose to assist them by transfiguring these forces. Probably the most influential of the strategies they have advocated have been labeling theory, social reform, and milieu therapy.

## Labeling Theory

Since the 1960s labeling theory has had a real vogue in sociology, though this now seems to be waning. Many empirical attempts have been made to validate it, but these have not been notably successful. Primarily the theory has been applied to deviance and mental health, and in the latter especially to the role problems induced by illnesses such as schizophrenia. Among those who contributed to its creation was Erving Goffman. His observations about mental hospitals being "total institutions" drew attention to the phenomenon of "institutionalization," a process which robs long-term patients of their individuality and transforms them into submissive and compliant inmates. He also researched the deleterious effects of stigmatization and documented the fact that recognizable signs of deviance themselves elicit rejection from others. He further observed that people with problems do not have to offend others with their behaviors in order to be ostracized, that being categorized as falling within a tainted category is usually sufficient.

Other research has pointed in a similar direction. Very influential was psychologist David Rosenhan's study, reported in an article titled "On Being Sane in Insane Places" (1973). He related what happened when a sane person faked his way into a mental hospital and was assigned a patient role, which then became difficult to shake. Telling others about what had happened proved insufficient to establish his sanity, for, as a diagnosed patient, his protests were interpreted as a confirmation of his illness.

It remained for Thomas Scheff to systematize these observations into a labeling theory specifically applied to the mentally ill. He proposed that residual rule breaking, that is, deviance not otherwise classified (e.g., as crime), is very common and occurs at rates even higher than mental illness. While most of this is of transitory significance, those who become stereotyped with a mental-illness label have their deviance converted into a stable social role. Once assigned such a role, according to Scheff, they are rewarded for playing it and punished for abrogating it. Because of their suggestibility, many people voluntarily agree to play such roles. He, and others, further hypothesized that assigning people a deviant role serves a function for the larger society by establishing and enforcing the boundaries of normality.

The solution to this dilemma was viewed as the reduction or elimination of invidious labeling. It was suggested that if society were to stop recruiting people for the mentally ill role, far fewer people would be mistakenly assigned to it. Also, if patients were allowed an easier exit from the role, many would take advantage of this. The kind of role change envisaged was a role transfer, in which a person could move as easily out of a defective role as he had moved into it. The significant condition for success then was not perceived as residing in the person, but with what others choose to let him do or not do. This conclusion, of course, supposes that there is enormous power in cognitive symbols and that by changing them, one can reliably change the behaviors they motivate. It further supposes that people have considerable control over the labels they use and the way they choose to use them. Unfortunately, these suppositions seem dubious.

Clearly, labeling theory does not propose a new psychotherapy. Nor does it assign a class of professionals to provide social support, socialization, or resocialization services for clients. Nevertheless, if adopted, and if it works as imagined, it might result in a more supportive world. It would encourage interpersonal negotiations that socialize normality and would reduce external interference in the resocialization efforts of individuals.

## Social Reform

Social reformers have an orientation similar to labeling theorists. They too want to change social roles by changing social institutions. They point to the voluminous documentation of the personal injury caused by iniquitous social arrangements, and they urge that if these are changed, fewer people will be hurt. They note that poverty can undermine a person's health, happiness, and outlook on life and that although some of the violence and disorganization of the poor is self-inflicted, even this results from their lack of life chances. It has also been observed that psychological maladies, like depression, follow from socially imposed losses, such as of a job or a marriage.

There exists within sociology a long reformist tradition (as exemplified by the Marxists) that espies oppression and exploitation everywhere and demands that society be reorganized on a more equitable basis. While this agenda has often assumed utopian overtones, programs advocating the more equal distribution of economic resources and the discouragement of unfair discrimination would seem to have some hope of success. Fairer patterns of socialization nurtured by an improved school system and expanded family-life education might make for a "kinder, gentler" world.

Like labeling theories, the proposals of reformers, if adopted and if successful, would encourage a more supportive society, with fairer role negotiations that prevent role dysfunctions before they arise.

### Sociotherapy/Milieu Therapy

Finally, among the sociological approaches, we must consider an actual therapy, namely sociotherapy (also called milieu therapy). It was designed primarily for application within social change institutions. For the most part, this has meant mental hospitals and organizations charged with socializing difficult children. Figures such as Marshall Edelson have noted the degree to which socialization occurs informally and have sought techniques for harnessing this resource. They have, for example, urged the more extensive use of organized groups to enforce therapeutic norms. They have also counseled that ordinary social interactions be arranged so that they will assume therapeutic value. It is suggested that if role problems are tackled when they occur, the chances of correcting them are increased. One would thereby take advantage of what has been called the "teachable moment."

Sociotherapy and milieu therapy concentrate on altering the social negotiations that create and maintain defective roles. In this they are socialization oriented, although a responsive social environment may also be expected to be a supportive one.

## COMMUNITY PSYCHIATRY

The same impulse that animates the sociological approaches has infiltrated medical circles. Physicians such as Gerald Caplan have also advocated a reformed world in which role problems are interdicted before they become established. To this end, Caplan talks about a population-oriented prevention model, a crisis model, and a support systems model, each of which has its separate applications. Operationally, they translate into child guidance clinics, family support organizations, and stress prevention programs. The object is to promote mother-child bonding, effective parenting skills, social empowerment, and self-esteem. Only if these prophylactic measures fail would clinicians try to repair the damage of failed roles. Community psychiatry thus specializes in socialization and social support. It too would suppress role dysfunction by helping individuals become strong enough to engage in fair negotiations.

## TEMPERAMENTAL FIT

The last of the ecological interventions we should discuss is that associated with the names of doctors Stella Chess and Alexander Thomas. Their persuasive longitudinal studies regarding the enduring effects of individual temperament have made it plain that certain aspects of personality must be accommodated rather than altered. They have distinguished three global patterns of childhood behavior that may well have genetic origins. In particular, they describe the "easy" child, the "difficult" child, and the "slow-to-warm-up" child. The easy child smiles readily, has positive responses to most novel experiences, and quickly complies with parental requests. The difficult child, in contrast, is easily upset, quick to anger, and a handful to control. The slow-to-warm-up child has the potential to be as cooperative as the easy child, but because he is wary of new experiences, he reacts negatively if pushed too hard. Each of these thus demands a different kind of parenting.

But, warn Chess and Thomas, there is no guarantee that life will provide a "goodness of fit" between parent and child. The easy child is a delight for most parents, while the difficult one, born to similarly disposed parents, may provoke a domestic war. Likewise, an impatient parent may not allow a slow-to-warm-up child the time and space to make adjustments, unintentionally precipitating many needless conflicts. A poor fit, therefore, is an invitation to disordered role negotiations. The wrong combination of parent and child temperament produces a coercive reaction that is unfair to parent and child alike.

In their clinical recommendations, Chess and Thomas are very socialization minded. They alert parents to the potential danger of a mismatch and encourage the kind of responsive parenting that allows for the development of personal roles that suit the child. Should difficulties already have developed, they counsel informing the child about what went wrong and explaining that he has no control over his temperament and hence is not to blame. They then encourage the child to be himself and adopt behavior patterns that harmonize with who he is. In short, they promote less coercive socialization, supervised either by the parent or child, depending upon which is most appropriate.

# 7

# *The Romantics*

The diverse therapies here being labeled "romantic" are not always linked together. Nor would some of their adherents appreciate the connotation of sentimentality inherent in the term. They would much prefer to see their therapies referred to as humanistic or philosophical; this would emphasize their roots in a person-oriented and value-committed tradition. Nevertheless, the word romantic has not been chosen lightly. Derived from literary sources, it implies that they share a strong emotional sensibility and calls attention to the fact that above all else they specialize in a fuzzy emotionality.

Romanticism, to be sure, implies more than a concern with the emotions; it also connotes a slightly irrational naïveté, even a touch of the quixotic. Since the emotions have a reputation of being irrational, it should not be surprising that those who celebrate them acquire a similar aura. There is also, however, a sense that these therapies, which include client-centered, gestalt, primal-scream, and existential therapies, and also transactional and Jungian analyses, partake of an overly simple view of human nature and interpersonal relations. There is a suspicion that they are excessively optimistic (or pessimistic) about people, often treating them like caricatures. The notion is that they share a "feel-good," "be all you can be" mentality that ignores social constraints and sometimes even denies human conflict. Some, like Jungian analysis, also embrace cosmic pretensions and more than a dollop of mysticism.

Several of these therapies, most notably existential therapy, have strong value commitments. They rely heavily on a philosophy of life and try to orient clients in a world the purposes of which are not always clear. There is sometimes a self-righteous quality about these therapies, based on assertions that they are self-evident and/or uniquely moral. While some, such as client-centered therapy, stress their scientific credentials, this can be misleading. Although they may have developed from scientific disciplines, as did gestalt psychology, or stress the utility of scientific research in assessing the effectiveness of their techniques, as do the Rogerians, this is apparently not their essence. Indeed, their scientism often seems more a bid for legitimacy than a determinant of their practice.

## CLIENT-CENTERED THERAPY

Carl Rogers was a psychologist who, like so many advocates of non-Freudian therapies, had received training in psychoanalysis. Moreover, as with many other innovators, much of his early professional life was spent practicing within the confines of a child guidance clinic. What sets him apart, however, is the many years he also spent in an academic environment. Although hardly a standard academic psychologist, he sought a change technology that was not mysterious and could easily be transmitted to students. In this, he succeeded admirably.

In contrast with Freud's archeological inclinations, Rogers emphasized a commonsense, here-and-now, problem-solving approach. He strongly encouraged clients to feel what they were feeling and to become what they were capable of being. His was an almost mystical faith in the ability of the "congruent" self to pursue its own destiny and solve its own problems. Nevertheless, or perhaps because of this, he was weak on the theory of how personal change occurs, and he left many of the details of change to the client's innate human genius. For him the client was central, and he indicated this by calling his therapy "client-centered" and later "person-centered."

The irony is that despite Rogers's emphasis on the client, his most noteworthy contributions concern the therapist and her activities. As a trainer of potential psychotherapists, Rogers was cognizant of their need to establish a solid therapeutic relationship with their clients. It was this toward which most of his research was directed and most of his writings addressed. Of the great founders of psychotherapy, Rogers has undoubtedly done most to make practitioners aware of the central importance of the therapeutic relationship. It is to him that we owe an understanding of relationship variables as the bedrock of all helping interventions.

## Levels of Intervention

### Social Support

"Perhaps the most fundamental and pervasive concept in person-centered therapy is trust" (Raskin and Rogers, 1989). So proclaimed Rogers toward the end of his career. He believed that every human being has "a constructive directional flow toward the realization of [her] full potential" and that this self-actualizing tendency must be respected. Therefore, the therapist does not solve the client's problems; he merely helps her solve her own. The essence of this philosophy is confidence in social support. The idea is that the helper enables the client to do something she did not know she could do, but with external encouragement discovers she can.

Because much of Rogers's professional life was spent in an academic environment, most of the clients to whom he had access were students. Like all students, they had problems adjusting to the demands of college life and their burgeoning social relationships. Problems with being able to study, conflicts with parents, decisions about their vocational directions, and ill-fated romances headed the list of troubles they brought to counseling centers. It was therefore these that Rogers and his disciples were called upon to solve. While the students' troubles were not characterized as role problems, and probably encompassed fewer serious role dysfunctions than are seen in private practice, they often concerned the shift from an adolescent role identity to that of an adult. It was disruptions in this progress that troubled the students and led them to seek aid in moving forward.

But instead of offering them sage advice and then sending them on their way, Rogers invited his clients to look inward and discover answers for themselves. His was the quintessential nondirective therapy. Although his clients undoubtedly sought answers, in his system their requests were gently parried. Despite this, however, it was necessary to retain them in therapy. The solution to this challenge turned out to reside in the helping relationship itself. He found that if this relationship could be made safe and supportive, clients would sustain their efforts at self-exploration and continue in treatment.

Central to the Rogerian relationship were empathy, unconditional positive regard, and congruence. Empathy is not sympathy. It is an emotional understanding of another human being, which best emerges from a role-taking posture in which a person is able to project himself imaginatively into another's shoes. This understanding is expected to be accurate, and not a reflection of the helper's own condition. If this is successfully accomplished, the client will feel understood, and less alone.

Unconditional positive regard is a kind of caring. The helper who takes this stance avoids making judgments about his client. But being non-judgmental is not equivalent to being uninterested. The helper cares, but does not foist his own standards onto the client. He lets the other be himself and does not freeze him out because of what he has done or because of the kind of life he seeks to live. Since Rogers believed that everyone is self-actualizing and basically good, he recommended that the therapist merely let the client be what he wants to be. The helper can afford to accept the client as he is, because the client is basically worthy of acceptance. And once he feels accepted, he will be able to relax. He will then not need to defend himself from the clinician, because the clinician is not one of those who are eager to condemn his misdeeds or force him in a more suitable direction.

Congruence is a concept unique to Rogers. It is the mark of a person who is integrated, whole, and genuine. The congruent person is someone who is aware of who she is and accepts herself as such. In consequence, she can be herself with others and allow them to see her as she is. As a therapist the congruent person does not burden her client with her own problems, but neither does she deny herself or her feelings, including those regarding the client and their relationship. She does not hide behind a mask of professionalism. In essence, the congruent person is open and honest with herself and others. And being so, she elicits congruence from others. She is therefore a model of what a client should become at the end of therapy; that is, clients too should aspire to be comfortable with themselves and able to trust themselves to be creative, dependable, and free.

It is remarkable what a compassionate and trustworthy clinician can accomplish. Although Freudians too have lauded the virtues of the thera-peutic alliance, it has been Rogers and his followers who have documented the functional aspects of a favorable relationship. Whether one is strug-gling to solve a current role difficulty or weathering the depths of resocialization, personal problems usually require courage to resolve. Adding new role skills, or relinquishing outmoded commitments, involves a risk that a troubled person may be reluctant to assume. A safe, caring relationship, however, can alter this equation by adding the strength that comes from being teamed with a trustworthy other. The therapist who encourages growth is doing something extremely useful, but the one who goes further and establishes an environment that is protective enough to make growth seem feasible does something essential. Without such confidence, people merely defend themselves; they don't solve problems or try to change. A Rogerian-style relationship, that is, one based upon trust, is now widely recognized as a nonspecific element fundamental to virtually all therapeutic endeavors.

### Socialization

Little need be said about socialization, for it is not one of the specialties of the Rogerians. They are not inclined to teach lessons about how to live, because they believe that most of what clients need to know is already accessible to them. Because everyone is assumed to be self-actualizing, the therapist's job is to stand back and let growth happen, not to teach it.

### Resocialization

Rogerians are apt to treat their clients as if they were "black boxes." That is, while they encourage change, both expecting it and being pleased when it appears, they are less clear about how it happens. Such change as does occur is viewed as within the provenance of the client. The therapist's task is merely to free him so that he can get on with the business of change, not to supervise its internal mechanics. Freudians have developed elaborate interpretations of their clients' inner dynamics, in the belief that this understanding enables them to oversee the changes they hope will take place. Rogerians, however, are more sanguine about the individual's inner resources and are content to help him understand his own situation. It is anticipated that once he does, he will be able to be congruent and solve his problems himself.

Nevertheless, persons in client-centered therapy do undergo resocialization. Because role change is a natural phenomenon, setting up the conditions under which it occurs can facilitate it, whether or not the facilitator realizes what he is doing. Yet Rogerians hardly seem to be aware of the painful process involved in relinquishing dysfunctional roles. Perhaps because much of Rogers's experience was with college-aged clients, who were more concerned with learning new roles than releasing old ones, his disciples have been optimistic about the ease with which change can occur. Still, when confronted with a therapist who genuinely encourages him to solve his problems, the client who is in need of role transformation may spontaneously tackle what needs to be done. And because the client-centered therapist is very concerned with being responsive, he may provide his client with much of what he needs in order to achieve this. In particular, he may help him identify and reexperience his dysfunctional roles and even break through some of the most egregious emotional barriers to change.

## Phases of Change

### *Reexperiencing/Identifying*

The client-centered therapist can be very skilled at the opening phases of resocialization. Since Rogerians are intent upon helping clients develop an accurate understanding of themselves and their situation, this effort is capable of being directed toward an understanding of dysfunctional role behaviors. Techniques designed to turn a client's awareness in on himself can effectively help him perceive what he is doing, and why. They also motivate the experiencing of who he is, and hence the reexperiencing of dysfunctional roles. Since feelings play a central part in the Rogerian universe, there is special attention paid to helping clients reexperience this aspect of their role scripts.

Because client-centered therapy assigns the responsibility for change to the client, she is expected to be able to communicate her problems to her therapist. It is believed that by talking about them she will realize what she is saying, and thereby become aware of her feelings and perhaps of the way they can be resolved. This places a burden on the clinician to be a skillful listener, who carefully follows what his client is saying and accurately reflects it back to her. Rogerian therapists are therefore active questioners, who frequently rephrase a client's statements so that they can be understood by her. Thus, someone who relates a story about a conflict with her parents may come to understand it as a "conflict" by having the statements she originally directed at her parents paraphrased to her by the clinician. Such interpretations as are offered are not of the Freudian variety, which offers insights about psychosexual fixations, but more commonsense syntheses of the client's behaviors and feelings. They might, for instance, bring together different parts of her story to help her understand why she was angry at her parents.

There is a kind of immediacy of interaction in the client-centered session that may be absent in psychoanalysis. The Rogerian is not supposed to be a tabula rasa upon which her client projects, but a human being who cares and is intent upon helping him make his own discoveries. This enables the clinician to validate the client's rights and perceptions. She is able to say to him, "Yes, you are angry," or, "That hurt you very much, didn't it?"

Such interventions do not merely clarify what the client is thinking; they verify its reality. Since a person in the throes of a role problem usually doubts himself, a trusted other can stabilize his perceptions of himself and others. This other can thereby counter the effects of coercive role partners who require that the person not see his role negotiations for what they are.

### Relinquishing

Client-centered therapy virtually ignores the relinquishing aspect of role change. Its here-and-now orientation tends to deny the reality of dysfunctional roles imported from childhood. Since its goal is to help the client become consistent with herself, there is little awareness that childhood conflicts can have established interpersonal behavior patterns that cannot be deactivated without a mourning process. Rogerians know that clients often become sad during the process of therapy, but the connection between this and role change tends to be overlooked.

### Renegotiating

The nondirective ideal of Rogerian counseling discourages utilization of the therapist as a negotiating partner. The clinician is supposed to be a helper who supports growth, not an interlocutor with whom improved roles are negotiated. Still, the ideal relationship is supposed to be a fair one, and the therapist is expected to be a responsive role partner, so a diluted model of fair negotiations is provided. Advice, however, is abjured, and the therapist avoids negotiation mistakes by not being too active. Nor is the Rogerian style calculated to foster mediation between the client and her other role partners. Being nondirective means not telling a client how to cope with unfair others. The clinician can, however, make it plain when a third person is being unfair and can give his client permission to resist.

## Barriers to Change

### Emotions

In practice, Rogers's system glorifies the emotions. Their elicitation and experience become the emblem of successful therapy. That client who is genuinely in touch with herself, who can genuinely feel her feelings, is thought to be making the most progress. The intense experience of emotions is itself taken as a curative factor. A catharsis is apparently supposed to occur that will free the person to reinvent herself. Conversely, not being able to tolerate a feeling is seen as preventing an accurate self-assessment, and hence as interfering with the ability to be self-consistent.

Yet the Rogerian views emotions in a rather undifferentiated fashion. Despite the importance attached to feelings, little effort is made to analyze them. Instead of exploring the goals of particular emotions or helping a client achieve these, raw feeling is celebrated. Emotions too, therefore, are treated as "black boxes." They may make change appear, but their mechanism is obscure.

## Volitions

Client-centered therapy does not specialize in reorganizing a person's values, the way existential and rational-emotive therapy do; however, it does incorporate deeply held beliefs, which are usually passed on to its clients. Its central trust in the human being therefore becomes a double-edged sword. On the one hand, the therapist is enjoined not to impose values on her client. The ability of the person's own organism to embrace a positive philosophy, and make suitable judgments, is supposed to be honored, and the therapist is only to assist in making the client's commitments evident to him. On the other hand, the Rogerian is not value neutral. She strongly believes in trust and personal congruence; indeed, the client's congruence is supposed to be the cynosure of her interventions. Yet the fully functioning (i.e., congruent) person is described as creative, dependable, and free: all value-laden terms. That the client who chooses such a counselor will reject this outlook is unlikely. But if it is adopted, it will sanction change that has hitherto been prevented by the less fair-minded commitments that have dominated his relationships with previous role partners. So perhaps imposing values does have some advantages.

## Cognitions

An emphasis on congruence has implications for a client's cognitive goals, too. The notion that a person should be self-consistent implies that his understandings of the world should also be consistent. While Rogerians are not notable for exploring the epistemological ramifications of client problems, their emphasis on encouraging people to express their thoughts tends to make internalized conflicts the property of the client, rather than a reflection of his previous interpersonal conflicts. Undoubtedly, Rogerians and their acolytes are aware of the etiological provenance of client understandings, but a here-and-now concern with the self looks more toward the cognitions themselves, rather than the social demands that prompted them.

## Social Demands

It is probably in the area of combatting unscrupulous external mandates that Rogerians perform worst. In their own words, they are "client centered," and hence they often leave it up to the client to resist unfair role partners by herself. Their bias against offering advice handicaps their efforts to mediate on a client's behalf. Instead of being coached on how to respond to unfair impositions, the client is allowed to discover for herself how to negotiate with others.

## GESTALT THERAPY

Gestalt therapy is another Romantic approach to helping people. It too stresses the significance of the emotions, and more than most, it dramatizes their experience. Gestalt techniques are primarily associated with the name of Fredrick Perls. Trained in Germany as a physician and psychoanalyst, Perls became the consummate showman of psychotherapy. And because he hated dogmatism, he introduced a large measure of rebellion into his system. For many, he and his methods seemed outrageous, and perhaps a bit immoral. Nevertheless, laymen loved his flamboyance and flocked to his standard. By encouraging them to participate in exercises that involved them in their therapy, he gave them a sense of opening new doors within their lives.

The term "gestalt," which means a configuration of elements, derives from a venerable psychological tradition that has its roots in Germany. Originally gestalt psychologists explored such phenomena as cognitive closure, but the therapy Perls derived from their work is ruthlessly emotional. Nevertheless, Perls was far more concerned with practice than theory. For better or worse, it is his practice, not his doctrine, that has been most influential. Even when training potential therapists, he utilized example and participation, rather than a rigorous theoretical exposition.

The gestalt approach has attempted to be "holistic" and stresses the importance of phenomenological awareness. Immediate experience is honored, and what the person perceives and feels in the current situation is taken as crucial. Gestalt therapists are militantly anti-intellectual. Insight is construed by them to mean awareness of one's feelings and perceptions, rather than Freudian-style interpretation. Again and again it is the client's here-and-now experience that is sought and extolled, not a successful expedition into his past. Gestalt therapy is associated with encounter groups, marathon therapy, and the Esalen Institute, not with sober explorations of the antecedents of personal distress.

### Levels of Intervention

*Social Support*

Those who saw Perls in action were often surprised by the degree to which he seemed to bully his clients. This impression, however, was belied by the fact that many people sought his attentions and testified to their effectiveness. In some sense, then, they must have found them comforting. Perls himself considered therapy an existential dialogue. He attempted to establish an "I-thou" relationship in which a genuine interaction occurred. Relative to psychoanalysis, his was an extremely active brand of therapy. He virtually demanded that clients respond in the way he desired, and as a result of their confidence in him, they often did.

Much gestalt therapy occurs within the encounter group. With its emphasis on exercises that enlist the client's emotions, it has proved a very involving form of therapy. By propelling people to identify with each other and with the group, it leads them to participate in a mutually supportive effort. The extensive use of gestalt techniques in nonprofessional settings is eloquent testimony to its power to be supportive. Gestalt technique engenders a here-and-now vibrancy that adds a dimension of reality to group relationships. Urging people to cry when they feel in pain, or to hug when they feel alone, creates at least temporary bonds that many seem to value.

*Socialization*

Gestalt modalities do not teach personal skills, except perhaps relationship skills. Despite their here-and-now orientation, they promote significant change rather than the addition of new roles. In practice, gestalt therapists' concern with eliciting emotions is best suited to effecting a radical reorganization of a person's life, rather than a tepid extension of existing roles.

*Resocialization*

The emotionalism of gestalt therapy favors substantial change, even though this isn't explicitly conceptualized as resocialization. Instead, its practitioners endorse personal growth. Exactly what this growth entails is, however, somewhat of a mystery. Although an analogy is drawn with the growing organism, and allusions are made to emotional and moral growth, just what these denote operationally is not altogether clear. The notion is, of course, that the person should be allowed to become all that she is capable of being, a view very similar to that of Rogers. What is actualized, however, and how this occurs, is not precise. Perls believed that a person must "allow" change to happen, as opposed to directing it through a series of well understood steps. Even though he recognized that some problem conditions are initiated by coercive parental maneuvers, the idea that dysfunctional roles must be relinquished was not made explicit; nor was the view that a form of mourning is necessary for letting them go. Still, the notion that people become trapped in conflicted roles from which they need to extricate themselves was unambiguous. It was expressed as a need to be freed from personal conflicts so that one's spontaneous self is allowed to become what it can.

## Phases of Change

### Reexperiencing/Identifying

Very much in the manner of the Rogerians, gestalt therapists concentrate on the identification and reexperience of client problems. It is essentially the emotional dimensions of these problems that excite their attention. But whereas Rogerians tend to be sedate and proper, the followers of Perls walk on the wild side. It is the very intense recapitulation of emotions that they seek. While they too focus on the client's problem areas, they are dramatic in the techniques they choose.

The gestalt therapist specializes in exaggeration and catharsis. Thus, when a client has begun to experience something important, he will likely be advised to "stay with it" until it becomes more vivid and real. He may even be encouraged to enact his thoughts and feelings through movement and verbalization. The object is for him to live out his internal experience, and thereby intensify it. One of the more modest efforts in this direction is "guided imagination," in which a client is urged to rehearse his experiences in his head. Externalized role playing can subsequently be used to give substance to his feelings by attaching them to the physical situation where they are ventilated.

Gestalt therapy is most famous for the personal and interpersonal exercises it employs to reinforce feelings. Perhaps the best known of these is the "two-chair dialogue" (sometimes called the "empty chair" technique). In this, the client is seated opposite an empty chair, in which he is to imagine another person, or part of himself, seated. He is then requested to initiate a dialogue with this other person. Next he is supposed to change seats and continue the dialogue from the other person's point of view. This, therefore, is a special form of role playing in which both parts are played by the same individual. It is especially well adapted to provoking role taking, because in order to carry it out, one has to have insight into the parts of both role partners. When relationships grounded in the distant past are at stake, the client can thereby gain a perspective on the motives of a specific role partner—a perspective he could not have had during their original role negotiation.

This method of gaining insight into another's role can be particularly fruitful in an adult's relationship with his parents. It is virtually impossible for a child to understand the true import of parental demands, for it is not given to a child to comprehend an adult's situation. Thus, projecting one's adult self into an earlier parental role can open up new vistas on what occurred, and why. It sheds light on one's contemporary role, because one finally realizes what part one had been asked to play. Not only does this make the current role more tangible, but it makes very clear what went wrong with it. If, for example, a parent demanded that a child be a caretaker, the child can, as an adult, realize why his parent wanted protection and also that such a role would have been dysfunctional for a child who was incapable of providing what was desired.

A variation on the two-chair exercise is the top dog–underdog dialogue. In this procedure, two specific aspects of the person's own personality are accessed. The part of his parents that has been internalized as a rigid, perfectionistic conscience is pitted against the weak, fun-loving child who still resides within him. This conflict, which almost surely reflects one that actually occurred between parent and child, has to be recognized as having an ongoing existence within the person. When it is, some kind of reconciliation may become possible.

In a group setting, it is also possible to engage in role plays with other group members. Because gestalt therapists recognize that intense emotional reenactments can be frightening, they utilize the special attributes of the group to establish islands of safety from which role explorations can be launched. As a means of introducing clients to intrapersonal pain or interpersonal conflict, the group experience affords a certain degree of indirection. Thus, within a group a client can be introduced to exercises that involve "making the rounds." He can, for instance, be asked to make statements about himself, and then, before the emotional intensity escalates, pass the buck to another participant. Each participant can also take a turn telling secrets or feeding sentences to others who are expected to complete them. In addition there are explicit role reversals and group-authorized withdrawals. The upshot is that dysfunctional roles can gradually be acted out and progressively accepted as belonging to the individual. The effect is to clarify the person's dysfunctions and import them into his current experience.

Because gestalt therapy places the responsibility for change squarely on the individual, it is she who is expected to best understand her situation. The drama inherent in games is designed to recruit her into playing her own part with gusto. It gives her an opportunity to explore her formative years, to discover where her role problems began, and to discern how they manifest themselves. The feelings that were initiated when she was originally socialized become available to her, and it is then possible to begin reworking them.

### Relinquishing

According to gestalt theory there is a paradox inherent in attempted change: the more one tries to make change happen, the less likely it is to occur. Change is something that is allowed, not forced. Although this is not a direct acknowledgment of the need to mourn lost roles, it permits a circumstance similar to that which exists in grief. When one endures the sadness provoked by a serious loss, one does not consciously cut one's ties with what is lost. Rather the loss is permitted to happen. Sadness is something that carries a person along, not something he actively manipulates. He must allow the feeling to exist; then it will do its work. As in Rogerian theory, this work occurs within the person even though it is not purposively implemented by him. Thus, it is ultimately his responsibility to change, not because he controls his destiny but because it is within his compass to prevent its unfolding.

### Renegotiating

The existential dialogue fostered in gestalt interventions contains the seeds of role renegotiation. While it does not incorporate a clear-cut dual-concern model, it does encourage a person to pursue his own interests. The concept of freeing one's spontaneous self to grow includes the possibility of discovering one's own interests and honoring them. People who have been exploited in their early socialization often lose touch with what they want or need. They are so busy resisting the impositions of others that they have no idea what will satisfy them. They surrender the capacity to dream and so don't know which way to head. Spontaneity can therefore be a magical gift when they try to renegotiate roles. Following one's own impulses to see where they lead, if pursued within safe bounds, opens up a world of possibilities. And since a dual-concern model requires a person to seek her own interests, permission to be oneself is also permission to assert one's personal entitlement, even in opposition to the claims of others.

Moreover, the gestalt emphasis on the negotiation processes that occur within the person, and the group, can provide excellent practice in negotiation tactics. Learning to be fair with oneself, or with group members, is an admirable rehearsal for the negotiations that occur with real-life role partners. Practice negotiations are almost as stressful and confusing as the genuine article. If one can meet the internalized demands of the self or the external demands of others without becoming overbearing or excessively submissive, this achievement can be generalized to other situations and one's capacity for fair bargaining significantly expanded.

## Barriers to Change

### Emotions

The centrality of emotions for gestalt therapy has already been sufficiently emphasized. By all accounts, it is a very "touchy-feely" enterprise. Thus, when it is emotions that are preventing change, gestalt techniques can be an excellent avenue for exposing and disarming them. Its stress on a phenomenological awareness of one's feelings sanctions the utilization of catharsis as a mechanism for dismantling barriers to change. Yet, as happens with so many catharsis-oriented techniques, the mode through which catharsis works is not well documented. It seems probable that encouraging the passionate reexperiencing of problem emotions desensitizes a person to them. Feeling them within the confines of a protective social environment should produce an incremental tolerance to them, which in turn should create the possibility of reevaluating their underlying goals and using their inherent power to achieve their objectives.

Still, the expressive nature of gestalt methodology is a turnoff to many people who feel emotionally constrained. Its wide-spread touchy-feely reputation makes it unlikely to appeal to those who are afraid of their feelings. Even though it emphasizes safety, its stress on intense catharsis makes it less applicable to those who need a sheltered, long-term form of resocialization.

## Volitions

There is also a very antimoralistic strain in gestalt circles. Perls's rebelliousness was manifest in his insistence that people should not be constrained by "shoulds." Autonomy and self-determination became paramount, with the emphasis being on neutralizing unfair moral constraints imposed by coercive parents. A client's preferences were considered important, but not themselves classified as shoulds. The result has been that gestalt therapy often authorizes a degree of autonomy that is unrealistic. There are some moral imperatives to which people simply must subscribe, and from which no degree of spontaneity can protect them. While a strident proclamation that there are "no shoulds" can give a person the backing he needs to resist unfair moral standards derived from childhood, it does less well at preparing her to be a competent adult moral negotiator.

## PRIMAL-SCREAM THERAPY

If the catharsis fostered by gestalt interventions is beneficial, then how much better might be an even more vehement expression of emotion. This is the logic behind primal-scream therapy, psychologist Arthur Janov's version of psychotherapy, which builds upon Freud and his successors and was very trendy in the 1970s. It promises a way of speeding up traditional psychoanalysis by intensifying the emotional release through which it presumably works. Primals pledge to free clients from the extreme pain they experienced in childhood, and thereby rid them of their need for the defenses that cramp their adult lives.

Primal therapy has always been conceived of as promoting radical change. It is supposed to help people overcome their neuroses and improve their general ability to function. Problems with indecision, phobias, anxieties, and depressions are all grist for its mill. In this, it takes a resocialization approach. By promoting the reliving of core experiences from childhood, people are presumably enabled to relinquish debilitating aspects of their past. Memories of injustice, suppressed along with the pain imposed by coercive childhood relationships, are to be reopened for inspection once the pain itself has lost its sting, and thenceforth reworked.

It is evident that primal therapy specializes in cultivating the reexperiencing of a painful past and in spurring emotional release. By providing an intensive catharsis, which can last for days or weeks, and by furnishing a cocoon of safety in which regression is encouraged, it allows clients to move backwards and feel as they did when they were very young children. Typically, a subject winds up on the floor, screaming out pain he repressed years ago. Long-forgotten rages and terrors come flooding to the front of his brain and pour out in an orgy of sound and fury. The object is to liberate real feelings and delegitimize false ones. Success is measured by the amount of deep, wracking pain that is elicited.

What sets primal therapy apart is its determined assault on a person's emotional defenses. While it also encourages a working through of problems, it glorifies the efficacy of emotional release. Whatever its success in this, it is even less dignified than gestalt practice. Moreover, it is weakest in those areas of resocialization that depend upon the renegotiation of roles.

## EXISTENTIAL THERAPY

Existentialism is not a form of psychotherapy per se. It is more a philosophical movement that some have adapted for therapeutic purposes than a specific change technology. In consequence, existential approaches can assume an abstract, slightly transcendental quality. They claim to be the proper prescription for today's alienating world, but they sometimes seem a bit alienated from the day-to-day problems of ordinary people.

Existentialism began as a European intellectual fashion that was associated with such names as Jean-Paul Sartre and Martin Heidegger. It was then adapted, largely by psychiatrists, to the objectives of therapy. Here the names of Ludwig Binswanger, Viktor Frankl, Rollo May, and Irvin Yalom stand out. Overall, existentialists take a dim view of the modern world. They lament the wars and depressions that have torn apart the fabric of so many lives, and they bemoan the impersonality of mass societies, which heartlessly ignore the needs of the individual. Most of all, they are distressed by a human condition that leaves each person alone to cope with the irrationalities of an uncertain universe.

Existential theorists have explored the nature of human experience in depth. They have been impressed by the anxiety, depression, grief, loneliness, isolation, and anomie that beset people. In particular, they are aware of the guilt that drastically circumscribes the personal options of many individuals. A person is described by them as an "I am" who has a "being in the world." But this being is limited, for the world ends in death for all of us. The only things we may have to hold on to are our meaningful relationships, our selves, and our human ability to transcend the immediate situation through thought.

## Level of Intervention: Resocialization

Existential approaches are designed to effect major changes. Even though they seek to support the individual in a forbidding universe, existential therapists are more concerned with freeing him to cope with that universe more effectively. Still, existentialism is not a well developed methodology. There are few training programs that specialize in it, and most of its practitioners are apt to have other professional allegiances as well. Existentialism is more a point of view that colors the implementation of therapy, than a therapy in itself. As a framework for understanding the meaning of the world, it purports to provide insight into the problems people face and to offer philosophical answers to troubling conundrums.

## Phase of Change: Reexperiencing/Identifying

Existential therapists are dedicated to exploring human experience. Theirs is a phenomenological orientation. They wish to establish a secure relationship with their clients in which they can together face the world as it is. By at least partially piercing the aloneness of the individual, they hope to explore life's challenges in tandem with him. The assumption is that in sharing their joint human condition, the therapist and client can gain greater access to the client's personal dilemmas.

When the therapist begins looking for what is specifically troubling his client, his expectation is not of finding conflicts with particular individuals, but of finding quarrels with life itself. Such role problems as the client may experience are seen as emerging more from the absurdities of human existence, and less from his peculiar circumstances. Thus, one's original conflicts are not perceived as fundamentally with coercive role partners, but with the givens of a universe that embraces death, freedom, isolation, and meaninglessness. It is these that are supposed to give rise to the anxieties from which people neurotically protect themselves.

Identifying problems of the human condition within the client's own experience is the central task of existential therapy. It is recognizing and feeling the power of these that is supposed to set the client on the road to accepting them. When he is able to correctly apprehend his situation, he will presumably be able to acquiesce in his limits and deal with the unavoidability of death and aloneness. In the meantime, he will be better able to make decisions and commitments and enjoy the bounded relationships that life does allow. All this is said to lie within his responsibility. The therapist helps him see what is going on, but it is up to him to act.

### Barriers to Change

*Emotions*

Not unlike psychoanalysis, existentialism stresses the role of anxiety in trapping people in unsatisfying behavior patterns. Yet it expands the therapeutic horizon to encompass emotions not always dealt with by other perspectives. In particular, the loneliness, guilt, and fear of death that haunt many people are decisively acknowledged. So too are the despair and confusion that attend living in a world that has no intrinsic meaning. Accepting and tolerating these debilitating emotions can make it possible to interact with reality and with those others who inhabit this world with us.

*Volitions*

Of the various psychotherapies, existentialism is the most stridently value oriented. It openly announces its value commitments, proclaiming them a worthy guidepost for anyone confused about how to live. By building upon what many therapies take for granted, namely a person's reasons for living, existentialism erects its own raison d'être. It recognizes meaninglessness as the central fact of existence and sets out to establish an authentic form of meaning.

In emphasizing the need of the individual to take responsibility for his life, even in the face of death and aloneness, existentialism acknowledges our human need to make decisions and to enter commitments with others despite the limits of the human condition. It says, in effect, that we human beings must make plans for living while we are alive, and that despite our uncertainties, we have to act. Life is conceived as more than a congeries of facts; of necessity, it embraces human purposes that are no less valid for being imperfect and vulnerable. Though sometimes people feel guilty for not living up to their potential, existentialism tells us that this is inevitable. Guilt must nonetheless be surmounted, and life must move on. A person's potential may not always be obvious, but it is worth exploring.

Those who do not share an existentialist worldview can still benefit from its moral outlook. Thus, while a role-problem perspective may deemphasize the burdens imposed by the human condition and play up the effects of coercive role negotiations, it too has to admit that role negotiations are bounded by the limits of our individual being. The uncertainties we have about our purposes, and our aloneness when making decisions, may frighten many of us into abdicating vital responsibilities. Yet abandoning our interests in favor of the interests of others is not an adequate rejoinder.

It only replaces our anxiety about mistakes with an even less trustworthy reliance on the good will of sometimes biased role partners.

## TRANSACTIONAL ANALYSIS

Transactional analysis (TA) has been incorporated within this chapter on romantic therapies, not because it is either unduly emotional or deeply philosophical, but because it may represent an overly simplified version of psychoanalysis. In popularizing Freud, it introduces a naïveté about change processes that must be explored. Eric Berne, the founder of TA, was a Canadian-born psychiatrist who did much of his most important work in San Francisco. Trained in psychoanalysis, he hoped to devise a more rapidly effective system which could be easily understood by a broad spectrum of mankind because it was conveyed in simple language.

Berne became a household name after writing his little book *Games People Play*, a runaway best-seller that held out the prospect that personal problems might be fun to solve. This was followed by other works, such as his *What Do You Say After You Say Hello?* and Thomas Harris's *I'm OK, You're OK*. The latter expanded Berne's work to include a discussion of so-called "life positions."

Transactional analysis, perhaps unfairly, has been perceived as providing easy answers capable of being readily incorporated into any popular guide to living. Whether used in a business setting or in lay therapy, it introduces a lively jargon the meaning of which seems immediately apparent. Nor does it hurt that TA is filled with exercises inviting participation. Still, its perspective is distinctly different from traditional Freudian therapy, or from approaches with a more emotional bias, and it deserves a sympathetic hearing. When such a hearing is extended, it reveals that TA is compatible with a social role perspective and that it specializes in the negotiation processes occurring within and between people.

### Levels of Intervention

#### Social Support

Although not intended by Berne for this purpose, TA's simple format adapts it for use in support groups. People can make a game of identifying ego states, life scripts, and ulterior communications and then use them to give direction to their interactions. Those who do not wish to endure the rigors of role change can thereby convince themselves that they are engaged in a worthwhile enterprise that will make them feel better.

### Resocialization

Berne's objective in simplifying Freudianism was not to make it less effective, but to make it more accessible. The idea was to promote role change, not inhibit it. He firmly believed that TA would enable clients to obtain the benevolent reparenting that they need. They would then be able to revise their life scripts to do justice to themselves and others. After obtaining a better understanding of themselves, they would be empowered to treat themselves and others differently. The therapist's job was thus to interrogate a client about her life situation, confront her with its reality, explain why she acts as she does, and provide her with an opportunity to practice acting differently.

While Berne's was not precisely a role perspective, concepts such as the "ego-state" and "life script" are capable of being translated into one. There are, according to Berne, three prime ego-states: the child, the parent, and the adult. These correspond loosely to Freud's id, superego, and ego. They might, however, be interpreted as roles that are activated at different times and in different ways. These ego-states are at least patterns of feeling, experiencing, and behaving. Life scripts are more complex sets of transactions that set the tone for an entire life and pattern the way that ego-states are implemented.

Everyone is said to enact the full panoply of ego-states, but to do so in different combinations and with different accents. People are part "critical parent" and part "nurturing parent," part "free child" and part "adapted child." These composites come close to what is meant by roles, while the person's specific role would depend upon how his particular ego-states are implemented. Changing the typical balance of these might therefore be a reasonable facsimile of role change. Still, it would be a form of change in which the relinquishing of the defective role is not seen as a critical event.

## Phases of Change

### Reexperiencing/Identifying

TA sometimes seems consumed with a need to identify each and every ego-state or transaction in which a person participates. It recommends that clients engage in "structural analysis" to identify ego-states, in "transactional analysis" to clarify communication patterns between ego-states, in "pastime" and "game analysis" to unearth the specific types of transactions that cause difficulties, and in"analysis of life scripts" to achieve a longer-term view. Given all these analyses, a TA session can sound like a contest aimed at naming whatever it is that its participants are doing. The reexperiencing of defective states is given a far lower priority. Reexperience is virtually assumed, and stress is placed instead on the presumably more difficult task of being clear about what one is experiencing.

### Renegotiating

Now we come to an area that makes TA distinctive. It is asserted that when two people occupy different ego-states, the transactions between them may be smooth or conflicted. If they are complementary, if for instance the "parent" of one person is talking to the "child" of another and the "child" of the second person is responding to the "parent" of the first, the communications can be completed without incident. But if the first person's "parent" speaks to the second's "child," while the second's "parent" addresses the first's "child," the communications will be crossed, and they are likely to be frustrated and confused. Another possibility is that two people interacting for what seems to be one purpose may both really have another goal in mind. These transactions (called games) are complementary but have ulterior motives, which involve payoffs and ego-state communications not immediately apparent. Games such as "Now I've Got You, You SOB" and "Kick Me" seem to be between two adult selves, but really engage parent and child ego-states and permit opportunities for revenge and self-punishment that are not openly acknowledged.

Transactional analysis attempts to cultivate improved role negotiations by uncrossing crossed transactions and exposing ulterior ones. The partners are thereby freed to engage in straightforward complementary transactions. These then improve their opportunity to achieve mutually beneficial bargains.

The life positions of which Harris wrote further clarify this situation. These positions are the standard approaches a person can take in entering transactions with others. In the "I'm OK; You're OK" position, two adults negotiate as equals, with the interests of both considered. In the "I'm OK; You're not OK" stance, the other's interests are discounted. With the "I'm not OK; You're OK" option, it is the other person's interests that are considered paramount. Finally, in the "I'm not OK; You're not OK" permutation, no one's interests count. Obviously, this is but another way of stating Pruitt's dual-concern model. That this model comes up in so many guises, in such a wide variety of therapies, would seem to indicate that it contains an important truth. The alternatives it enumerates apparently delineate real boundaries for role negotiations.

### Barriers to Change

*Cognitions*

With so many successors to Freud emphasizing emotional experience, it is surprising to find Berne harking back to the earliest days of psychoanalysis. His stress on naming what people are doing is an echo of Freud's belief that the correct interpretation of a person's problems provides the proper avenue for solving them. Berne glides over all the subsequent discoveries, which have indicated that there are emotional barriers to change that cannot be breached without being experienced. This bias, however, is probably a factor in TA's popularity. By not insisting on an emotional reiteration of past events, it embraces those individuals who are distinctly uncomfortable with their own emotionality.

## JUNGIAN ANALYSIS

At one time Carl Jung was the golden-haired boy of psychoanalysis. Indeed, Freud, for a while, thought of him as his intellectual heir and groomed him to take over the movement. In many ways theirs was almost a father-son relationship. Yet many important differences separated them, including the fact that Jung, as a Christian in a predominantly Jewish movement, chafed at being in Freud's shadow. He had many ideas with which he knew Freud would not agree, nor was he completely comfortable with Freud's psychosexual emphasis. Eventually the friction between the two became too great to conceal and an acrimonious break ensued.

Earlier we discussed several of the lineal descendants of Freud, and Jung was not listed among them. Jung's name was omitted because he is decidedly not in the cultural tradition. Rather, he has been appended to the romantics because of his mystical turn of mind. Therapists with a religious propensity often find themselves attracted to his exotic concepts and his affinity for the mythological and uncanny. Technically Jung was not very different from Freud, but his explanations of why people get in trouble were very different.

### Level of Intervention: Resocialization

Not unlike Freud, Jung believed that his clients were trapped by their unconscious motivations, and that unless they could understand these, they would remain enthralled by them. This suggested a far-reaching therapy in which dramatic change was attempted. In fact, Jung was well respected as a clinician and his services eagerly sought. Since he believed that people are in a constant state of trying to become what they are capable of being, his goal was to free their potential and allow them to succeed.

## Phase of Change: Reexperiencing/Identifying

Although Jung believed that experience is essential to client progress, much of his therapeutic effort was devoted to identifying what was happening in his client's unconscious. For this reason, again not unlike Freud, he relied heavily on dream analysis. Yet what he read in his clients' dreams was very different from what Freud read. Where Freud encountered sexual symbols, Jung found evidence of archetypes. Since Jung believed everyone participated in a collective unconscious, which manifested itself in behavior and thought, he expected universal ideas from this unconscious to evidence themselves in dreams. It was in part because of this difference, and because of the passionate, yet inconclusive way in which the adherents of Freud and Jung defended their views, that dream analysis has fallen into disrepute. If Freudian clients have Freudian dreams and Jungian clients Jungian ones, categorical interpretations of these dreams are subject to doubt.

Jung's archetypes are unconscious, instinct-like ideas that organize a person's behavior patterns. They are transpersonal and represent inherited memory traces accumulated in mankind's distant past. Therefore, for Jung there exist some universal symbols, like the hero, God, or the wise old man, that show up in dreams and serve as guides to what the person is trying to do. Some of these archetypes, such as the *persona*, the *anima*, the *animus*, and the *shadow*, are so important that they warrant being treated as separate systems of the personality. Thus, the masks one wears, one's masculine and feminine propensities, and one's derivations from the lower animals are fair game for Jungian analysis. It is the operation of these (and not of roles per se) that is identified in his therapy. Nevertheless, these concepts appear to be symbolic representations of widely distributed roles.

## Barrier to Change: Cognition

Despite Jung's insistence on the experience of his clients, his was a cognitively oriented methodology. His emphasis on interpreting the symbolic messages emanating from the unconscious puts a premium on intellectual understanding. Indeed, the therapist's unique skill lies in interpreting these. Penetrating the meaning of symbolic images, and following the goals they suggest, is the challenging aspect of his system. The archetypes are forms of thought, and so to alter them is to alter one's thoughts.

# 8

# *The Academics*

Since its inception, academic psychology has promised an understanding of the human psyche that would provide a key to solving personal problems. Many illustrious names, such as Kurt Lewin, George Kelly, Henry Murray, Gordon Allport, and Raymond Cattell, have been associated with theories that have been turned to clinical purposes. Field theories, trait theories, and personal construct theories have all been employed to shed light on the difficulties of the individual. Nowadays, however, the mantle of academic psychology has passed almost entirely to learning theory and its derivatives. Cognitive/behavioral therapies have burgeoned, to become a formidable rival to the more established modalities. Using the cachet of science to validate their interventions, those who practice these therapies proclaim that their theories are more solidly grounded than are humanistic approaches.

The irony of this is that for years academic psychologists denied the validity of personal experience. Under the leadership of theorists like John B. Watson, they sought to emulate the tactics of physicists. What happened inside an individual's head was deemed inaccessible to measurement, and so of no scientific value. What counted was observables, like behavior, which could be precisely calibrated, and the interrelationships of which could be accurately ascertained. A stimulus-response orientation evolved from this, in which the ways behavior was learned, or unlearned, became paramount. The person's head was triumphantly treated as a black box, having measurable inputs and outputs, but with inner workings that would forever remain beyond the ken of science.

Behaviorists were sure this was an advantage. They insisted that spec-ulations concerning consciousness would inevitably lead to mystical accounts about why individuals acted as they did. Instead, they put their faith in describing actual performances. Theorists such as Clark Hull were confident that behavioral observations were capable of translation into mathematical descriptions of constructs such as "habit strength," which would then accurately predict a person's actions. Watson earlier had been so convinced that this approach would work that he asserted that if given access to a young child, his psychological knowledge would enable him to condition the child to become whatever Watson wanted. Later behav-iorists retained this optimism, and it was to form the foundation of their behavioristic therapies.

For half a century, any psychologist who proposed the study of intra-personal experience was suspect. It took a veritable revolution to establish the significance of cognitive factors. After the black box of stimulus-response had led to a dead end in Hullian theory, psychologists began to recognize that the way people understand their world is accessible to study, and that thought has profound implications for action. In consequence, academicians began to query the nature of beliefs, to determine how these are established and how they affect behavior.

Behaviorism, in fact, might have died out completely had it not been saved by its application to clinical phenomena. Ironically, a science that had denied the relevance of human feelings began asserting that it held the answer to emotional problems. And when, against all odds, it came to enjoy meaningful success, it would credit this to learning theory. Mean-while, cognitivists also applied their discoveries to the clinical arena and claimed a comparable success. Even though one might have supposed that practitioners who espoused actively competing theories would be mutu-ally antagonistic, their joint academic roots melded them into a common approach. Subsequently, advocates of desensitization and stress reduction would join their club, and today they are collectively referred to as behaviorists. While many rightly complain that this is not an accurate appellation, it has stuck. Nevertheless, we might more accurately call them "academics," for although not all are strictly learning theorists, most do derive their legitimacy from academic sources.

The scientific origins of the academic therapies manifest themselves in the way they tackle client difficulties. Cognitive/behaviorists are decid-edly not role-problem oriented. Rather, they seek to handle discrete personal difficulties by matching them with discrete change technologies. Thus, if a client's distress is diagnosed as deriving from an excess of stress, the goal will be to treat him with a technique specifically designed to alleviate stress. Behaviorists, therefore, have separate approaches for phobias, obsessive-compulsive disorders, substance abuse, eating disorders, sleep disturbances, sexual dysfunction, mental retardation, hyperactivity, anxiety, affective disorders, and antisocial behaviors.

Academic therapists also tend to be problem solvers. While they have appropriated the term "psychotherapy," they abstain from time-honored therapeutic strategies and seek short-term solutions to here-and-now problems. Many of them dismiss psychoanalytic-type therapies as enmeshed with an irrelevant past, while they, in contrast, attempt to manipulate the more substantive cognitive and behavioral present. Nevertheless, their ministrations sometimes do resolve the same difficulties as the more traditional therapies, and hence they function as equivalents to them.

In general, it can be asserted that cognitive-behavioral therapies specialize in socialization techniques. Because of their learning bias, they perceive themselves as possessing a special expertise in the inculcation of appropriate behaviors. Whether dealing with responses to authority, drinking problems, difficulties with being assertive, or inappropriate reactions to stress, behaviorists try to teach people how to act and think differently so that they won't repeat their former errors. Essentially, they specialize in role transfer, that is, in moving clients directly from one social role to another. They simply do not treat their subjects as being trapped in dysfunctional roles that have to be relinquished before alternative roles can be adopted. While they may try to extinguish some problem behaviors, they do not seek to mourn them, and they often proceed to develop enhanced role skills without reference to the past.

It should be noted that the problem-solving approach of cognitive/behaviorism has distinct bureaucratic virtues that have contributed to making it the darling of mental health systems and insurance companies. Because it is time limited and promises inexpensive results, it appeals to organizations operating under financial constraints. Also, because of its emphasis on measurable interventions, it is ideal for the record-keeping and accountability requirements inherent in bureaucracy. Though it may not issue the sweeping promises of some other therapies, it documents tangible changes that can be both controlled and demonstrated. This is ideal for the third parties who fund most institutions. One finds, therefore, that academic therapies are frequently offered to poor and helpless clients who cannot fund their own therapies. One also finds them imposed upon those who have not voluntarily sought change. Prisons, mental hospitals, and chemical dependency programs have a fondness for them because they do not depend upon the cooperation of the subject.

## BEHAVIOR MODIFICATION

The first type of behavior therapy to gain wide acceptance was behavior modification. It is derived primarily from operant conditioning and assumes that people have problem behaviors, not problem roles. The particular activities in which people engage are seen as discrete, not as bundled together into gestalts having a peculiar reality of their own. Where role theory finds comprehensible patterns of interpersonal behavior that organize the ways people live, behaviorists perceive smaller pieces of activity that may or may not be related to other pieces. Because separate, it is assumed that these distinct behaviors can be separately altered. The thesis is that one can change particular reactions without having to modify interactions with role partners. In short, behaviorism was founded on a reductionism that is open to question.

Behavior modification interprets most problem behaviors as learned, and therefore capable of being relearned. In its universe, actions are either learned or instinctive; there is no third alternative. It does not recognize the existence of an intermediate form of constructed behavior. Ordinarily one thinks of learning as the acquisition of information or skills, and of this material as having been transmitted from one person to another the way a mother might teach her child how to eat with a fork. Roles such as that of caretaker are not, however, acquired in this way. Because they are negotiated with others, they gradually emerge from a social give-and-take. Both parties to the interchange have interests and ideas they try to implement, and it is not merely a case of one person foisting fixed patterns on another. Far from embodying an orderly transmission of preformed information, the result may be something neither party initially envisioned. A teaching paradigm misses this and attempts to replace it with a one-way, nondynamic model that does not do justice to the facts.

The roots of academic learning theory are to be found in classical and operant conditioning. Both of these depict the person as at the mercy of an unyielding environment. In classical conditioning, an organism learns to associate one stimulus with another, then responds to the second as it would to the first even when the first is not present. This kind of learning, which was originally investigated by Ivan Pavlov, is demonstrated by the dog who salivates at the sound of a dinner bell because the sound has always been followed by food in the past. In operant conditioning, an animal learns by observing the consequences of its actions. Edward L. Thorndike, the originator of this paradigm, noticed that cats would learn to escape from a cage by recognizing what freed them. B. F. Skinner refined this idea and showed how particular actions could be reinforced by rewarding them, while others could be extinguished by withholding the rewards. The animal learned what worked and what didn't, and adopted the former.

The psychologists who developed behavior modification sought to concretize the principles of learning theory. They proposed that all human activities were merely complex strings of conditioned behavior. Therefore, to correct a particular problem, all that is needed is a set of reinforcement contingencies designed to elicit the desired behavior. Behavior modifiers consequently became concerned with such nuts-and-bolts activities as toilet training and speech development, where the outcomes and contingencies are easily visible. This work ultimately proved very useful with mentally retarded and autistic clients. Such techniques were further expanded by applying them to normal populations who had difficulties with smoking or overeating. They were also imported into institutional settings through the use of token economies and individual behavior plans. In a token economy, clients are paid for desired behaviors, while a behavior plan tailors specific reinforcements and "consequences" to a particular client's needs. In each of these instances, it is the clinician who decides which outcome is desirable, then engineers the reinforcement schedule expected to bring it about.

Historically, behaviorists have stressed the need for positive reinforcers. They have regularly cited research to prove that these are more effective than negative ones. Punishment, therefore, is discouraged, except in the instance of aversive conditioning. Aversive conditioning is intended for use only with adult subjects who voluntarily agree to accept it (e.g., problem drinkers or overeaters). In practice the reality, unfortunately, has been that in order to find appropriate reinforcers, clinicians frequently determine what a client likes, remove it from him, then dole it back as a reward. In this, they inadvertently reintroduce the punishment they supposedly abhor.

The extinction of problem activities is also a frequent objective of behavioral procedures. The idea here is to give clients an opportunity to relinquish undesirable responses by not rewarding them. In practice, this often amounts to giving the client a "time out" in which he is forced to do nothing, except perhaps to review his misdeeds and accept the necessity of compliance.

## Level of Intervention: Socialization

Behavior modification is almost never used for social support or resocialization. It might be assumed that an approach with a problem-solving orientation would provide the means through which clients could solve their own problems, but behavior modification is usually very directive and concerned with teaching new ways to behave. Initially, many behaviorists even failed to recognize the significance of their relationships with clients. Praise might be acknowledged as a useful social reward, but the relationship itself was assumed to be neutral. The behavioral practitioner took as her role model the disinterested scientific investigator, and worried more about the technical design of her intervention than about her bedside manner.

Resocialization was neglected because its validity was doubted. Uncovering a client's childhood history was considered an interesting diversion, but basically irrelevant to correcting contemporary problems. Since the past was deemed to no longer exist, it was held to be beyond manipulation. The notion that there were unconscious determinants to current behaviors was dismissed as a myth, for behaviorists were certain that changing today's actions would deal with all that needed to be addressed. Unlike role theory, which is concerned with the personal scripts that guide behavior, the behavioral paradigm assures practitioners that they must modify palpable behaviors, not ephemeral internal conditions.

The behavioral credo insists that correcting a person's behaviors is tantamount to correcting his problems. If learning to be more assertive, or learning how to clean a house, will better adapt him to his situation, he will be made happier, and that is what matters. Since socialization is the process of refashioning the person to fit his social environment, behavior modification exemplifies it admirably. It does not consciously concern itself with learning social roles, but appropriates the post of an expert and impartial social arbiter whose task it is to impart proper behavior to sometimes recalcitrant individuals.

## Phases of Change

### *Reexperiencing/Identifying*

Those who practice behavior modification exhibit little interest in the reexperiencing of dysfunctional roles. If anything, they would like clients not to experience their dysfunctional roles at all, but to move directly to enacting more satisfying behavior patterns. Nevertheless, like most therapeutic perspectives, behavior modification finds it mandatory to assess the nature of the person's problems. Indeed, because the intent is to match interventions with particular problems, anything less than a precise identification is not considered sufficiently scientific.

Still, relative to other therapies, behavior modification devotes little attention to the identification process. Because its proponents are eager to get on with the business of modifying behaviors, they assume that these are readily observable. Often merely asking a client what is troubling him, and/or observing him in action, is believed sufficient to make this evident. Where clinicians in the psychoanalytic tradition will expend many years in peeling the onion of the client's unconscious, behaviorists, who are in any event skeptical about the existence of the unconscious, have no qualms about dealing with the surface. They wish to establish a therapeutic goal as quickly as possible, and then proceed to implement the proper mechanisms for achieving it.

Many behaviorists fail to appreciate that frequently clients either will not, or cannot, reveal the nature of their interpersonal difficulties. If the pain of childhood socialization has driven the recognition of how a person is behaving from her awareness, she may not be able to share what is really troubling her. A clinician who then establishes a therapeutic goal based solely upon freely accessible materials will be diverted from more important objectives. He may even be fooled into believing he has achieved therapeutic success when the most important work remains to be done. If, for instance, a student identifies her problem as a lack of classroom assertiveness, whereas in fact she is struggling with the aftereffects of sexual abuse, even becoming more assertive won't make her feel better.

This said, it must be acknowledged that behavior modifiers often do zero in on salient problems. Moreover, they often facilitate role change in clients who are ready for it. Thus, the sexually abused client discussed above may in the course of describing her lack of assertiveness be encouraged to explain why she is so preoccupied. Talking about this with the clinician may then allow for ventilation and catharsis, and perhaps even some mourning. So despite a lack of recognition of why these factors are beneficial, the therapy may still be consummated.

### Renegotiating

Since behaviorists are intent on teaching new behaviors, they place little emphasis on renegotiating them. There is scarcely any recognition that the relationship between clinician and client is a form of social negotiation. Nor is there a recognition that this negotiation influences the configuration of the role behavior the client adopts. Instead, the conviction is that the clinician is a neutral bystander who merely shares his special expertise with the client.

Yet negotiations are at work during behavior modification. The clinician, in imposing particular goals and specific reinforcement schedules, plays the part of an active role negotiator. He makes many decisions about acceptable client behaviors and about how they will be sought. The reinforcers he arranges are, in effect, demands for compliance. They are merely more conscious and consistent than the often confused expectations put forward during ordinary role negotiations. When a psychologist runs rats through a maze, it is he who designs the maze and he who decides when success has been achieved. The rats have relatively little say in the matter. The disparity in their social power is such that the investigator hardly has to consider the rats' perspective. When this paradigm is transferred to the clinical situation, the client may be treated as less than a complete person. Instead of according him the dignity of an equal bargaining partner, the clinician assumes her own superiority and presupposes that the client's job is to go along with the program. The client's assignment is simply to respond properly to the reinforcements introduced by the clinician and to change his behaviors.

Behavioral therapists have long been sensitive to the charge that they manipulate their clients. In defense, they point out that it is the task of any therapist to influence clients. They argue that if the charge is that they are competent at promoting change, it is one they will not deny. Yet the real question may be the degree to which behavioral techniques are coercive. Setting aside, for the moment, the question of how well these techniques work (the evidence here is equivocal), there is the problem of deciding whether influence and manipulation are equivalent phenomena. The form of influence that occurs in behavior modification often is very different from that which passes between fairly equal partners. Hence, if the power behavior modification employs is too compelling, it may justly be subject to limitation.

Behaviorists themselves acknowledge this difficulty and introduce mechanisms for circumventing it. One of these is the written contract between the clinician and the client. It is argued that if a client knowledgeably accepts a specified procedure, coerciveness is avoided. The problem with this strategy is that not all clients are sufficiently knowledgeable and that some are manipulated by the clinical situation into committing themselves to objectives they would not otherwise seek.

### Barriers to Change

One of the earliest, and most prominent, attempts at applying learning theory to individual problems sought to explain how psychoanalysis works. John Dollard and Neal Miller were impressed with Freud's theories and agreed that clients trapped in neurotic behaviors were acting in ways that kept them from changing. They then argued that this neurotic unhappiness was caused by learned drives and confusions and that, if these were removed, clients would be better able to utilize their adult rationality. In effect, they accepted such Freudian concepts as repression and tried to make them more scientifically respectable. This allowed psychotherapy to be reformulated as a mechanism for lifting learning-based repressions.

### Social Demands

Like most behavior modifiers, Dollard and Miller conceived of themselves as providing counterconditioning. But this implied that many of their clients might be living within coercive social environments. Moreover, while they wanted to be able to reward desirable behaviors, they were forced to note that if the therapeutic relationship itself was coercive, this might be impossible. They therefore recommended a permissive therapeutic attitude that would refrain from perpetuating the demands of unfair role partners. In this, they attempted to ameliorate unfair social demands impeding change.

### Emotions

Dollard and Miller described emotions as "drives" that motivate behavior. Some of these, such as fear, were presumably learned and consequently might be altered. Indeed, they identified the anxiety Freud described as interfering with change as being an acquired reaction. This interpretation suggested that clients might abstain from satisfying behaviors because of their fears, and hence that dislodging these might make it possible for them to act differently. The object was to reeducate them. A clinician might, therefore, teach clients that certain situations they have learned to associate with danger are no longer hazardous. The clients might, for example, be exposed to circumstances in which their old fears are no longer reinforced and hence should gradually melt away.

### Cognitive Barriers

Lastly, Dollard and Miller proposed the removal of neurotic stupidity. They believed that the way people understand their world is itself a learned phenomenon. In addition to the confusions imposed by fear, a neurotic client has learned the wrong labels with which to comprehend her world. She may therefore be led into believing a danger exists where it doesn't. The solution is to reward proper labeling. Moreover, because a neurotic client is thought to overgeneralize from problem situations, it is necessary to help her learn finer discriminations. If, for instance, she can be made to recognize that a new person, although a male, is not automatically dangerous in the way her father was, the path to establishing a productive relationship may be opened.

## COGNITIVE STRATEGIES

As one might suppose, cognitive therapists tend to construe client problems as caused by cognitive mistakes. They elevate these to the pivotal position in therapy. The way a person thinks, they assert, determines how he will feel or behave. Change the former and one automatically changes the latter. Whether the alterations a client needs to make are modest or profound, this one strategy holds the key to success.

In a sense, cognitivists believe in resocialization without the resocialization. They detect no inherent problem in relinquishing dysfunctional behaviors, believing instead that changes to a person's thought patterns transfigure his other difficulties fairly easily. Though they tackle one of the more significant barriers to role change, they assert that another, namely the emotions, is but an epiphenomenon. Consequently, one might be tempted to conceptualize cognitive therapy as merely a variety of socialization dedicated to teaching new thinking skills—except that cognitivists assure us that irrational, nonempirically based thoughts have to be replaced before change can occur.

For our purposes, two cognitivists will be taken as representative of the approach. These are Albert Ellis and Aaron Beck. Ellis, however, is not a typical academic. Very much an independent soul, he was emphasizing the importance of cognitive factors long before cognitive psychology successfully challenged the academic supremacy of behaviorism. While we might have classified him as a romantic therapist who takes a simplified approach to client problems, or as an educator intent upon reindoctrinating people, his ideas so clearly foreshadowed those of the cognitivists that including him anywhere else seemed a sacrilege. Beck, on the other hand, despite his roots in medicine, has been an exemplar of academic psychology. Where Ellis focuses much of his effort on proselytizing among the laity, Beck has stressed the necessity of psychological research to establish the validity of his therapeutic proposals. Although he too has courted the public, this has not been Beck's starting point.

### Albert Ellis

Albert Ellis has long championed rational-emotive therapy (RET). A Ph.D. in psychology, he spent his early career in the private practice of marriage, family, and sex counseling. While he had some training in psychoanalysis, in later years he claimed that he was never able to make the approach work with his clients. Instead, he developed his own method of helping people, one he has strenuously promoted. In this he has had great success; his commonsense, yet provocative, methodology has broad appeal.

While the propositions of RET are straightforward, its name is misleading. A therapy that includes the word "emotive" in its title might be expected to stress the importance of the emotions, but this is far from the case. Problem feelings are finessed by Ellis; they are not addressed on their own. Rather, he propounds an "ABC" model of personal problems to account for the way people get in trouble. The "A" in this formula is an activating event, and the "C" is an untoward consequence, like inappropriate anger or anxiety. These are mediated, however, by an intervening variable: the "B," which stands for belief. No matter what the initiating cause of a person's feelings or behaviors, their form is determined by what he thinks. Thus, a single stimulus might elicit very different responses depending upon what is going on inside the person's head.

The ABCs of RET stand behaviorism on its head. Instead of exalting behaviors and treating the psyche as an impenetrable black box, RET treats a person's thought processes as the causal factor and hypothesizes that these must be corrected if someone is to be helped. Irrational thoughts, and desires, become the culprit, not confused reinforcement schedules. If a person can be persuaded to change the way he thinks, the pain caused by his misguided demandingness will evaporate, and so will his problem.

### Level of Intervention

Few observers have accused RET of being a supportive therapy. Neither Ellis nor his creation have been noted for their warmth. Their object is not to be kind to people or to help them cope with the world's irrationalities, but to modify fundamental patterns of thinking. Nor is socialization the main endeavor. While RET strives to teach correct ways of viewing the world, the idea is to change beliefs, not merely add new ones. Resocialization, therefore, is the goal, even if the notion of role dysfunction is foreign to Ellis. Whatever his rationale, he consistently tries to remove cognitive barriers to change, so the relinquishing of dysfunctional patterns is a regular by-product of his efforts.

### Phases of Change

Ellis and his followers do not identify dysfunctional roles as such. Nonetheless, one aspect of the dysfunctional role script does concern them, namely its cognitive components, and they are at pains to unearth these.

As we shall shortly see, there is considerable concern with volitions too, but this is barely acknowledged. The relinquishing of a person's role losses, however, is thoroughly neglected. Since it is thoughts that are believed to determine feelings, it would be difficult to acknowledge that mourning, and not intellectual change, is the sine qua non of personal growth.

When it comes to the renegotiation of problem roles, Ellis has a very active style. Believing as he does that it is irrational ideas that disrupt lives, he is determined to extirpate them and replace them with more rational ones. He is not content merely to dramatize the irrationality of a client's present ideas or to placidly suggest possible alternatives. To the contrary, he and his disciples celebrate their disputatiousness. They vigorously argue with their clients, trying to talk them out of their cognitive errors. In essence, RET therapists act like negotiating partners who are not afraid to bully their clients into changing their minds. While much of this effort is clever, and often based upon a sound understanding of the way the world works, their use of ridicule and intransigence can give their undertaking a coercive cast. As role renegotiators, RET therapists are less partners who cooperate in constructing new role structures, than discussion leaders who orchestrate predetermined directions.

### Barriers to Change

As has been remarked, while RET purports to deal with feelings as well as cognitions, it is thoughts that it attempts to manipulate. What is less evident is that RET concentrates more on volitions than cognitions. In reality, it is far more concerned with values than with facts. This tends to be disguised by Ellis's use of the word "belief." Nevertheless, he does confess that within the compass of beliefs are to be found values and norms. The purpose of these latter is to help people make judgments about the world and to evaluate their relationship with it. In short, RET therapists assist people in deciding what they will do in their attempt to meet their needs. While there is, to be sure, a reciprocity between cognitions and volitions, in which each can influence the shape of the other, they are distinct in a way RET fails to acknowledge.

Ellis usually talks about beliefs as if they were incontestable facts. In his colorful yet tendentious vocabulary, beliefs get people in trouble by being "irrational," not by being mistaken. From reading his tracts, one might almost suppose that knowing something is a poison must reflexively lead to its rejection—that is, if one is rational. In essence, he denies the possibility that a person might reasonably decide to commit suicide, and therefore that the facts of the world can have very different implications, depending on one's purposes. Even though facts are an important determinant of action, the journey from "is" to "ought" is never as reflexive as Ellis implies. In making it seem so, he glosses over the differences between the cognitive and volitional and denies people an opportunity to conscientiously debate the merits of particular commitments.

For the most part, Ellis's value judgments are unexceptional, and they would be acceptable to most people. Thus, his observation that it is unwise to expect love from everyone is well taken; persons who seek love everywhere are indeed setting themselves up for failure. If this orientation is part of someone's role structure, that person's behaviors are bound to be dysfunctional, and moving on to more satisfying patterns does presuppose its modification.

Yet other of Ellis's judgments are deservedly more controversial. Perhaps the reason for this is to be found in his underlying attitude toward life. Ellis readily admits to having made philosophy a personal hobby, and more specifically to having been impressed with the works of the Stoic philosopher Epictetus. This turn of mind persuades him to accept many situations that most people would reject. For instance, in a book on anger aimed at the general public, *Anger: How to Live with and without It* (1977), he asks how someone should feel if a friend, after solemnly promising to share an apartment with him, suddenly backs out. Ellis suggests that the proper response is disappointment, not anger—that the only reason someone would have for getting angry is the irrational belief that the other person owes him something. The person who gets angry is accused of having convinced himself that what has happened is "awful," whereas it is really not; of believing that he won't be able to stand the affront, whereas he can; of thinking that the other person "shouldn't" behave that way, whereas "shoulds" are irrelevant; and of judging that the friend is a terrible person for having acted thus, whereas in fact it is his own judgment that is at fault. Ellis warns against "catastrophizing" the situation or engaging in "mustification." Anger, he tells us, is usually a wasted emotion. Better to change the way we look at the situation than get upset about it.

But many people, myself included, fail to share this assessment. When a promise is broken without sufficient cause, we do get angry. While this may not change the other person's mind, we do not deem the feeling a waste of time, or irrational. Dismissing all "shoulds" out of hand, merely because the other may not comply, does damage to the concept of moral value and is too stoical for most of us. In fact, Ellis is not afraid to promote values of his own. His strategy really amounts to disqualifying the commitments of others—that is, when he disagrees with them. It is, after all, the shoulds of clients, not his own, that are discounted. This tactic can be a useful device for persuading persons attached to counterproductive values to surrender what needs to be surrendered. In other situations, however, where a client's values are positive, it is less than fair.

### Aaron Beck

As were many psychiatrists, Aaron Beck was trained in psychoanalysis. One of his earliest professional endeavors, however, was to test Freud's assertion that depression is anger turned inward. When his research seemed to show that this was not the case, Beck turned in a different direction. Influenced by work such as that of Ellis, he rejected the validity of the unconscious and emphasized the role of cognitive processing errors in keeping people unhappy. This in turn led him to proselytize for short-term therapies directed at solving specific client problems, such as depression.

Beck hypothesizes that unhappy people are caught in cognitive distortions that prevent them from solving their problems, and that in their unhappiness they are victimized by "automatic thoughts" that perpetuate their misery. The solution to this dilemma was to lead them to correctly perceive their situation and stop sabotaging their own efforts. As a cognitivist, he believes that the key to reducing emotional distress lies with correct thinking. Unlike Ellis, however, he clearly distinguishes this from value commitments and stresses reality testing, rather than eliminating irrationality.

Central to Beck's therapeutic strategy is the conviction that the road to the emotions invariably leads through cognitions. His belief is that feelings are reactions to judgments of fact and that when these latter are changed, the former must also. Thus, if depression results from an interpretation that a loss has occurred, a different interpretation should occasion a different feeling. Similarly, construing a situation as dangerous provokes fear, whereas perceiving it as safe is reassuring.

On the face of it, this theory has an intuitive appeal and considerable experimental support. It should be noted, however, that there are equally plausible counterproposals. Robert Zajonc, for instance, has questioned whether preferences derive from cognitive inferences. He doubts that the way a person feels about something results from a logical operation performed on what the person consciously understands. Instead, Zajonc suggests that there are separate neurological channels for cognitions and emotions, and that therefore an intuitive recognition of danger may be part of the mechanism of fear. If this is so, a person need not self-consciously engage in cognitive judgments before reacting. The apparent immediacy of our emotional reactions, as well as recent research, suggests that this may well be so.

### Levels of Intervention

Beck's work has a definite bias toward socialization. He conceives of himself as teaching clients correct ways of thinking. His stress on short-term interventions is partial evidence of this. If it is indeed a cognitive skill that is being transmitted, one would expect it to be absorbed with relative speed. Presumably, the client whose thoughts are changed will quickly acquire the competence to construct improved roles for himself.

Beck talks about helping people with depression or anxiety, not those with dysfunctional roles, yet his notion that maladaptive thinking causes maladaptive behavior does not contradict the possibility of dysfunctional role playing. And because Beck's interventions are so concerned with correcting painful emotions, they can be useful to implementing resocialization. If depression or fear prevent the renunciation of unsatisfying role behaviors, reducing the intensity of the depression or fear can permit change to proceed. Beck himself recognizes that improved cognitive processing allows a person to risk new possibilities, and presumably this applies to the creation of new roles, too.

### Phases of Change

The special expertise of cognitive therapy lies in identifying and correcting cognitive errors. Thus, if a person is having automatic thoughts (e.g., "I am worthless. I will never succeed."), the cognitive therapist considers it imperative to recognize the thoughts' existence. To achieve this he will instruct his client to monitor her thoughts and see what she is saying to herself. He will then ask the client to recognize the connections between her thoughts and feelings. If the client is talking herself into unhappiness, the clinician wants her to be aware of this. (Whether or not thoughts of this sort exist, clients in cognitive therapy regularly discover them, much, it must be said, as clients in RET find irrational thoughts behind their problems and psychoanalytic patients dream Freudian dreams.)

While no direct effort at renegotiating roles is attempted by cognitive therapists, they assume a collaborative stance with their clients that is decidedly less confrontive than that taken by their RET counterparts. It is expected that both client and clinician will be examining the same facts, and hence that there is no need for the therapist to badger the client into submission. As with so many other types of therapy, the example provided by the relationship can serve as a template for other role negotiations. The responsibilities assigned to the client can, therefore, form the kernel of a more assertive attitude relative to his other role partners.

### Barriers to Change

More than anything else, cognitive therapy emphasizes the removal of cognitive barriers to resocialization. Whether or not role change is contemplated, correcting cognitive distortions and their contingent emotional distress opens the road to relinquishing dysfunctional roles. In challenging depression, anxiety, or anger, cognitive therapy confronts the very factors most capable of impeding change.

Of course, it does so utilizing cognitive strategies. It does not, for example, try to desensitize bothersome emotions in the manner of Wolpe, but looks to reform thought processes. When it is discovered that someone is making arbitrary inferences, is engaging in overgeneralizations, is participating in the maximization or minimization of her problems, or is addicted to dichotomous thinking, these offenses are attacked root and branch. The client is then urged to engage in reality testing. The evidence of the real world is examined to see what is logical and what is true. Instead of being allowed to catastrophize, she is guided in the investigation of her hypotheses regarding reality and encouraged to weigh their validity dispassionately. If the categories in which she analyzes the world are distorted, she will be encouraged to redefine them.

Cognitive therapy goes about correcting cognitive processing errors in a very businesslike manner. Much of this occurs in conversations between the client and clinician, but since learning is judged to be at stake, the client is held responsible for mastering his own lessons. It is not unusual, therefore, for a cognitivist to assign homework, in a way Freudians rarely do. The client is also asked to practice skills, such as thought stopping, in order to gain a proficiency at them.

Nor is Beck's approach entirely insensitive to volitional concerns. As with the emotions, however, he believes that value determinations proceed from observations of fact. Thus, the person who believes that happiness is a direct consequence of economic success is apt to value success. Likewise, if she believes that a lack of love automatically engenders misery, she will desperately seek love. "Ought" is thus held to be a consequence of "is," and the person who feels she "should" know everything, believes this because she is certain she will be rejected if she doesn't.

## AFFECTIVE STRATEGIES

If cognitivists treat emotions as but an adjunct to cognitions, there is a school of academic therapists who assign them a greater dignity. These therapists do not concur in the hypothesis that emotions can only be changed by manipulating thoughts; their therapy deals directly with the emotions. Although they are no less systematic, or research minded, than the cognitivists, they find a different sort of intervention more effective.

Perhaps the most important names associated with this orientation are Joseph Wolpe and Hans Selye. Wolpe is associated with the techniques of desensitization and assertiveness training, while Selye can be credited with almost inventing stress reduction. Between them, they have made elimination of anxiety and anger the central tasks of psychotherapy. It is when these are out of control that people are believed to suffer.

### Desensitization and Assertiveness Training

Wolpe, a psychiatrist of South African origin, is yet another example of a therapeutic innovator whose efforts were spurred by disenchantment with psychoanalysis. Like behavior modifiers, he too proposed the use of counterconditioning to relieve psychic distress. Because he believed that fears are learned, he attempted to reverse them through relearning. His major contribution in this direction, namely systematic desensitization, is a method of gradually reducing the power of intense emotions. It outlines a set of procedures for making a strong emotion less intimidating. In helping to launch the assertiveness training movement, Wolpe also promoted a mechanism for controlling problem anger. The assertiveness paradigm, which is essentially a model for fair negotiations, also affords a means of channeling rage in more appropriate directions.

#### Level of Intervention

As with the cognitive approaches, Wolpe's work has a decided socialization bias. It too is concerned with teaching vital skills. Learning to be less anxious or more assertive are treated as abilities to be acquired, rather than impediments to be removed. Given this orientation, there is considerable emphasis on homework and practice. Yet once freed from the grip of emotional incompetence, a client is expected to reorganize his life on a sounder footing. Resocialization, therefore, can be a corollary of successful emotional learning.

#### Phases of Change

Since resocialization is not recognized as the proper objective of desensitization or of assertiveness training, neither the relinquishing of dysfunctional roles nor the renegotiation of superior replacements is explicitly attempted. Most of the emphasis is placed on identifying what the person is afraid of or how he tries to make his needs known. A client's fears, for example, will be expressly ranked in terms of their power to frighten him. Both his past and present will be ransacked to unearth examples of debilitating terrors, which will then be codified and prepared for use in a desensitization sequence.

In assertiveness training, an effort is made to determine how a person asserts herself relative to others. A distinction is made between passive, aggressive, and assertive interactions. In the first instance, a person abdicates her own needs and allows things to happen as they will. In the second, she is demanding in the extreme and energetically pursues her own goals without any reference to the needs of the other; in this case, injury becomes probable. The last alternative, the recommended one, entails clearly and vigorously staking one's claims, all the while being careful not to ignore the legitimate claims of the other. Assertiveness is, therefore, very like the firm flexibility that Pruitt recommends, and the assertiveness paradigm is not unlike the dual-concern model.

Wolpe was firm in suggesting that people should learn to aim for a golden mean. Considering only the self, or only the other, was to be eschewed in favor of considering first the self, while not excluding the other. We, therefore, have here another method of imparting fair negotiation skills. The client is to learn how to recognize his interests and advocate them in a straightforward manner. Within the therapeutic setting, he will be taught what his interests are, how he typically asserts them, and how he can change his style to promote them more effectively. Being direct, and non-offensively telling the other person what is desired, is strongly advocated, and the client is afforded an opportunity to practice this technique.

### Barriers to Change

In desensitization programs, anxiety is the designated villain. It is a person's inability to tolerate this feeling that is identified as the wellspring of his difficulties. Presumably, were he less fearful, he wouldn't have to avoid doing things that are in his interest. The agoraphobic person, for instance, would not have to lock himself in his bedroom in order to forestall the terrors of the street. Could he but live with his fears, he wouldn't have to cower tremulously at home. The recommended strategy is therefore to inoculate the person against his fears. By exposing him to his anxieties in a step-by-step fashion, beginning with his most modest fears and progressing toward his most distressing, it is expected that he will gradually become used to them.

Wolpe's rationale for this procedure was that substituting an incompatible response for fear eliminates it as a viable alternative (reciprocal inhibition). The idea is that if a person can relax when afraid, the relaxation will supplant the fear. In practice, desensitization has proven to be a moderately effective mechanism. Whether accomplished in the setting feared by the client, within a clinical setting, or in the person's own imagination, it does result in fear reduction. What is not so clear is whether Wolpe's explanation is correct. It is equally plausible to ascribe therapeutic success to an incremental tolerance achieved by a progressive exposure to increasingly more serious fears or to a gradual reevaluation of the dangers to which one is exposed. In any event, desensitization is a welcome tool in disarming the anxieties that prevent resocialization.

If we look again at assertiveness training, we see that while it is a means of teaching negotiation skills, it can also be understood as a mechanism for controlling dangerous anger. Aggression is not merely a form of coerciveness; it is also a sign of anger gone wild. An objectionably aggressive person pursues only his own interests, not merely because he is selfish but because when he is frustrated his anger escapes its bounds and he charges unthinkingly ahead. The result is that teaching assertiveness skills reins in unsuitable anger, while simultaneously substituting techniques that reduce frustration.

Assertiveness training is also admirably suited to teaching people how to counter inappropriate social demands. When role partners prevent change by demanding that a person be what they want, an ability to actively articulate one's own interests is invaluable. Typically, those who come to assertiveness classes are very aware of being oppressed by unfair role partners, and when the time comes to practice assertiveness skills, the scenarios they choose reenact incidents with real persons. The therapist in this case is well positioned to encourage self-defense.

## Stress Reduction

The concept of stress is an interesting one. It combines a biological, psychological, and social dimension. Selye has defined it as "a nonspecific response of the body to any demand" (1980, p. 127). Thus it refers to physiological and psychological reactions to both social and physical stimuli. In common parlance, however, stress often refers to the demand made, rather than the response to it. The effects of divorce, of abusive role partners, and of war are all said to be stressful. There are even popular scales that purport to measure the degree to which specific events engender stress (Holmes and Rahe, 1967).

Indeed, "stress" often seems to be used as a nonthreatening alternative for "anxiety." In our culture, admitting to being fearful is a confession of weakness; it is to acknowledge that one is not capable of managing events that an adult should be able to handle. By introducing an ambiguity between the internal response and the external stimulus, it becomes possible to project one's own weakness onto the outside world. The precipitating event therefore comes to be regarded as stressful, not the person as discombobulated. The concept also allows one's internal focus to be on the biological rather than the psychological. If it is merely one's endocrine system that has been turned on, rather than a fear that has been activated, one seems less culpable.

In consequence, when stress is incriminated, the treatment of choice is to reduce its external precipitants or to alter one's biological response. Indeed, it has been by effecting the latter that stress reduction has chiefly gained renown. Although medications too have been employed to tamp down fear reactions, relaxation techniques have come to be regarded as a superior nonchemical alternative. Thus physiology is harnessed to achieve a psychotherapeutic result.

It should also be noted that the concept of a "nonspecific response" dilutes the particularity of fear. When people are afraid there is usually a specific danger at work. How best to prepare for it generally depends upon what is anticipated. In a sense, then, "stress" takes the dread out of fear by obfuscating its source. If "anxiety" were being removed, one might inquire into what had aroused it, whereas with "stress" it is deemed sufficient to institute a procedure for making the person feel more relaxed. Similarly, "stress" can be used to remove the particularity of anger by obscuring the frustration that instigated it.

*Level of Intervention*

More than most behavioral approaches, stress reduction aims at providing support. Thus, when relaxation techniques are effective, they help a person deal better with life problems. By portraying the individual as a hostage to external pressures, the concept of stress provides a rationale for coping with them. The stimuli with which he is said to have difficulty are not conceived as deriving from role demands, but these are not pointedly excluded. Stress reduction can, in fact, provide someone with the courage to persevere. When his fears (however labeled) are quieted, it will be easier for him to think more clearly and act more competently. Although relaxation techniques may be taught as a skill, they can lay the foundation for engaging in more adequate role negotiations.

## Phase of Change

Because stress reduction is usually a short-term intervention not aiming at drastic modifications, it does not emphasize any particular phase of resocialization. Indeed, it is often persons who are not seeking major change who find it most congenial. Nevertheless, stress reduction strategies do help individuals identify and experience their stress. Questions about when and why it arises are often asked and answered. The assumption is that a person who understands the origin of his distress will be able either to elude or to combat it.

## Barriers to Change

Since stress reduction techniques are not specifically designed to foster resocialization, it should be surprising to find them removing barriers to change. Yet they are engineered to counter unmanageable fear. Because stress and anxiety are parallel concepts, reducing stress can make a person less fearful. And for the less fearful person, many things become possible, including role change.

Among the mechanisms used to reduce stress are progressive relaxation, transcendental meditation, biofeedback, and exercise. It is believed that there exists a relaxation response, which if activated will interfere with the stress. In progressive relaxation, a person learns to tense parts of his musculature systematically, then release them and experience the subsequent ease. Once this feeling of release has been identified and the person has a reliable way of producing it, the response can be summoned up to dispel tension. Likewise, a mantra repeated quietly to oneself can institute a state of mind that is incompatible with stress. So, apparently, can exercises such as jogging.

Biofeedback is a means of applying science to the problem of stress. When it was discovered that people can exercise control over primarily autonomic responses (e.g., heart rhythm), using this approach to manage stress was an obvious extrapolation. What was needed, however, was a dependable technique for identifying someone's internal responses. When it was found that the measurement of the galvanic skin response and muscular tension could provide this, machines were developed that could be used by clients. They could then be instructed on how to teach themselves to be calm.

Therapists who specialize in stress reduction also work with the social demands impinging on their clients. They counsel people to avoid stressful interpersonal situations and steer them toward supportive relationships.

## ECLECTIC BEHAVIORAL STRATEGIES

The diversity among behavioral/cognitive approaches might have sparked intense rivalries, but because therapists found that no one technique answered all of their needs, it became necessary to be eclectic. Consequently, the application of academic theories to personal distress demanded pragmatism and flexibility. The result has been an attempt to match specific techniques with specific client problems, thereby converting a potential liability into an asset.

It was in an attempt to make eclecticism more effective and more respectable that Arnold Lazarus created multimodal therapy. Dissatisfied with the scattershot approach many clinicians had been taking, he aimed at developing a comprehensive methodology that could provide guidance on when to institute particular techniques. These, of course, did not include those of the psychoanalysts or the client-centered therapists. The primary concern was with identifying when particular cognitive, behavioral, or affective strategies would be appropriate.

### Multimodal Therapy

Lazarus's approach is distinctly problem solving in its outlook. It therefore concentrates on social support and socialization, rather than resocialization. Since it does not add new change techniques, it says nothing unique about removing barriers to change. The amendment it makes to previously described therapies is that it is more systematic in its identification of client problems. Specifically, it directs clinicians to scrutinize a variety of factors before deciding what is wrong with a client.

To summarize his broad conceptualization of client problems, Lazarus offers the acronym BASIC ID (behavior, affect, sensation, imagery, cognition, interpersonal relations, and drugs). This obviously encompasses all of the standard categories of the behavioral spectrum, plus a few additional ones. Besides behaviors, cognitions, and emotions, a social category, two biological ones, and a psychological one are added. In essence, this is a checklist to make sure that nothing is left out. It aids in the identification of client problems by reminding the therapist what to monitor. Also, when formalized into a bureaucratic system, it provides the headings necessary for comprehensive record keeping.

# 9

# *Antitherapies*

Not all clinicians who work with clients having role problems are comfortable with the notion of psychotherapy. As we have seen, many academics deny the necessity of relinquishing dysfunctional roles. Strict behaviorists even describe the traditional therapies as mumbo jumbo. Questions about a client's past, or attempts to elicit emotional responses, are considered irrelevant at best. It is only direct efforts to solve client problems that they believe to have scientific merit. In essence, they are reductionists who insist on describing everything in the molecular terms of behavior, and hence they fail to distinguish the larger patterns of role problems and role change. Although they prize the honorific "psychotherapy," they distrust its substance.

Many other putative therapists are even less comfortable with the historic forms of psychotherapy. It turns out that they are fundamentally hostile to the concept of resocialization. Their therapies may be employed as an equivalent for, or an adjunct to, psychotherapy, but they consciously abjure role change. They would rather use their techniques as a substitute for, rather than an improvement upon, the traditional approaches. Some even go so far as to denounce role change as a myth.

To the degree that they solve role problems, most antitherapies are social-support and socialization oriented. They share with the behavioral approaches a conviction that if one modifies a client's problem behaviors, one thereby solves her problem. For them there is nothing beyond what the client is doing or feeling, and so altering these becomes central. Moreover, change is almost always therapist imposed. Rather than helping the client engage in an internal process of change, the clinician determines what is wrong, then attempts to induce the client to act or feel differently. Persuasion and manipulation are held in great esteem, and the client's responsibility for personal growth is derogated.

What are here being classified as antitherapies constitute a very diverse assemblage. While they enjoy a widespread and probably expanding acceptance, they employ very different strategies. The first set of approaches we must discuss is the medical interventions. Versions of psychiatry that are biological in their orientation almost automatically reject role change methodologies. They find pharmacotherapy far more congenial and are convinced that it is more effective than mere talk.

A second set of antitherapy strategies includes strategic therapy and hypnotherapy. Clinicians employing these related methodologies are willing to fool the client into doing what they believe needs to be accomplished. They distrust the client's willingness, or ability, to change, and as long as he can be maneuvered in desirable directions, they declare themselves satisfied.

A third type of strategy is reality therapy. It is education and problem-solving oriented and explicitly rejects traditional talk therapies. While it demands that clients act responsibly, it casts the clinician almost in the role of an enforcer.

A fourth antitherapy, or, more properly, non-therapy, is vocational rehabilitation. This procedure refuses to acknowledge the negative impact of buried roles and seeks to inculcate improved role behaviors directly. Even more educationally oriented than reality therapy, it assumes that new patterns of living can compensate for client disabilities.

We should also mention the brief therapies. Although these do not constitute a separate class of intervention, they modify other therapies in directions away from resocialization. By limiting the amount of time allotted for change, they often prevent its realization. Clients are promised all the benefits of role change, then arbitrarily terminated at the clinician's insistence. Like many other antitherapies, they aim at solving circumscribed problems and prefer to deal with later manifestations of deferred distress as they arise.

The recent boom in the antitherapies is probably a consequence of financial and institutional factors. In the early days of psychoanalysis, patients had to be sufficiently affluent to pay a physician for five or six visits a week. When the apparent success of this form of treatment markedly increased the demand for therapy, many potential clients found they could not afford the out-of-pocket expense. Instead, they turned to governmental agencies or insurance companies for relief. Initially these obliged, but the burgeoning public appetite for therapy stretched their resources past the breaking point. Rather than explicitly turn people down, these third-party payers sought quicker and cheaper interventions. They found these in the antitherapies. Although these methodologies cloak themselves in the mantle of psychotherapy, by prescribing drugs or limiting the number of client sessions, they effectively neutralize the more expensive attributes of traditional therapy. Potential clients are nevertheless persuaded that they are being provided with the genuine article and that, moreover, they are receiving what they need. The upshot is that the antitherapies constitute a special instance of Gresham's law, with a devalued therapeutic currency driving out the more expensive ones.

## MEDICAL INTERVENTIONS

Even though the word "therapy" derives from a Greek word meaning "to cure or to nurse," its incorporation in the term "psychotherapy" does not preordain a medical process. Indeed, there is reason to believe that what most therapists do is distinctly nonmedical. Certainly the core instances of role change are not similar to those of medical cure. Role dysfunction may be painful, and its correction may benefit from professional interventions, but it is not a disease requiring a biological treatment.

It is ironic, then, that medicine was first into the field of psychotherapy. Whether in the guise of a Sigmund Freud or an Adolf Meyer, the fact is that physicians pioneered the talk therapies. Moreover, as we have repeatedly seen, psychiatrists have figured prominently among their most influential innovators and skilled practitioners. Many doctors have been so competent at promoting personal change that they merit our respect. It is also true that biologically oriented psychiatry has been a valuable supplement to role-change procedures. Utilization of medications can, for instance, make it possible for a person to tolerate a talk therapy that would not otherwise be feasible. Still, medicine is fundamentally antithetical to resocialization. It places the locus of fault in an entirely different location and so usually discourages role-change efforts.

The essence of medicine is the prevention and treatment of physiological problems. Ever since Hippocrates proposed that people in pain were suffering from physical disorders rather than spiritual ones, the hypothesis that a disrupted biology causes illness has proven fruitful. It has laid the foundation for the many modern advances in understanding how the body works and how it can be manipulated to function more satisfactorily. Surgery, antibiotics, or a changed diet have all been employed, with spectacular results. Indeed, today, for the first time in history, someone who seeks medical help actually increases the prospect that she will get well. The success rate of physicians has risen to such heights that people feel cheated when a doctor is unable to cure them.

Unfortunately, this enviable record does not guarantee that the medical analogy is applicable to personal problems. If a role problem paradigm is valid, then biology is not the cause of all personal pain. One will need a very different hypothesis to explain why the adult victim of childhood abuse remains in pain and is unable to change. Such an explanation is more likely to be found in the facts of role conservation than in those of biological transmission. The fault will lie in dysfunctional interpersonal behavior patterns, not in the quantity of neurotransmitters in the brain. While both the role-conservation and biological transmission theories have scientific credibility, they cannot both be correct, and our wager is that the former comes closer to the truth.

To be sure, there exist real mental illnesses that can disrupt a person's role performances (Thomas Szasz notwithstanding). There is ample evidence to suggest that schizophrenia has both genetic and chemical precursors. For this reason, in some instances biological treatments are not only appropriate but virtually mandatory. Psychotropic medications can be absolutely essential in enabling a mentally ill person to function with any semblance of normality. Yet even in the case of schizophrenia, some of the difficulties a person experiences do derive from role dysfunction. In recent years, physicians have become aware that "expressed emotion" can elicit schizophrenic symptoms. They have, however, been less cognizant of the fact that intense emotions are an integral part of most role negotiation processes. They fail to realize that it is when a schizophrenic person is confronted with the challenge of emotionally demanding role partners that he retreats into illness. His sensitivity to such demands virtually insures that he will be an incompetent role negotiator. And because he is not able to defend his interests effectively, he is forced into role behaviors that are grossly unsatisfying.

The solution therefore may be a combination of medical treatment and resocialization. Pharmacotherapy is indispensable for controlling the worst symptoms of the illness, but resocialization may be necessary to open the possibility of a reorganized interpersonal life. There need be no automatic division between the two, and a cooperative approach to solving a patient's problems is not excluded. In practice, however, a real breach does exist. Many medicalists, such as Dr. Paul Wender, assail psychotherapy as a romantic delusion and assert that chemical solutions are overwhelmingly best. They suggest that it is unnecessary to explore or correct role problems, because underlying physical failings are responsible for almost every client affliction.

The real difficulty with the medical perspective becomes apparent when it is applied to normal problems in living. When a dispute between spouses, or the distress of a vocational crisis, are reconceptualized as disease-like entities, their role-failure origin is disguised. In effect the patient is told that part of his body is not functioning properly, when he is in fact enacting a role that is not meeting his needs. If he is convinced by the physiological explanation, the responsibility for improving his situation will be perceived as residing with the doctor, not himself. He will reason that a disordered physiology requires the intervention of a trained physician, rather than that of a layman who initiates his own change. His solution may consequently be discerned in taking a pain-reduction pill, rather than in undergoing a process of relinquishing a dysfunctional role.

The pharmacotherapy option not only denies the validity of resocialization, but it can also interfere with its implementation. A person who is taking a psychotropic medication may have difficulty in executing the several stages of role change. When on a drug, it may be next to impossible to reexperience a failed role or to renegotiate it. The point of many psychotropics—such as the anxiolytics—is to reduce, and if possible eliminate, the distress a person experiences. They numb him and do not clarify why he is hurting. They are, therefore, well suited to masking the nature of role problems. Yet if a person doesn't know that he is suffering from a role problem, he is scarcely likely to seek a role change solution. To the contrary, he is more apt to become dependent upon a drug and a physician. As long as he is led to believe that a medication is achieving all that can be expected, his motivation to reconstruct his problem behaviors will be nil.

## Levels of Intervention

### Social Support

Medication-oriented therapies specialize in social support, albeit without the social element. They are symptom oriented, identifying the distress a person experiences as his problem. They therefore propose to suppress his symptoms and cure, or at least control, his disorder.

When psychotropic medications are properly prescribed, they function as a powerful tool for helping people cope with debilitating circumstances. Tranquilizers, for example, can calm someone during his worst interpersonal crises. It may be impossible for him to reason with his temperamental boss or to tame his unruly children, but a pill can make these predicaments less intolerable. He will then be able to continue interacting with these others without precipitating a disaster. Because he feels less agitated, he isn't compelled to tell off his boss or hide under the bed covers. In short, he will be able to enact his current roles more effectively, even if he isn't able to change them. Such an outcome is not to be sneered at, although it may discourage more sweeping efforts at self-help.

### Socialization

Medical interventions are not aimed at teaching new role behaviors. Since roles are deemed irrelevant, no conscious attempt is made to substitute new ones. If social learning does occur, it is a by-product of reduced anxieties, not of a medical strategy.

### Resocialization

Role change is the greatest casualty of the medical model. An emphasis on symptom relief is antithetical to long-term processes of change. Role problems are not identified, reexperienced, relinquished, or renegotiated; they are only papered over. Often they are not even denied, but merely ignored.

## Phase of Change: Identification

Medically oriented psychiatrists do make efforts to identify client problems, albeit not as role problems. Personal distress is conceptualized in strictly medical terms. Since doctors are most familiar with disease categories, the framework they invoke classifies instances of distress as quasi-diseases. The American Psychiatric Association's *Diagnostic and Statistical Manual of Mental Disorders* (1980) is nothing less than a compilation of such categories. It groups together congeries of symptoms, labels them disorders, and in the process hypostasizes them. Instead of remaining collections of problem behaviors, these assemblages are conflated with biologically grounded disorders and take on a solidity they would not otherwise possess. While such a procedure may be justifiable with physiologically based conditions like schizophrenia, it is extremely misleading when applied to personality or adjustment disorders.

One may also speculate that a diagnostic enterprise is inherently antagonistic to a role perspective. Although social roles may themselves be labeled, these designations allow for considerable variation and do not pigeonhole people in inflexible categories. The clinician who attempts to identify a dysfunctional role engages in an ongoing process of determining the contours of his client's distinctive interpersonal behavior patterns. These are recognized by him as particular and complex. A diagnostic category, however, confuses an individual's situation with those of others. After all, persons given the same diagnosis presumably have the same problem. This is certainly the case with normal diseases: two people suffering from measles are expected to be infected by the same microorganism. The consequence is that medical diagnoses often dehumanize clients and convert them from individuals with unique problems to interchangeable bearers of biological maladies.

## Barriers to Change

### Emotions

It might seem that the psychotropic medications that reduce anxiety would thereby remove it as an impediment to role change. Yet the situation is more complicated. It is true that for some people the chemical control of an unbearable emotion can pave the way for psychotherapy. Some clients, after being reassured that a drug can restrain the worst of their terrors, do gain the confidence to embark on a therapeutic enterprise. When this occurs, use of the medication is to be applauded and can function as a valued adjunct to psychotherapy.

The rub is that for most people psychotropics do not reduce the intensity of a problem emotion; they simply disguise its presence. A person coping with anxiety through the medium of tranquilizers may not feel distressed while she takes her pills, but once she stops, the old fears will reappear with a vengeance. They will clearly not have been reduced in the way that a program of desensitization might have reduced them. However much these fears are controlled, the person will know that they have not been disarmed, and she will consequently avoid reexperiencing the dysfunctional role of which they are a part. She will instinctively recognize that reanimating her role entails reliving emotions she was so afraid of feeling that she has been compelled to employ medication to shield herself from them. Since the reexperiencing of a dysfunctional role is a requirement for launching resocialization, change will be aborted. The person is thus ensnared in a contradiction: in employing medication to make therapy possible, she allows herself to aggravate the very emotion she has sought to contain; yet if she chooses more medication to counteract what she has initiated, she will forestall further therapy.

## STRATEGIC INTERVENTIONS

Strategic therapy has emerged from two traditions. On the one hand it derives from family therapy and on the other from hypnosis. The central personalities in its evolution are Jay Haley and Milton Erickson. Haley, it will be recalled, worked with Bateson and the Palo Alto group. He shared with them an interest in communications and family research. Along the way, he also became impressed with the work of Erickson, a charismatic physician with a reputation as a gifted practitioner of hypnosis. Haley subsequently adopted, and popularized, many of Erickson's techniques, most notably the paradoxical intervention.

In reading the works of those influenced by strategic therapy, one is impressed by the almost magical quality of the cures they record. They seem to assure us that by pointing a client in an unexpected direction, a barrier will suddenly be breached and the person will rush pell-mell into a totally revised life circumstance. Furthermore, the impression one receives is that the clinician must outwit his client and trick him into solving his problem. This is especially so for the paradoxical techniques. When I was in high school, paradoxical approaches were called "reverse psychology," and they had a slightly disreputable reputation. Strategic therapists, however, celebrate their ability to issue instructions that upon being disobeyed, actually further the intentions of the therapy. This tactic is considered both pragmatic and clever. It is also deemed an unavoidable corollary of the fact that psychotherapy entails influencing client actions. The indirection of the paradox is interpreted as merely an effective means of persuasion with people who are inclined to resist change.

Strategic therapy is here being classified as an antitherapy, not for what it attempts to achieve, but for how it attempts to achieve it. The problems of its clients are recognized as emerging from faulty relationships and might even be conceived of in role terms, yet the form of change advocated bypasses the labyrinthine intricacies of resocialization and moves straight to the imposition of amended roles. More importantly, this is achieved not with the cooperation of the client, but in opposition to him. Strategic therapists simply don't trust their clients. They are convinced that people can correct their problem behaviors if they choose to, but that since they don't, they must be manipulated for their own good. The implication is that resocialization is generally impossible because people won't implement it. The only viable alternative is for a clinician to assess the client's problem, devise a reasonable solution, and then concoct a strategy for circumventing the resistance. Therapy, therefore, becomes something that is done to the client, rather than something he is helped to do for himself.

## Level of Intervention: Resocialization

Sometimes strategic therapists help clients make small changes in their lives that might be construed as social support or as socialization oriented. A modest change in the way a person interacts with his parents, or in his eating patterns, can help him cope with life and/or develop new role scripts. Nevertheless, most strategic interventions aim at more drastic revisions. Strategic therapists want their clients to stop living in their unproductive old ways and adopt dramatically new ones. Furthermore, they recognize that, because significant change can arouse significant opposition, large-scale change is rarely easy. Though they fail to appreciate the significance of mourning in achieving the letting go of what is lost, they have a real sense of there being a barrier that must be surmounted, and they are determined to clear it.

## Phase of Change: Renegotiation

Strategic therapists are both indirect and directive. Dedicated as they are to manipulating the client into doing what is best for her, they negotiate with her in a deceptive yet energetic manner. The very name "strategic" gives a clue to the approach taken. A strategy is a plan for making something happen, but in this case it is usually a covert plan. It is almost as if the client were an enemy who must be outmaneuvered, rather than a negotiating partner with whom a mutually satisfactory bargain can be effected.

Peggy Papp has graphically described the way these therapists conceive of clients. She notes that people in therapy can either be compliant or defiant. If they are compliant there will be no problem, for they will readily go along with the suggestions of their therapist; if they are defiant, however, the clinician must be like a jujitsu master and turn the clients' efforts against them. The situation, therefore, seems clear, and the justification for paradoxical tactics unimpeachable.

Yet the dichotomy between compliance and defiance is ill-conceived. It includes two false assumptions about the nature of therapeutic negotiations. The first is that a therapist must impose something on a client, whose sole task is to accept or reject it. This fails to account for the possibility that the two may engage in a joint enterprise, in which both make contributions to the final outcome. The second false assumption is that the therapist and client are irredeemable rivals, and that the alternative to capitulation is interminable warfare. This misses their potential for problem solving. It converts Pruitt's dual-concern model into a single-concern version in which contending and yielding are the only options.

As importantly, this dichotomy thoroughly misconceives the nature of client resistance. Intransigence is represented as a response to the therapist, rather than a reaction to the role problem. As far back as Freud, psychotherapists have confused the difficulty clients have in changing with their attitude toward their helper. Of course, clients do resist change, but this is more from a fear of letting go than from a desire to frustrate the clinician. Thus, casting the problem in an us-versus-them framework diverts attention from the change process, where the attention belongs.

Many critics have charged that paradoxical interventions are basically unfair and dishonest, that by making a policy out of fooling the client, they do more than influence; they manipulate. The gravamen of this charge is that paradoxical strategies sabotage therapeutic negotiations. In effect, they epitomize the worst sort of negotiation tactics. Certainly the client who takes them seriously and attempts to use them with role partners outside of therapy will alienate more people than he influences. Yet if paradox is meant only for the therapeutic setting, does this indicate that the clinician is somehow superior? Alternatively, if it is meant for the client's use too, does this disclose a cynical worldview? Either way, the implication is disquieting.

A more charitable interpretation of the paradoxical intervention might explain it as an effort at subtly relieving the demands made upon the client, and thereby encouraging him to implement a more assertive negotiation policy. Suppose, for instance, that a young adult refuses to leave home because he feels a need to protect his mother. If the therapist tells him he must leave because it will help him become more independent, he may demur and cling tenaciously to his long-standing duties. Should he, however, be encouraged to continue in his ministrations, he may more easily be able to let go and move on. The former suggestion may be taken as adding another demand to that of his own internal voice, thereby making the two so potent that he will fear that his only recourse is to leave immediately and traumatically. Removing the external demand, however, may reduce the internal coercion as well, and give him an opportunity to establish a more gentle transition. This interpretation converts the therapist's action from a coercive external mandate into permitting the client to be less coercive with himself. Instead of being deceptive, the therapist is understood as honestly encouraging his client not to do what he is not ready to do.

This latter interpretation of the paradoxical intervention removes its paradoxical element. Instead of advising the client to remain with his mother because one expects him to disobey, one truthfully suggests that staying, when he is not ready to leave, is in fact best. Such a statement can reduce his internal coercion by implying that what he demands of himself is not necessary. It is then by easing up on himself that he will be emotionally free to move on, rather than by defying the therapist and paradoxically doing what is secretly wanted. The inner dynamic of this process is a negotiation in which the clinician quietly allies himself with the client against the client's internalized coercion and/or against continued external pressures, for example from the client's mother.

### Barriers to Change: Social Demands

If the above interpretation is correct, then strategic therapies also specialize in countering social demands. If the therapist is the secret ally of his client, he may be giving him the courage to resist unfair others. Assuming that it is the covert demands of role partners that prevent change, the effect may indeed be to breach the barriers to resocialization. The fact that paradoxical strategies are so closely allied to family therapies gives one the suspicion that this is so, that the therapist is in fact inserting himself into continuing negotiations and is doing so on behalf of the identified client.

## REALITY THERAPY

The subtitle of William Glasser's best-selling book *Reality Therapy* (1965) is *A New Approach to Psychiatry*. In this he vigorously expresses his opposition to conventional psychotherapy as practiced by the Freudians and their progeny. In contrast with what Glasser imagines psychoanalysis to be, his creation aims at dealing with the real world in a realistic way. The tenets of his approach are clear-cut and simple and allow the therapist to demand change of the client. Usually this makes the approach problem-solving with a vengeance. Yet it is precisely because of this quality that reality therapy has been popular with governmental agencies mandated to impose change on dependent and/or deviant clients. Counselors in penal institutions, public welfare programs, and adolescent group homes all find it congenial. Instead of encouraging them to spend months or years probing the depths of their clients' despair, it directs them to get on with the business of imposing social responsibility. Since this is just what their employers wish, it simplifies their job enormously.

Glasser makes no bones about his antitherapeutic attitude. He vigorously attacks the idea that clients in therapy are suffering from mental illness, openly derogates the utility of exploring their past difficulties, and considers an examination of unconscious motivation utterly unnecessary. In dismissing orthodox psychiatry, he, by implication, also rejects a role-problem interpretation. Certainly he rejects the notion that because some individuals are entangled in problem behaviors adopted in their past, they must be allowed to mourn these behaviors in the present. As part of its hard-eyed realism, reality therapy is consumed with the here and now. The past is viewed as a tempting diversion and the unconscious as little more than a booby trap. Consequently, they are treated as rationalizations mustered to avoid change, rather than as necessary adjuncts to a change process.

Reality therapy is instead almost obsessed with the morality of client behaviors. If it does not see its clients as mentally ill, it does perceive them as morally impaired. Many of their difficulties are attributed to a lack of personal responsibility. Their pain is interpreted as deriving from unfulfilled needs, and these needs are unfulfilled precisely because the person has not accepted her obligations to herself or society. The prescription is therefore to acknowledge one's responsibility and set about the task of acting in ways that bring satisfaction. It is, however, recognized that a past abdication of responsibility may have left a person with gaps in her education. Having renounced her obligations, she will not have attempted to learn the skills she must possess to meet her current needs. This implies that, in Glasser's words, "therapy is a special kind of teaching or training which attempts to accomplish in a relatively short, intense period what should have been established during normal growing up" (1965, p. 24).

As described by Glasser, reality therapy is direct almost to a fault. A client is to admit her responsibility, develop a plan for meeting her own needs, then act upon this plan. Glasser informs us that one of his favorite questions is, What is your plan? Generalized complaints are simply not tolerated. The object is to do something, not merely talk about it. The clinician's function is to inspire action and monitor its implementation. Changed behaviors rather than altered attitudes are what impress him. Only secondarily is he a teacher who fills in the discontinuities in the client's knowledge. Though reality therapy is said to entail a special kind of teaching, this is achieved through action rather than pedagogy.

## Levels of Intervention

### Social Support

As a problem-solving approach, reality therapy is more concerned with helping clients cope with role problems than with changing their roles.

Although the reality therapist is supposed to be supportive, it is the degree to which he is directive that distinguishes him from other clinicians. He helps his clients cope by pushing them to do so. His no-nonsense, no-excuses attitude exerts a steady pressure toward action. For clients unsure of their own willpower, this can be a welcome service. For adolescents, it can be particularly beneficial. Since they are engaged in the development of an adult identity, judiciously applied external pressure can help them overcome their normal tendency to procrastinate and temporize.

## Socialization

Despite Glasser's commendation of teaching, whether reality therapy has a socialization dimension is largely a function of the type of client being served and the problem-solving strategy being adopted. If the plan that a client develops has as its goal the construction of a new role, socialization will occur. Certainly if new role behaviors require new skills, these must somehow be learned. The therapist, however, is likely to offer advice and inspiration, not information. The client will therefore have to arrange learning experiences for himself. When the client is an adolescent, the learning of new role skills may be the centerpiece of the therapy process. When an adult is involved, there will usually be fewer changes to his role repertoire.

## Resocialization

With its antipathy to traditional psychotherapy, not surprisingly, reality therapy is little concerned with resocialization. Indeed, it flatly denies the validity of the therapeutic enterprise and aims, at best, at a kind of role transfer. Nevertheless, this very tenacity can be of value to many individuals. Adolescents, who are in the process of formulating their adult roles, can be disoriented by attempts at role change. Even if their efforts at growth are stymied by dysfunctional roles deriving from childhood, their preoccupation with the present may make it difficult to explore the past or relinquish the irretrievably lost. These tasks may prove necessary, but usually need to be delayed until the person begins to feel like an adult. In the meantime, the best plan is to prevent additional problems from developing. Since an adolescent will in any event resist resocialization, pushing for it will only introduce a new element of coercion. Encouraging the reexperiencing of traumatic role negotiations that a person has not yet learned to combat, can have a negative impact by forcing her to lose once more. In contrast, reality therapy's strategy of pressing for action gives a teenager something constructive to do that makes sense to him and is achievable. The plans he is asked to develop and execute lie well within his competence.

## Phases of Change

### *Identifying*

It is difficult to imagine how reality therapy could be less congenial to the reexperiencing of dysfunctional roles. Its insistence on dealing with the present is an expression of its hostility to reliving the past. Nevertheless, like all therapies, it must engage in identification of client problems, although it does not have an elaborate methodology for achieving even this. Because the reality therapist is intent upon action, his concern with the hows and whys of a client's distress is less developed than his demand for action. It is assumed that the client must have a problem, or he wouldn't be in therapy. Lingering too long over the details of the problem is construed as opposition to change, rather than as laying a foundation for it.

### *Renegotiating*

The directive nature of reality therapy makes for a confrontational, often acerbic, species of negotiation. When it is new roles that are being negotiated, the therapist plays a demanding and sometimes coercive role partner. Within the therapeutic relationship there is no question about who is the dominant figure. Although the client may be encouraged to be innovative, the helping relationship does not itself provide a model for flexible negotiations. The new patterns of action advocated by the therapist may be suitable, but it is questionable whether the client will be learning how to solve future role negotiation problems when they arise.

## Barriers to Change

In spite of Glasser's aversion to resocialization, his therapy can remove some barriers to role change. For instance, its emphasis on personal responsibility can correct particular volitional errors. The person who fails to solve a problem because she is committed to the proposition that others owe her a better life can be helped by recognizing that her fate is in her own hands. If she continues to demand that past role partners recompense her for their mistakes, it will be difficult for her to let go and move on to other roles. Similarly, when a client makes cognitive mistakes, a reality therapist is commissioned to point them out and insist on their rectification.

If this is done effectively, it may not be necessary for the client to understand the derivation of these mistakes. Simply correcting her perceptions can avert errors that will interfere with her personal growth.

Surely one of the weakest aspects of reality therapy is its neglect of the emotional dimensions of personal problems. Its action orientation relegates emotional reactions to the status of excuses to be eschewed, rather than barriers to be extirpated. The attitude is almost, Don't feel, just do.

## REHABILITATION

Also action oriented is vocational rehabilitation. It, however, is almost the epitome of an educational approach. Rehabilitation programs are dedicated to teaching clients new ways of living and, in particular, new occupational roles. These are intended to compensate for the role deficiencies conceived of as "disabilities."

Rehabilitation joins threads from both medicine and social welfare. Although not associated with a specific founder, it has a venerable pedigree in the United States, having been among the first federally sponsored attempts to help persons in trouble. Originally rehabilitation was addressed to the difficulties of veterans wounded in the "Great War," but during the course of this century it has expanded to include civilians injured on the job, persons born with developmental disabilities, and patients afflicted by mental illness. Indeed, in recent decades it has almost functioned as a substitute for psychotherapy with psychiatric clients not deemed suitable for therapy. For instance, persons suffering from severe schizophrenia, who are considered too fragile to endure "uncovering" strategies, are referred for rehabilitation, which provides them with a measure of help while simultaneously distracting them from their underlying distress. Since it is not considered possible to cure their illness, the hope is that they will at least be able to function more effectively.

While clients undergoing rehabilitation may also be in conventional psychotherapy, the two are somewhat antagonistic. Certainly, a client in rehabilitation will not be asked to explore the etiology of his dilemmas. Instead the focus will be on his current limitations and on potential techniques for compensating for them. Both the client and his counselor will avoid emotional turmoil and concentrate on skill training. Together they will agree on a specific goal and specific techniques for achieving it. Moreover, both will perceive the client as acquiring important information. In the end, it is expected that the client will have accumulated knowledge that will be useful in living.

The paradigm for rehabilitation remains the injured worker who has lost his job because his physical skills no longer allow him to perform in his accustomed manner. The rationale for helping him is that the development of alternative skills that are commensurate with his current abilities will enable him to function satisfactorily without his having to change who he is. The roles addressed by this endeavor are usually not basic, personal ones, but secondary and impersonal ones, generally those needed for employment. Yet when applied to clients with psychiatric or developmental difficulties, this pattern remains the same. Even though clients suffering from mental illness have had their most basic roles disrupted, rehabilitation efforts focus on less emotionally charged roles aimed at the marketplace. It is assumed that if the client can at least appear to function normally, both he and society will benefit.

The justification for this gambit is that teaching a disabled person a viable new role thereby empowers him. In the term popularized by Wolf Wolfensberger with respect to the mentally retarded, the client achieves "normalization." It is alleged that many of the difficulties of the disabled result from social stigmatization, and that therefore teaching them to behave in ways that attract less censure will relieve them from external constraints. Moreover, a sense of competence that derives from being able to perform satisfactorily is expected to generalize to the person's self-esteem and help her function in the world.

Rehabilitation techniques occur within many settings, most of which are very different from the traditional therapeutic interview. Vocational workshops, day treatment centers, group homes, education programs, and on-the-job enclaves are all used to deliver services. One-on-one counseling and job coaching may be part of the rehabilitation process, but efforts to get "too deep" are avoided. Indeed, rehabilitation often occurs in situations that discourage resocialization. Role change usually requires a degree of privacy for self-examination, but in a workshop, for instance, coworkers and the exigencies of the job divert attention from internal factors. The person will be asked to keep his mind on the task at hand, not to relive some distant upheaval from the long-forgotten past.

### Level of Intervention: Socialization

Without a doubt, rehabilitation is socialization oriented. While it may provide some supportive services, the focus of its efforts is to instill new roles. The assumption is that one can learn such roles without having to relinquish past ones, that is, that they are a form of role transfer. In traditional vocational rehabilitation the client's previous role has already been lost because he can no longer perform it. The notion that he may also have to mourn it is not entertained, and it is believed that an impersonal rationality should prevail. It is assumed that the client will understand where his interests lie and will be able to apply himself satisfactorily to a new task. Nowadays, however, rehabilitation professionals have become more aware of the vicissitudes of client motivation. They have learned that people who have sustained grievous losses often need a period of adjustment before they are ready to dedicate themselves to new projects. Still, most of them see this as a preparatory process best supervised by psychotherapists, rather than as an integral part of rehabilitation. They would rather stick to the teaching of new skills.

## Phases of Change

### *Identification*

Despite helping clients acquire new roles, rehabilitation programs are usually oriented toward specific skills. Clients are not assessed in terms of role deficits, but skill deficits. Influential theoreticians, such as William Anthony, have developed elaborate technologies for determining particular limitations. Very often the heart of a rehabilitation treatment is this evaluation process. All sorts of tests are administered, some involving paper and pencil, others hands-on manipulations. Everything from the person's IQ to his manual dexterity is considered. In the end, a profile of his talents emerges that is supposed to guide a reasoned selection of appropriate training. The client's interests are also considered, but these too are judged accessible to testing. The possibility that it may take time and further experience for the client to decide what he wants to do is sometimes admitted, but rarely respected. Instead of being perceived as a pattern of life to be negotiated with others, the client's new role is treated as an assemblage of skills optimally selected by an appropriate assortment of tests. The professional's skill is demonstrated in the selection and interpretation of these, not in his ability to facilitate change.

### *Renegotiation*

The training programs in which rehabilitation specializes are not understood as involving role negotiations. Because the paradigm on which they are based is an educational one, it is believed that the professional teaches and the client learns. Ideally, this relationship is supposed to be unequal, and often impersonal. Any counterdemands made by the client are treated as a disruption in services, not as a valuable part of the process. In rehabilitation, clients do influence their own programs—indeed, if they are to develop viable new roles, they must be able to make individual accommodations—but this occurs almost in secret. Overtly, a kind of "oversocialized" view prevails in which society is conceived as transmitting precious cultural materials to the receptive individual. In practice, the reality of a two-way process is accommodated, but hardly ever welcomed.

### Barriers to Change

*Volitions*

Much rehabilitation is based on the intrinsic value of work. A kind of Protestant ethic is invoked that celebrates the virtue of productive labor. Although many of the skills that the clients are taught are menial and poorly remunerated, work itself is supposed to have redemptive power. The self-respect that it is supposed to generate is itself believed worthy of pursuit. In fact, when people decide to dedicate themselves to work, many do feel better. They are able to base their identities upon and organize their lives around it. Consequently, when someone is stuck in a dysfunctional role because he has committed himself to resist productive activity, a work ethic can be a liberating instrument. It can give him permission to get on with life.

*Emotions*

As with reality therapy, rehabilitation is especially weak in the area of the emotions. Because it exalts a business-like approach, it often tries to implement the impersonality of business. Work is work, and feelings belong in one's private life, not on the job. When they are manifested within the training setting, the client may be asked to control herself or, failing this, be referred to a psychotherapist who will be asked to control them for her.

# 10

# *Conclusion*

A role-problem/role-change paradigm turns out to be a useful instrument. In the best tradition of science, it brings order to enormous diversity. It permits a grand synthesis that demonstrates the connections between apparently antagonistic perspectives. While it cannot resolve all of the disputes (as the various therapies continue to differ in emphasis), it enables the more disinterested observer to locate particular therapies in terms of their specialties. This should allow a better evaluation of their successes, as well as of their applicability to particular problems.

It must also be clear that no one therapy is best suited to all problems, and that the wide diversity of current treatment strategies encompasses a broad range of virtues and faults that fit them for very different purposes. A judgment about which is superior will depend upon the difficulty at hand and on the resources available to solve it. I have a bias toward resocialization, but must reluctantly admit that it is not suitable for everyone or for all problems. And even resocialization can be accomplished in different ways. The steps through which it is achieved may be clear-cut, but the techniques for effecting these are not easily ranked according to their potency. Different individuals, with different backgrounds and motivations, may respond differently to them. What is more confusing, but perhaps equally hopeful, is that despite their differences in rationale, in practice most brands of therapy perform similar tasks. Both research and anecdotal evidence suggest that they share underlying commonalities, which a role change perspective can make visible.

Psychotherapy is a complex enterprise with room for divergent orientations. A role-change model, however, provides a basis for making judgments and comparisons, regardless of one's starting point. Its synthesis establishes a framework for evaluating the particular strengths and weaknesses of individual therapies. It also allows for the inclusion and integration of the many phenomena that appear during therapy. By making room for social support, socialization, and resocialization, as well as for the different phases of role change and for cognitive, emotional, volitional, and social barriers to change, it creates a comprehensive pattern that can give meaning to the parts.

Given this power, role theory deserves a better hearing than it has traditionally received. Moreover, because it is inherently psychosocial and intuitively comprehensible, it is accessible to both professionals and clients. Furthermore, it does not raise false hopes or assign unfair blame. Neither the client nor the clinician is held responsible for things beyond his control. In particular, the client is not blamed for being an inadequate person, but is understood as the victim of dysfunctional roles that were adopted during the press of coercive role negotiations and that subsequently proved difficult to change, while the therapist is seen as an expert facilitator of change, not an omnipotent guarantor of personal happiness or the purveyor of a medical cure.

It would be a shame if the advantages of role theory were overlooked due to the prior commitments of therapists. All is well known, the vagaries of professional turf building are in part responsible for the Tower of Babel presently obfuscating the field; how much sadder if entrenched interests preclude the achievement of a worthwhile rapprochement. Most practitioners are well aware of the convergences between their work and that of others. It will be gratifying if this realization can be ratified on the neutral conceptual ground of role theory.

# Bibliography

Abt, C. E., and Stuart I. R. 1982. *The Newer Therapies: A Sourcebook*. New York: Van Nostrand Reinhold.

Ackerman, N. W. 1958. *The Psychodynamics of Family Life*. New York: Basic Books.

Adler, A. 1931. *What Life Should Mean to You*. Boston: Little, Brown.

———. 1954. *Understanding Human Nature*. Greenwich, Conn.: Fawcett.

———. 1963. *The Practice and Theory of Individual Psychology*. Paterson, N.J.: Littlefield, Adams.

Alexander, F. 1948. *Fundamentals of Psychoanalysis*. New York: W. W. Norton.

Alexander, F., and French, T. 1946. *Psychoanalytic Therapy*. New York: Ronald Press.

Allport, G. 1985. "The Historical Background of Social Psychology," In *Handbook of Social Psychology*, ed. Lindzey, G., and Aronson, E. 3d ed. New York: Random House.

American Psychiatric Association Task Force on Nomenclature and Statistics. 1988. *Diagnostic and Statistical Manual of Mental Disorders*. 3d ed., rev. Washington, D.C.

Anthony, W. (ed.). 1980. "Special Issue: Rehabilitating the Person with a Psychiatric Disability: The State of the Art." *Rehabilitation Bulletin*, vol. 24, no. 1.

Ausubel, D. 1967. "Personality Disorder Is Disease." In *Mental Illness and Social Process*, ed. Scheff, T. New York: Harper & Row.

Auxline, V. A. 1969. *Play Therapy*. New York: Ballantine.

Baars, B. J. 1986. *The Cognitive Revolution in Psychology*. New York: Guilford.

Bach, G. R., and Wyden, P. 1968. *The Intimate Enemy*. New York: Avon.

Barlow, D. H. 1988. *Anxiety and Its Disorders: The Nature and Treatment of Anxiety and Panic*. New York: Guilford.

Basch, M. 1980. *Doing Psychotherapy*. New York: Basic Books.

Bateson, G. 1972. *Steps to an Ecology of Mind*. New York: Ballantine.

Bauer, G. P., and Kobos, J. C. 1987. *Brief Therapy: Short-Term Psychodynamic Intervention*. Northvale, N.J.: Jason Aronson.

Bavelas, J. 1978. *Personality: Current Theories and Research.* Monterey, Calif.: Brooks/Cole.

Beattie, M. 1987. *Codependent No More.* San Francisco: Harper & Row.

Beck, A. 1967. *Depression: Clinical, Experimental and Theoretical Aspects.* New York: Harper & Row.

————. 1976. *Cognitive Therapy and the Emotional Disorders.* New York: International Universities Press.

Beckham, E. E., and Leber, W. R. (eds.). 1985. *Handbook of Depression: Treatment Assessment and Research.* Homewood, Ill.: Dorsey.

Beitman, B. D. 1987. *The Structure of Individual Psychotherapy.* New York: Guilford.

Berger, D. 1987. *Clinical Empathy.* Northvale, N.J.: Jason Aronson.

Berger, M. M. (ed.). 1978. *Beyond the Double Bind.* New York: Brunner/Mazel.

Berne, E. 1961. *Transactional Analysis in Psychotherapy.* New York: Grove.

————. 1964. *Games People Play.* New York: Grove.

————. 1972. *What Do You Say After You Say Hello?* New York: Grove.

Bettleheim, B. 1983. *Freud and Man's Soul.* New York: Knopf.

————. 1990. *Freud's Vienna and Other Essays.* New York: Knopf.

Biddle, B. 1979. *Role Theory: Expectations, Identities and Behaviors.* New York: Academic Press.

Blanck, R., and Blanck, G. 1986. *Beyond Ego Psychology: Developmental Object Relations Theory.* New York: Columbia University Press.

Bloom-Feshbach, J., and Bloom-Feshbach, S. (eds.). 1987. *The Psychology of Separation and Loss.* San Francisco: Jossey-Bass.

Blumer, H. 1969. *Symbolic Interaction: Perspective and Method.* Englewood Cliffs, N.J.: Prentice-Hall.

Boszormenyi-Nagy, I., and Krasner, B. 1986. *Between Give and Take: A Clinical Guide to Contextual Therapy.* New York: Brunner/Mazel.

Bowen, M. 1978. *Family Therapy in Clinical Practice.* New York: Jason Aronson.

Bowlby, J. 1969. *Attachment.* New York: Basic Books.

————. 1973. *Separation: Anxiety and Anger.* New York: Basic Books.

————. 1980. *Loss: Sadness and Depression.* New York: Basic Books.

Bratter, T. E., and Forrest, G. G. 1985. *Alcoholism and Substance Abuse: Strategies for Clinical Intervention.* New York: Free Press.

Breuer, J., and Freud, S. 1957. *Studies on Hysteria,* trans. Strachey, J. New York: Basic Books.

Brim, O., and Kagen, J. (eds.). 1980. *Constancy and Change in Human Development.* Cambridge, Mass.: Harvard University Press.

Brissett, D., and Edgley, C. 1990. *Life as Theater: A Dramaturgical Source Book.* New York: Aldine de Gruyter.

Brown, G., and Harris, T. 1978. *Social Origins of Depression.* New York: Free Press.

Brownell, K. D., and Foreyt, J. P. 1986. *Handbook of Eating Disorders: Physiology, Psychology, and Treatment of Obesity, Anorexia, and Bulimia.* New York: Basic Books.

Bullar, D. (ed.). 1959. *Psychoanalysis and Psychotherapy: The Selected Papers of Frieda Fromm-Reichmann.* Chicago: University of Chicago Press.

Caplan, G. 1964. *Principles of Preventive Psychiatry.* New York: Basic Books.

Carkhuff, R. 1969. *Helping and Human Relations.* New York: Holt, Rinehart and Winston.

Carkhuff, R., and Berenson, B. 1977. *Beyond Counseling and Therapy*. New York: Holt, Rinehart and Winston.

Chess, S., and Thomas, A. 1986. *Temperament in Clinical Practice*. New York: Guilford.

Chessick, R. D. 1974. *The Technique and Practice of Intensive Psychotherapy*. New York: Jason Aronson.

Choca, J. 1980. *Manual for Clinical Psychology Practicums*. New York: Brunner/Mazel.

Clausen, J. (ed.). 1968. *Socialization and Society*. Boston: Little, Brown.

Clinard, M. 1968. *Sociology of Deviant Behavior*. New York: Holt, Rinehart and Winston.

Connaway, R. S., and Gentry, M. E. 1988. *Social Work Practice*. Englewood Cliffs, N.J.: Prentice-Hall.

Cooley, C. H. 1956. *Human Nature and the Social Order*. Glencoe, Ill.: Free Press.

Corsini, R. 1966. *Roleplaying in Psychotherapy: A Manual*. Chicago: Aldine.

———— (ed). 1981. *Handbook of Innovative Psychotherapies*. New York: Wiley.

Corsini, R., and Wedding, D. (eds.). 1989. *Current Psychotherapies; Fourth Edition*. Itasca, Ill.: F. E. Peacock.

Cotter, S., and Guerra, J. 1976. *Assertion Training*. Chicago: Research Press.

Dean, A., Kraft, A., and Pepper, B. (eds.). 1976. *The Social Setting of Mental Health*. New York: Basic Books.

Dewald, P. A. 1972. *The Psychoanalytic Process*. New York: Basic Books.

Dietrich, D. R., and Shabad, P. C. 1989. *The Problem of Loss and Mourning: Psychoanalytic Perspectives*. Madison, Wis.: International Universities Press.

Dollard, J., and Miller, N. E. 1950. *Personality and Psychotherapy: An Analysis in Terms of Learning, Thinking and Culture*. New York: McGraw-Hill.

Dorpat, T. L. 1985. *Denial and Defense in the Therapeutic Situation*. New York: Jason Aronson.

Durkheim, E. 1933. *The Division of Labor in Society*. New York: Free Press.

Edelson, M. 1970. *Sociotherapy and Psychotherapy*. Chicago: University of Chicago Press.

Eisdorfer, C., Cohen, D., Kleinman, A., and Maxim, P. (eds.). 1981. *Models for Clinical Psychopathology*. New York: Spectrum.

Ellis, A. 1962. *Reason and Emotion in Psychotherapy*. Secaucus, N.J.: Lyle Stewart.

————. 1973. *Humanistic Psychotherapy*. New York: McGraw-Hill.

————. 1977. *Anger: How to Live with and without It*. New York: Citadel.

English, H., and English, A. 1958. *A Comprehensive Dictionary of Psychological and Psychoanalytic Terms*. New York: David McKay.

Erikson, E. 1950. *Childhood and Society*. New York: W. W. Norton.

————. 1968. *Identity: Youth and Crisis*. New York: W. W. Norton.

Eysenck, H. J. 1986. "A Critique of Contemporary Classification and Diagnosis." In *Contemporary Directions in Psychopathology: Toward the DSM-IV*, ed. Millon, T., and Klerman, G. L. New York: Guilford.

Fairbairn, W. R. D. 1954. *An Object Relations Theory of Personality*. New York: Basic Books.

————. 1963. "An Object Relations Theory of Personality." *International Journal of Psychiatry* 44: 224–25.

Fein, M. 1988. "Resocialization: A Neglected Paradigm." *Clinical Sociology Review* 6: 88–100.

————. 1990a. *Role Change: A Resocialization Perspective*. New York: Praeger.

————. 1990b. "Dysfunctional Role Maintenance." *Clinical Sociology Review* 8: 87–99.

Fenichel, O. 1941. *Problems of Psychoanalytic Technique*. New York: Psychoanalytic Quarterly.

Fine, R. 1979. *A History of Psychoanalysis*. New York: Columbia University Press.

Fishman, H. C. 1986. "The Family as a Fugue." In *Evolving Models for Family Change*, ed. Fishman, H. C., and Rossman, B. L. New York: Guilford.

Fishman, H. C., and Rossman, B. L. (eds.). 1986. *Evolving Models for Family Change*. New York: Guilford.

Ford, D. H., and Urban, H. B. 1963. *Systems of Psychotherapy*. New York: Wiley.

Frank, J. 1973. *Persuasion and Healing; A Comparative Study of Psychotherapy*. Baltimore: Johns Hopkins University Press.

Freud, A. 1966. *The Ego and the Mechanisms of Defense*. New York: International Universities Press.

Freud, S. 1953–74. *The Standard Edition of the Complete Psychological Works of Sigmund Freud*, ed. and trans. Strachey, J. London: Hogarth Press and Institute for Psychoanalysis.

————. 1959. *Beyond the Pleasure Principle*, trans. Strachey, J. New York: Bantam.

Frijda, N. H. 1987. *The Emotions*. Cambridge: Cambridge University Press.

Fritz, J. 1985. *The Clinical Sociology Handbook*. New York: Garland.

Fromm-Reichmann, F. 1950. *Principles of Intensive Psychotherapy*. Chicago: University of Chicago Press.

Gallagher, B. 1980. *The Sociology of Mental Illness*. Englewood Cliffs, N.J.: Prentice-Hall.

Gay, P. 1988. *Freud: A Life for Our Time*. New York: W. W. Norton.

Glass, J. 1979. "Renewing an Old Profession." *American Behavioral Scientist* 22, no. 4: 513–29.

Glass, J., and Fritz, J. 1982. "Clinical Sociology: Origins and Development." *Clinical Sociology Review* 1: 3–6.

Glasser, W. 1965. *Reality Therapy*. New York: Harper & Row.

Glassner, B., and Friedman, J. 1979. *Clinical Sociology*. New York: Longmans.

Goffman, E. 1963. *Stigma*. Englewood Cliffs, N.J.: Prentice-Hall.

Goldberg, A. (ed.). 1980. *Advances in Self Psychology*. New York: International Universities Press.

Goldenberg, I., and Goldenberg, H. 1980. *Family Therapy: An Overview*. Monterey, Calif.: Brooks/Cole.

Goldenson, R. 1978. *Disability and Rehabilitation Handbook*. New York: McGraw-Hill.

Goslin, D. (ed.). 1969. *Handbook of Socialization Theory and Research*. Chicago: Rand McNally.

Gove, W. (ed.). 1982. *Deviance and Mental Illness*. Beverly Hills, Calif.: Sage.

Greenberg, L., and Safran, J. 1987. *Emotion in Psychotherapy*. New York: Guilford.

Grinker, R. 1961. "A Transactional Model for Psychotherapy." In *Contemporary Psychotherapies*, ed. Stein, M. New York: Free Press of Glencoe.

Gurman, A. S., and Kniskern, D. P. (eds.). 1981. *Handbook of Family Therapy*. New York: Brunner/Mazel.

Haley, J. 1973. *Uncommon Therapy: The Psychiatric Techniques of Milton H. Erickson, M.D.* New York: W. W. Norton.

Hall, C., and Lindzey, G. 1978. *Theories of Personality*. New York: Wiley.

Hamilton, N. G. 1988. *Self and Others: Object Relations Theory in Practice.* New York: Jason Aronson.

Harris, T. 1969. *I'm OK, You're OK.* New York: Harper & Row.

Harrison, J. 1976. *Hume's Moral Epistemology.* Oxford: Clarendon.

Hartmann, H. 1964. *Essays on Ego Psychology: Selected Problems in Psychoanalytic Theory.* New York: International Universities Press.

Helle, H. J., and Eisenstadt, S. N. (eds.). 1985. *Micro Sociological Theory.* Beverly Hills, Calif.: Sage.

Herink, R. (ed.). 1980. *The Psychotherapy Handbook.* New York: Meridian.

Hersen, M., Kazdin, A., and Bellack, A. (eds.). 1983. *The Clinical Psychology Handbook.* New York: Pergamon.

Hinsie, L. E., and Shatsky, J. 1947. *Psychiatric Dictionary.* New York: Oxford.

Hobbes, T. 1956. Leviathan, Part I. Chicago: Henry Regnery.

Hollingshead, A., and Redlich, F. 1958. Social Class and Mental Health. New York: Wiley.

Hollis, F. 1972. Casework: A Psychosocial Therapy. New York: Random House.

Holmes, T. H., and Rahe, R. H. 1967. "The Social Readjustment Scale." *Journal of Psychosomatic Research* 11: 213–18.

Horney, K. 1939. *New Ways in Psychoanalysis.* New York: W. W. Norton.

———. 1942. *Self-Analysis.* New York: W. W. Norton.

———. 1945. *Our Inner Conflicts: A Constructive Theory of Neuroses.* New York: W. W. Norton.

Horowitz, M. J. 1988. *Introduction to Psychodynamics: A New Synthesis.* New York: Basic Books.

Ivey, A., and Authier, J. 1978. *Microcounseling: Innovations in Interviewing, Counseling, Psychotherapy and Psychoeducation.* Springfield, Ill.: Charles Thomas.

Jacobson, E. 1964. *The Self and the Object World.* New York: International Universities Press.

Janov, A. 1970. *The Primal Scream, Primal Therapy: The Cure for Neurosis.* New York: Putnam.

Jourard, S. M. 1964. *The Transparent Self: Self Disclosure and Well Being.* Princeton, N.J.: Van Nostrand.

Jung, C. G. 1953–78. *Collected Works,* ed. Read, H., Fordham, M., and Adler, G. Princeton, N.J.: Princeton University Press.

Kanter, J. S. (ed.). 1985. *Clinical Issues in Treating the Chronic Mentally Ill.* San Francisco: Jossey-Bass.

Kennedy, D. B., and Kerber, A. 1973. *Resocialization: An American Experiment.* New York: Behavioral Publications.

Kernberg, O. F. 1984. *Severe Personality Disorders: Psychotherapeutic Strategies.* New Haven, Conn.: Yale University Press.

Klerman, G. L., Weissman, M. M., Rounsaville, B. J., and Chevron, E. 1984. *Interpersonal Psychotherapy of Depression.* New York: Basic Books.

Kohut, H. 1977. *The Restoration of the Self.* New York: International Universities Press.

Kottler, J. 1986. *On Being a Therapist.* San Francisco: Jossey-Bass.

Krasner, L. 1963. "Reinforcement, Verbal Behavior, and Psychotherapy." *American Journal of Orthopsychiatry* 33: 601–13.

Kübler-Ross, E. 1969. *On Death and Dying.* New York: Macmillan.

Kuhn, T. S. 1970. *The Structure of Scientific Revolutions.* 2nd ed. Chicago: University of Chicago Press.

Kutash, I., et al. (eds.). 1980. *Handbook on Stress and Anxiety*. San Francisco: Jossey-Bass.

Laing, R. D. 1960. *The Divided Self*. London: Tavistock.

Lazarus, A. A. 1981. *The Practice of Multimodal Therapy*. New York: McGraw-Hill.

Leary, M. 1983. *Understanding Social Anxiety: Social, Personality and Clinical Perspectives*. Beverly Hills, Calif.: Sage.

Lennard, H., and Bernstein, A. 1960. *The Anatomy of Psychotherapy*. New York: Columbia University Press.

Lewin, K. 1935. *A Dynamic Theory of Personality*. New York: McGraw-Hill.

―――. 1951. *Field Theory in Social Science: Selected Theoretical Papers*, ed. D. Cartwright. Chicago: University of Chicago Press.

Lewis, M., and Saarni, C. (eds.). 1985. *The Socialization of Emotions*. New York: Plenum.

Lindzey, G., and Aronson, E. (eds.). 1985. *Handbook of Social Psychology*. 3d ed. New York: Random House.

Linton, R. 1936. *The Study of Man*. New York: Appleton-Century-Crofts.

London, P. 1964. *The Modes and Morale of Psychotherapy*. New York: Holt, Rinehart and Winston.

McHugh, P. 1966. "Social Disintegration as a Requisite of Resocialization." *Social Forces* 44, March 1966, pp. 355–63.

Mahler, M., Pine, F., and Bergman, A. 1975. *The Psychological Birth of the Human Infant: Symbiosis and Individuation*. New York: Basic Books.

Malcolm, J. 1982. *Psychoanalysis: The Impossible Profession*. New York: Knopf.

Malinowski, B. 1929. *The Sexual Life of Savages*. New York: Harcourt, Brace & World.

Maslow, A. 1954. *Motivation and Personality*. New York: Harper & Row.

Maslow, A., and Mittleman, B. 1951. *Principles of Abnormal Psychology*. New York: Harper.

Matthews, A. M., Gelder, M. G., and Johnston, D. W. 1981. *Agoraphobia: Nature and Treatment*. New York: Guilford.

May, R. 1950. *The Meaning of Anxiety*. New York: W. W. Norton.

―――. 1979. *Psychology and the Human Dilemma*. New York: W. W. Norton.

Mead, G. H. 1934. *Mind, Self and Society*. Chicago: University of Chicago Press.

Mendelson, M. 1975. *Psychoanalytic Concepts of Depression*. New York: Spectrum.

Menninger, K. 1958. *The Theory of Psychoanalytic Technique*. New York: Harper & Row.

Meyer, A. 1908. "The Problem of Mental Reaction-Types, Mental Causes and Diseases." *Psychological Bulletin* 5: 245–61.

Miller, G. A., Galanter, E., and Pribram, K. 1960. *Plans and the Structure of Behavior*. New York: Holt, Rinehart and Winston.

Miller, J. 1978. *The Body in Question*. New York: Vintage.

Millon, T., and Klerman, G. L. (eds.). 1986. *Contemporary Directions in Psychopathology: Toward the DSM-IV*. New York: Guilford.

Minuchin, S. 1974. *Families and Family Therapy*. Cambridge, Mass.: Harvard University Press.

Mischel, W. 1968. *Personality and Assessment*. New York: Wiley.

Moreno, J. 1953. *Who Shall Survive?* New York: Beacon House.

Murray, H. A., et al. 1938. *Explorations in Personality*. New York: Oxford University Press.

Neilson, W. A. (ed.). 1952. *Webster's New International Dictionary of the English Language*. Springfield, Mass.: Merriam.

Nicholi, A. (ed.). 1978. *Harvard Guide to Modern Psychiatry*. Cambridge: Belknap.

Nichols, M. P. 1987. *The Self in the System: Expanding the Limits of Family Therapy*. New York: Brunner/Mazel.

Norcross, J. C. (ed.). 1986. *Handbook of Eclectic Psychotherapy*. New York: Brunner/Mazel.

Nye, F. I. 1976. *Role Structure and the Analysis of the Family*. Beverly Hills, Calif.: Sage.

Obermann, C. E. 1968. *A History of Vocational Rehabilitation in America*. Minneapolis, Minn.: T. S. Denison.

Papp, P. 1983. *The Process of Change*. New York: Guilford.

Patterson, C. H. 1986. *Theories of Counseling and Psychotherapy*. 4th ed. New York: Harper & Row.

Perls, F. 1969. *Gestalt Therapy Verbatim*. New York: Bantam.

Perls, F., Hefferline, R., and Goodman, P. 1951. *Gestalt Therapy*. New York: Delta.

Pruitt, D. G. 1981. *Negotiation Behavior*. New York: Academic Press.

———. 1983. "Strategic Choice in Negotiation." *American Behavioral Scientist* 27, no. 22: 167–97.

Raskin, N. J., and Rogers, C. 1989. "Person-Centered Therapy." In *Current Psychotherapies*, 4th ed. Corsini, R., and Wedding, D. Itasca, Ill.: F. E. Peacock.

Redlich, F., and Freedman, D. 1966. *The Theory and Practice of Psychiatry*. New York: Basic Books.

Reisman, J. 1971. *Toward the Integration of Psychotherapy*. New York: Wiley-Interscience.

Rice, L., and Greenberg, L. (eds.). 1984. *Patterns of Change*. New York: Guilford.

Richards, M. 1974. *The Integration of a Child into a Social World*. London: Cambridge University Press.

Rieff, P. 1961. *Freud: The Mind of a Moralist*. Garden City, N.Y.: Doubleday Anchor.

Riley, M. W., et al. 1969. "Socialization in the Middle and Later Years." In *Handbook of Socialization Theory and Research*, ed. Goslin, D. Chicago: Rand McNally.

Rogers, C. 1951. *Client Centered Therapy*. Boston: Houghton Mifflin.

———. 1961. *On Becoming a Person*. Boston: Houghton Mifflin.

———. 1970. *Encounter Groups*. New York: Harper & Row.

Roman, P., and Trice, H. (eds.). 1974. *The Sociology of Psychotherapy*. New York: Jason Aronson.

Romano, J. 1947. "Psychotherapy." In *Teaching Psychotherapeutic Medicine*, ed. Witmer, H. L. New York: Commonwealth Fund.

Rosenhan, M. 1973. "On Being Sane in Insane Places." *Science* 179, January, pp. 150–58.

Ruesch, J. 1961. *Therapeutic Communication*. New York: W. W. Norton.

Rushing, W. 1964. *The Psychiatric Professions: Power, Conflict and Alienation in a Psychiatric Hospital Staff*. Chapel Hill: University of North Carolina Press.

Sager, C. J., and Kaplan, H. S. (eds.). 1972. *Progress in Group and Family Therapy*. New York: Brunner/Mazel.

Sarbin, T., and Allen, V. 1968. "Role Theory." In *Handbook of Social Psychology*, ed. Lindzey, G., and Aronson, E. 3d ed. Reading, Mass.: Addison-Wesley.

Satir, V. 1977. *Peoplemaking*. Palo Alto, Calif.: Science and Behavior Books.

Scheff, T. 1966. *Being Mentally Ill: A Sociological Theory*. Chicago: Aldine.

——— (ed.). 1967. *Mental Illness and Social Process*. New York: Harper & Row.

————. 1979. *Catharsis in Healing, Ritual, and Drama.* Berkeley: University of California Press.

Selye, H. 1956. *The Stress of Life.* New York: McGraw-Hill.

————. 1980. "The Stress Concept Today." In *Handbook on Stress and Anxiety,* ed. Kutash, I., et al. San Francisco: Jossey-Bass.

Sennett, R., and Cobb, J. 1972. *The Hidden Injuries of Class.* New York: Vintage.

Shapiro, D. 1989. *Psychotherapy of Neurotic Character.* New York: Basic Books.

Silverman, H. 1972. *Marital Therapy: Psychological, Sociological and Moral Factors.* Springfield, Ill.: Charles Thomas.

Stein, M. (ed.). 1961. *Contemporary Psychotherapies.* New York: Free Press of Glencoe.

Storr, A. 1979. *The Art of Psychotherapy.* New York: Methuen.

Straus, R. (ed.). 1969. "Clinical Sociology." *American Behavioral Scientist,* 22, no. 4, special issue: 473–608.

———— (ed.). 1985. *Using Sociology: An Introduction from the Clinical Perspective.* New York: General Hall.

Strean, H. 1985. *Therapeutic Principles in Practice: A Manual for Clinicians.* Beverly Hills, Calif.: Sage.

Stryker, S., and Statham, A. 1985. "Symbolic Interaction and Role Theory." In *Handbook of Social Psychology,* ed. Lindzey, G., and Aronson, E. 3d ed. New York: Random House.

Sullivan, H. S. 1940. *Conceptions of Modern Psychiatry.* New York: W. W. Norton.

————. 1953. *The Interpersonal Theory of Psychiatry.* New York: W. W. Norton.

————. 1954. *The Psychiatric Interview.* New York: W. W. Norton.

Szasz, T. 1961. *The Myth of Mental Illness: Foundations of a Theory of Personal Conduct.* New York: Dell.

Thomas, W. I., and Thomas, D. S. 1928. *The Child in America: Behavior, Problems and Progress.* New York: Knopf.

Truax, C. B., and Carkhuff, R. R. 1967. *Toward Effective Counseling and Psychotherapy: Training and Practice.* Chicago: Aldine.

Turner, F. 1978. *Psychosocial Therapy: A Social Work Perspective.* New York: Free Press.

Turner, R. H. 1962. "Role Taking: Process vs. Conformity?" In *Human Behavior and Social Processes,* ed. Rose, A. M. Boston: Houghton Mifflin.

————. 1978. "The Role and the Person." *American Journal of Sociology* 84: 1–23.

————. 1985. "Unanswered Questions in the Convergence between Structuralist and Interactionist Role Theories." In *Micro Sociological Theory,* ed. Helle, H. J., and Eisenstadt, S. E. Beverly Hills, Calif.: Sage.

Turner, S. M., Calhoun, K. S., and Adams, H. E. 1981. *Handbook of Clinical Behavior Therapy.* New York: Wiley.

University of the State of New York. 1961. *Psychology.* Handbook 51. Albany: State Education Department.

Vandenbos, G. (ed.). 1980. *Psychotherapy: Practice, Research, Policy.* Beverly Hills, Calif.: Sage.

Viorst, J. 1986. *Necessary Losses.* New York: Fawcett.

Walker, C. E. (ed.). 1981. *Clinical Practice of Psychology.* New York: Pergamon.

Watson, J. B. 1914. *Behavior: An Introduction to Comparative Psychology.* New York: Holt.

Wegscheider-Cruse, S. 1980. *Another Chance: Hope and Health for Alcoholic Families.* Palo Alto, Calif.: Science and Behavior Books.

Weiss, R. S. 1975. *Marital Separation*. New York: Basic Books.

Wender P. H., and Klein, D. F. 1981. *Mind, Mood, and Medicine: A Guide to the New Biopsychiatry*. New York: Farrar, Straus, & Giroux.

Wentworth, W. 1980. *Context and Understanding: An Inquiry into Socialization Theory*. New York: Elsevier.

Wirth, L. 1931. "Clinical Sociology." *American Journal of Sociology* 37: 49–66.

Wolberg, L. 1967. *The Technique of Psychotherapy*. New York: Grune & Stratton.

———. 1982. *The Practice of Psychotherapy*. New York: Brunner/Mazel.

Wolfensberger, W., with Nirje, B., et al. 1972. *The Principle of Normalization in Human Services*. Toronto: National Institute on Mental Retardation.

Wolman, B. (ed.). 1973. *Handbook of General Psychology*. Englewood Cliffs, N.J.: Prentice-Hall.

——— (ed.). 1976. *The Therapist's Handbook: Treatment of Mental Disorders*. New York: Van Nostrand Reinhold.

Wolpe, J. 1973. *The Practice of Behavior Therapy*. New York: Pergamon.

Wrong, D. 1961. "The Oversocialized Conception of Man in Modern Sociology." *American Sociological Review* 26, no. 2 :183–93.

Wynne, L. C., Cromwell, R. L., and Matthysse, S. 1978. *The Nature of Schizophrenia: New Approaches to Research and Treatment*. New York: Wiley.

Yalom, I. D. 1970. *The Theory and Practice of Group Psychotherapy*. New York: Basic Books.

———. 1980. *Existential Psychotherapy*. New York: Basic Books.

Zajonc, R. B. 1980. "Feeling and Thinking: Preferences Need No Inferences." *American Psychologist* 35: 151–73.

Zander, A., Cohen, A., and Stotland, E. 1957. *Role Relations in the Mental Health Professions*. Ann Arbor: University of Michigan Press.

Zeig, J. K., and Munion, W. M. (eds.). 1990. *What is Psychotherapy? Contemporary Perspectives*. San Francisco: Jossey-Bass.

# Index

ABC model, 177
aborted roles, 7, 20–22, 35. *See also* dysfunctional roles
abuse. *See* coercion
academic psychology, 9, 167–69, 176, 188
Ackerman, Nathan, 58, 74, 122
Adler, Alfred, 11–12, 60, 98–105
adolescence, 114, 201
Adult Children of Alcoholics (ACOA), 136–38
advice giving, 91, 149
affective strategies, 182–88
aggression, 185. *See also* assertiveness training
Alcoholics Anonymous (AA), 55, 63, 64, 135–37
alcoholism counseling, 135–38
Alexander, Franz, 62, 93
anal stage, 84–85, 113
anger, 179, 185. *See also* emotions; emotional barriers
Anna O. *See* Pappenheim, Bertha
antitherapy, 189–91, 196, 199–200
anxiety, 47, 93, 111, 186; basic, 106, 107–8, 160; signal, 93
anxiolytic. *See* pharmacotherapy
archetypes, 165–66

"as if," 104
assertiveness training, 32, 56–57, 68, 71, 183–85
attachment behavior, 114–15
authority figures, 9
automatic thoughts, 180–81
aversive conditioning, 171

bargaining, 38–39, 40. *See also* negotiations
barriers to change, 38–42, 51, 68–75, 92–95, 103–5, 107–9, 111–12, 116–17, 149–52, 156–57, 160, 174–75, 178–80, 182, 184–85, 187–88, 195, 202–3, 206. *See also* cognitive barriers; emotional barriers; social barriers; volitional barriers
BASIC ID, 188
basic mistakes, 99, 103
basic personal roles, 6, 17. *See also* roles, social
Bateson, Gregory, 124, 196
Beck, Aaron, 57, 176, 180–82
behavior modification, 56, 67–69, 170–76
behavioral interventions, 9, 10, 65, 167–69
behavioral problems, 9

beliefs, 177–78
Berne, Eric, 66, 161–62, 164
biofeedback, 187
Bowen, Murray, 123–24
Bowlby, John, 39, 114–15, 116, 117
Breuer, Joseph, 78, 81
brief therapy, 190

Caplan, Gerald, 141
caretaker role, 21, 36–37, 44, 81
castration fears, 85–86
catastrophizing, 179
catharsis, 92–93, 149, 156
change processes. *See* resocialization;
  role change
character, 8
chemotherapy. *See* medical interventions; pharmacotherapy
Chess, Stella, 142
client-centered therapy, 54–55, 62, 70,
  144–51
codependence, 136–38
coercion, 12, 18, 174, 198–99. *See also*
  negotiations; renegotiating
cognitive barriers, 41, 92, 103, 111,
  164, 176, 181–82
cognitive therapy, 57, 65, 72–73, 168,
  176–82
cohesion, group, 130
communication: crossed, 66, 163; family, 124–26; ulterior, 66, 163
community psychiatry, 55, 141
compliance, 197
conditioning: aversive, 171; classical,
  170; operant, 170–71
conflicts, 48
confusion, personal, 19–20, 47–48
congruence, 144, 146, 150
consequences, 171
contending, 43. *See also* dual concern
  model
coping. *See* support, social
corrective emotional experience, 62, 93
Corsini, Raymond, 6, 12
counseling, 14, 73, 204
counterconditioning, 175
countertransference, 89
courage, 101

covering therapy, 29. *See also* uncovering therapy
cultural therapy, 60, 66, 74, 98–112,
  119

defective roles, 15, 18–23, 80–83
defense mechanisms, 113
defiance, 197
demands, social. *See* social barriers
demoralization, 46–47
denial, 38
depression. *See* grief; mourning; sadness
desensitization, 57, 71, 183–85
detachment, 39
developmental stages: Freudian, 83–86;
  Sullivanian, 112; Eriksonian, 113–14
diagnosis, psychiatric, 194–95
directive therapy, 200–201
disabilities, 203–4
disengagement, 126
disorder, mental, 46. *See also* mental illness
dispute resolution. *See* negotiations
Dollard, John, 174–75
Dora, 81–82
double bind, 124
dramatizations, 112
dramatizing, 38, 134, 153–55
dream analysis, 79, 165
drives, 175
dual concern model, 45, 66, 107, 125,
  156, 184, 198. *See also* negotiations;
  renegotiating
dynamisms, 111
dysfunctional role maintenance, 18–19.
  *See also* demoralization; trapped,
  feelings of being
dysfunctional roles, 15, 18–23, 80–83.
  *See also* role problems

eclectic behaviorism, 188
ecological therapy, 119–20
Edelson, Marshall, 141
educational interventions, 30, 200, 203
ego, 8; autonomy, 113, 116; defenses,
  113
ego psychology, 99, 113, 116, 120, 127

ego states, 58, 161–63
Ellis, Albert, 57, 67, 72, 176–79
emotional barriers, 41, 70–72, 92–93, 107–8, 116–17, 149–50, 156–57, 195
emotions, 15, 40–41, 47, 177, 180, 183; disarming intense, 41
empathy, 54, 145–46
"empty chair" dialogue, 153
English, Horace, and English, Ava, 5, 6, 11
enmeshment, 126
Erickson, Milton, 196
Erikson, Erik, 113–14
errors (cognitive, volitional). *See* barriers to change; mistakes, basic
existential therapy, 60, 67, 74, 158–61
expressed emotion, 192

failed roles, 7, 20–22, 35. *See also* dysfunctional roles
Fairbairn, Ronald, 114
family communications, 124–26
family genius, 21
family hero, 20, 137
family romance, 85–86. *See also* Oedipus complex
family therapy, 58, 67, 71, 74–75, 120–28
fear. *See* anxiety
feedback loops, 124, 130
Fenichel, Otto, 90, 93
fictional finalism, 104
firm flexibility, 43
Fishman, Charles, 127–28
fixations, 83, 85, 87
force. *See* coercion; power
Frank, Jerome, 12–13, 46, 50
Frankl, Viktor, 158
free association, 79, 88–89
Freud, Anna, 81, 113, 116–17
Freud, Sigmund, 37, 59–60, 62, 77–79, 80–95, 97, 99, 117, 164–65, 191; self-analysis, 79, 92
Freudian therapy, 2. *See also* psychoanalysis
functional disorder, 193

games, 66, 162–63

genius, family, 21
genuineness, 54, 146
gestalt, 151
gestalt therapy, 2, 62–63, 70, 144, 151–57
Glasser, William, 199–202
goals. *See* values
goals of change, 5–11
Goffman, Erving, 139
grief, 23, 90. *See also* mourning; sadness
group therapy, 10, 128–35, 152
growth, personal, 152–53
guilt, 93, 94, 160

Haley, Jay, 124, 196
Harris, Thomas, 66, 161, 163
Hartmann, Heinz, 99, 113
Harvey, William, 45
hero, family, 20, 137
homeostasis, family, 124
Horney, Karen, 60, 66–67, 74, 99, 105–9
Hull, Clark, 168
Hume, David, 72
hypnosis, 81, 92, 190, 196
hysteria, 78, 80–81

"I-thou" relationship, 152
id, 87, 98
identification with aggressor, 113
identifying role dysfunctions, 36–38, 102, 110, 137, 148, 153, 159, 162–63, 172–73, 177–78, 181, 188, 194–95, 202, 205
identity formation, 17, 114
illness, mental. *See* mental illness
"I'm OK, You're OK," 66, 163
imagination, guided, 153
impediments to change. *See* barriers to change
inaction. *See* dual concern model
individual psychology, 100–105
individuation, 14
infantile sexuality, 78–79, 81–82, 92
inferiority complex, 100, 105
influence, 12–13. *See also* manipulation of clients

intense emotion, 19; disarming, 41. *See also* emotions
intentions, 103
interests, 43–44
interpersonal therapy (IPT), 64, 71, 117
interpretation: Freudian, 89, 90; Rogerian, 147
interview techniques, 110
irrational ideas (thoughts), 57, 177–78, 181
isomorphic behavior patterns, 127–28

Jackson, Don, 124
Janov, Arthur, 157
Jung, Carl, 164–65

Klerman, Gerald, 64, 117
knowledge: self-, 44; of other, 44
Kohut, Heinz, 116
Kübler-Ross, Elizabeth, 38–43

labeling theory, 56, 75, 139–40, 175
Lazarus, Arnold, 188
learning, theory of, 13, 170–72, 174–75
letting go, 117. *See also* relinquishing
levels of intervention, 27–33, 51, 52–61, 100–101, 152–53, 161–62, 181, 193–94, 200–202. *See also* resocialization; socialization; support, social
Lewin, Kurt, 132
libido, 79, 83, 87, 92, 112
life positions, 66, 163
life scripts, 162–63
life-style. *See* style of life
locus of fault, 7
loss, 34–36, 115, 116
loss curve, 33

Mahler, Margaret, 114
"making the rounds," 154
Malinowski, Bronislaw, 86
manipulation of clients, 174
masculine protest, 100
May, Rollo, 158
Mead, George Herbert, 109
meaninglessness, 158–59
medical interventions, 10, 55, 190, 191–95

melancholia, 93
mental illness, 10, 27, 192, 204
Meyer, Adolph, 109, 191
milieu therapy, 141
Miller, Neal, 174–75
Minuchin, Salvador, 126
Mischel, Walter, 7
mistakes, basic, 100, 103
modeling of roles, 132
morality (moralism) 93–94, 157, 160, 200. *See also* values
Moreno, Jacob, 3, 133–34
mourning, 23, 38–42, 115. *See also* grief
multimodal therapy, 188

needs fulfillment, 16, 18
negotiated products, 17
negotiations: social, 13; strategies, 43, 146, 184
neurosis, 78, 106, 108
neurotic needs, 108
neurotic stupidity, 111, 175
Nichols, Michael, 127
nondirective therapy, 145, 149
nonjudgmental relationships, 146
nonspecific responses, 185. *See also* stress
normalization, 204
norms, social, 131–32

object relations therapy, 99, 112–17, 129
Oedipus complex, 79, 85–86, 92, 106, 113–14
oral stage, 83–84, 113
overgeneralizations, 103, 182

pain of change, 22–23. *See also* barriers to change
Palo Alto group, 124–25, 196
Papp, Peggy, 197
Pappenheim, Bertha, 81
paradoxical interventions, 196, 197–98
passivity. *See* assertiveness training
Patterson, C. H., 14
Pavlov, Ivan, 170
penis envy, 85–86
Perls, Fredrick (Fritz), 63, 151–53

persona, 165
personality, 6–8, 109; disorders, 6, 7;
  dysfunction, 6–8
personifications, 111
persuasion, 12
phallic stage, 85. *See also* Oedipus
  complex
pharmacological therapy. *See* pharmacotherapy
pharmacotherapy, 192–95
phase of change, 51, 61–68, 87–91,
  101–3, 106–7, 115–16, 137–38, 148–
  49, 153–56, 159, 162–64, 172–74,
  177–78, 181, 183–84, 194–95, 197–
  99, 202, 205–6. *See also* identifying
  role dysfunctions; reexperiencing; relinquishing; renegotiating
power, 102–3, 104–5
primal scream therapy, 60–61, 63, 71–
  72, 157–58
problem-solving, 169, 200–201
problems: in living, 11, 193; personal,
  27–28
protest phase, 38–40, 90
Pruitt, Dean, 43
psyche, 6
psychoanalysis, 59–60, 62, 64, 66, 74,
  77–95, 97, 120, 174–75
psychodrama, 3, 63, 133–34
psychosexual theory, 78–79, 81–82, 92
psychosocial construct, 7–8, 16
psychotherapy, 1, 2, 6, 169, 189; definition of, 4–15, 191; varieties of, 128–29

rational disputation, 58, 178
rational-emotive therapy (RET), 57–58,
  67, 72, 73, 176–79, 181
reality principle, 94
reality therapy, 55, 74, 190, 199–202
reciprocal inhibition, 185
reexperiencing (dysfunctional roles),
  22, 36–38, 62–63, 88–89, 133–34,
  148–49, 153–55, 157–58, 163
reflecting, 62
reform, social, 140–41
reframing, 125
regression, 89
rehabilitation, vocational, 58, 68, 73,
  190, 203–6

reinforcement schedules, 171, 173–74
Reisman, John, 4
relationship, therapeutic, 144, 145–47.
  *See also* trust
relationship factors, 53–54; problems, 19
relaxation techniques, 186–87
relinquishing (roles), 38–42, 63–65, 89–
  90, 116, 137–38. *See also* letting go
reliving losses. *See* reexperiencing
renegotiating (roles), 43–44, 65–68, 90–
  91, 102–3, 107, 123, 125, 126, 134,
  155–56, 163–64, 173–74, 178, 181,
  197–99, 202, 205
repetition compulsion, 37, 46, 88
repression, learned, 175
resistance, 90
resocialization, 24, 33–34, 50, 59–61,
  80, 87, 101, 115, 132–34, 147, 152–
  53, 162, 197, 201. *See also* role
  change
responsibility, 200, 202
responsiveness, 53–54
romanticism, 143–44
Rogerian therapy. *See* client-centered
  therapy
Rogers, Carl, 62, 144–45, 147
role change, 11–13, 19, 23–25. *See also*
  resocialization
role change curve, 33
role negotiations, 17, 83–86
role partners, 17
role problems, 15, 18–23, 80–83. *See*
  *also* dysfunctional roles
role repertoires, 17
role reversals, 153–54
role scripts, 7, 18, 68, 105
role theory, 3, 15–22
role transfer, 23–24, 140, 169, 204
role-making. *See* negotiated products
role-playing, 132–34, 153–55
role-taking, 28
roles, social, 15–23, 30; coherence, 18;
  conservation, 14, 17–19; defective,
  19–23. *See also* caretaker role; family genius; family hero; scapegoat
Rosenhan, David L., 139

sadness, 42, 114, 155. *See also* grief;
  mourning

Satir, Virginia, 124–25
satisfaction. *See* needs fulfillment
scapegoat, 58, 122, 136
Scheff, Thomas, 139–40
schizophrenia, 27, 29, 124, 192. *See also* mental illness
scripts, role, 18, 68, 105
seduction theory, 78–79, 95
self, 8
self-actualization, 146, 153
self-in-the-system, 127–28
self psychology, 8, 116, 127
Selye, Hans, 183, 185
shame. *See* emotions
"shoulds," 157, 179, 182. *See also* morality; values
signal anxiety, 93. *See also* emotions
Skinner, B. F., 170
social barriers, 42, 74–75, 94–95, 104–5, 109, 112, 185, 199
social demands. *See* social barriers
social reform, 140–41
social support. *See* support, social
socialization, 24, 30–31, 56–59, 100–101, 121, 131–32, 169, 171–72, 181, 183, 201, 204–5
sociological approaches, 75, 138–41
sociotherapy, 141
solidarity, social, 130
specializations, 49–52, 53–75
stigmatization, 139
strategic therapy, 65, 190, 196–99
stress, 185–86; reduction, 55, 185–89
structural analysis, 162–63
structural family therapy, 126–27
style of life, 101
Sullivan, Harry Stack, 60, 74, 99, 109–12, 138
superego, 93
support, social, 28–30, 54–56, 129–31, 136, 145–47, 161–62, 193–94, 200–201
symbolic interaction, 8, 109, 111
symptoms, 45–48, 194
systems theory, 10, 11, 120–21, 123
Szasz, Thomas, 11

T-group, 132
talking cure, 14, 81

teachable moment, 141
teleology, 103, 104
temperament, 7
temperamental fit, 59, 142
termination, 90–91
testing: aptitude, 205; IQ, 205; interest, 205
therapeutic alliance, 146
Thomas, Alexander, 142
Thorndike, Edward L., 170
time-limited therapy, 190
"time out," 171
toilet training, 85. *See also* anal stage
top dog–underdog dialogue, 154
traits, personality, 6, 17. *See also* personality
transactional analysis (TA), 58–59, 63, 66, 161–64
transference, 37, 62, 89, 91
translations, conceptual, 52
trapped, feelings of being, 20, 39–40. *See also* demoralization
triangulations, 123
trust, 53, 145–47
twelve-step process, 135, 137–38
"two-chair dialogue," 153–54

unblocking emotions. *See* emotional barriers
unconditional positive regard, 54, 146
unconscious, 79, 87, 89, 165, 200
uncovering therapy, 203
understanding (self, other). *See* knowledge

validation, 130
values, 44, 67, 72, 73–74, 150, 160, 178–79, 200, 202, 206. *See also* morality
ventilation, 131. *See also* catharsis
volitional barriers, 41, 73–74, 93–94, 104, 111, 150, 160
Von Bertlanffy, Ludwig, 124

warmth, 54
Watson, John B., 167
Weiner, Norbert, 124
Wender, Paul, 192
Wolfensberger, Wolf, 204

Wolpe, Joseph, 65, 71, 183–85
"working through," 60, 66, 90, 116

Yalom, Irvin, 158

yielding. *See* dual concern model

Zajonc, Robert B., 180

## ABOUT THE AUTHOR

MELVYN L. FEIN teaches applied sociology at Kennesaw State College, Marietta, Georgia. A certified clinical sociologist, he holds a doctorate from the City University of New York and has over twenty years' clinical experience in helping individuals solve their personal, relationship, and vocational problems. Dr. Fein recently published *Role Change: A Resocialization Perspective* (Praeger, 1990), and is completing a work dealing with anger management. Among his other research interests are the medical model of personal distress and the social negotiation of moral rules.